Modernism, Sex, and Gender

NEW MODERNISMS SERIES

Bloomsbury's *New Modernisms* series introduces, explores, and extends the major topics and debates at the forefront of contemporary Modernist Studies.

Surveying new engagements with such topics as race, sexuality, technology, and material culture, and supported with authoritative further reading guides to the key works in contemporary scholarship, these books are essential guides for serious students and scholars of Modernism.

Published Titles

Modernism: Evolution of an Idea
Sean Latham and Gayle Rogers

Modernism and the Law
Robert Spoo

Modernism in a Global Context
Peter J. Kalliney

Modernism's Print Cultures
Faye Hammill and Mark Hussey

Modernism, Science, and Technology
Mark S. Morrisson

Modernism, Sex, and Gender
Celia Marshik and Allison Pease

Modernism, War, and Violence
Marina MacKay

Forthcoming Titles

The Global Avant-Garde
Christopher Bush

Modernism and Its Media
Chris Forster

Race and Modernisms
K. Merinda Simmons and James A. Crank

Modernism, Sex, and Gender

Celia Marshik and Allison Pease

BLOOMSBURY ACADEMIC
LONDON · NEW YORK · OXFORD · NEW DELHI · SYDNEY

BLOOMSBURY ACADEMIC
Bloomsbury Publishing Plc
50 Bedford Square, London, WC1B 3DP, UK
1385 Broadway, New York, NY 10018, USA

BLOOMSBURY, BLOOMSBURY ACADEMIC and the Diana logo are trademarks of Bloomsbury Publishing Plc

First published in Great Britain 2019

Copyright © Celia Marshik and Allison Pease, 2019

Celia Marshik and Allison Pease have asserted their rights under the Copyright, Designs and Patents Act, 1988, to be identified as Authors of this work.

For legal purposes the Acknowledgments on p. x constitute an extension of this copyright page.

Cover design: Daniel Benneworth-Gray
Cover photograph: Suffragette Mabel Capper outside Bow Street Court, 1 January 1912

All rights reserved. No part of this publication may be reproduced or transmitted in any form or by any means, electronic or mechanical, including photocopying, recording, or any information storage or retrieval system, without prior permission in writing from the publishers.

Bloomsbury Publishing Plc does not have any control over, or responsibility for, any third-party websites referred to or in this book. All internet addresses given in this book were correct at the time of going to press. The author and publisher regret any inconvenience caused if addresses have changed or sites have ceased to exist, but can accept no responsibility for any such changes.

A catalogue record for this book is available from the British Library.

Library of Congress Cataloging-in-Publication Data
Names: Marshik, Celia, author. | Pease, Allison, author.
Title: Modernism, sex, and gender/Celia Marshik and Allison Pease.
Description: London, UK: Bloomsbury Publishing, 2018. |
Series: New modernisms series | Includes bibliographical references and index.
Identifiers: LCCN 2018012767 (print) | LCCN 2018013942 (ebook) |
ISBN 9781350020467 (ePub) | ISBN 9781350020474 (ePDF) |
ISBN 9781350020443 (pbk.) | ISBN 9781350020450 (hardback)
Subjects: LCSH: Modernism (Literature) | Feminism and literature. | Feminism in literature. | Women authors.
Classification: LCC PN56.M54 (ebook) | LCC PN56.M54 M375 2018 (print) | DDC 809/.9112–dc23
LC record available at https://lccn.loc.gov/2018012767

ISBN: HB: 978-1-3500-2045-0
PB: 978-1-3500-2044-3
ePDF: 978-1-3500-2047-4
eBook: 978-1-3500-2046-7

Series: New Modernisms

Typeset by Integra Software Services Pvt. Ltd.

To find out more about our authors and books visit www.bloomsbury.com and sign up for our newsletters.

For Laura

CONTENTS

List of Figures viii
Acknowledgments x

Introduction 1
1 Feminine Difference 13
2 Sexuality 51
3 Masculinities 91
4 Sex, Politics, and Law 123

Coda 163
Critical Bibliographies for
   Modernism, Sex, and Gender 166
Works Cited 174
Index 187

LIST OF FIGURES

1 From Bonnie Kime Scott, *The Gender of Modernism*. Courtesy of Indiana University Press 28
2 Intersections with the gender complex. From *Gender in Modernism: New Geographies, Complex Intersections*. Copyright 2007 by the Board of Trustees of the University of Illinois. Used with permission of the University of Illinois Press 46
3 Marguerite Radclyffe Hall and Lady Una Troubridge, August 1927. Getty Images 71
4 Claude McKay and Baroness Elsa von Freytag-Loringhoven, 1922. Library of Congress, Prints & Photographs Division 81
5 This 1933 illustration of Ernest Hemingway by Mexican artist Miguel Covarrubias, though never published, may have been intended for the *Vanity Fair* series "Private Lives of the Great"; herpicide in hand, the image clearly references Hemingway's dispute with Eastman. © María Elena Rico Covarrubias 105
6 "Your motherland will never forget" from *Canada in Khaki* (1916). British Museum 115

7 Glackens, L. M., Artist. "St. Anthony Comstock, the Village Nuisance" (1906). Library of Congress, Prints & Photographs Division 129
8 Harris and Ewing, photographer. "WOMAN SUFFRAGE." Library of Congress, Prints & Photographs Division 152

ACKNOWLEDGMENTS

There may be two names on the cover of this book, but *Modernism, Sex, and Gender* would not have come into being without the work of others. Our thanks are first to Gayle Rogers and Sean Latham, editors of the *New Modernisms* series, who gave us the opportunity to write this study and offered timely feedback as we worked. We also appreciate David Avital's encouragement and kindness; conversations with him helped us understand how to envision the project. The anonymous readers who reviewed our proposal shaped our work, and we appreciate their acuity.

As feminist critics, we benefited enormously from a circle of friends who pointed us to significant scholarship we might otherwise have missed. For reading drafts and offering feedback, we thank Melissa (Missy) Bradshaw, Tamar Katz, Elizabeth (Lily) Sheehan, Carey Snyder, and Julie Vandivere. We want to thank Adam McKible for the useful suggestions his wide reading afforded. When we prepared the manuscript for the press, Benjamin Blickle offered much appreciated assistance in pulling everything together. Funding for this work was provided by the Dean's Office in the College of Arts and Sciences, Stony Brook University, and a grant from the Office for the Advancement of Research at John Jay College.

Finally, this book is dedicated to Laura Frost, who introduced us many years ago. The three of us wrote our second monographs together, an experience that provided us with opportunities for raucous lunches. This would have been a funnier book if she had written it with us, but we hope she enjoys reading it in the California sunshine.

Introduction

It was all the books, all the literature in the world, right back to Juvenal .... Education would always mean coming in contact with all that.
—DOROTHY RICHARDSON, *PILGRIMAGE*, 1919

"She had, it seems, no difficulty in sustaining the different parts, for her sex changed far more frequently than those who have worn only one set of clothing can conceive" (220–1). Virginia Woolf, chronicling the many clothing changes of the protagonist of *Orlando*, presents readers with a puzzle. In the 1928 novel, Woolf's title character suffers a disappointment in love and travels to Turkey, where Orlando experiences a miraculous and unexplained change of biological sex. After her return to England, Orlando ponders the role of clothing in identity, noting (for example) that wearing a skirt makes her feel and act feminine. At the same time, she embraces the performance of gender identity clothing allows her, dressing alternately in masculine and feminine garments to play different roles in eighteenth-century London.

This much is clear. But what did Woolf mean by asserting that "her sex changed ... frequently"? Does she mean to suggest that Orlando adopts masculine or feminine characteristics as the mood strikes? Might she intend readers to think that the character's sexual orientation—the desire for men or women—depends on the clothing Orlando adopts? Or could Woolf be signifying that Orlando's biological sex is itself transformed to suit the garment, moment, and mood? All of these interpretations are possible because Woolf wrote decades before the term "gender" came to signify (in

1945) masculinity and femininity, and a few years before "sexual orientation" took on the meaning (in 1931) of same- or opposite-sex desire. Readers cannot tell whether the author is deliberately playing with us or lacks the terminology to make her meaning plain.

One conclusion is obvious: Woolf wanted her readers to think about biological sex *and* gender *and* sexual orientation as they read *Orlando*. In this she was like many of her contemporaries: D. H. Lawrence in his (in)famous tribute to the mutual, heterosexual orgasm in *Lady Chatterley's Lover*; Djuna Barnes in her playful accounts of lesbian social circles in *Ladies Almanack* and *Nightwood*; E. M. Forster's fantasy of cross-class male romance in the posthumously published *Maurice*; or T. S. Eliot's oblique references to abortion, homosexual pickup lines, and *The Waste Land*'s transgender Tiresias. These examples are just a few of the many that might be offered as evidence of the modernist fascination with sex, gender, and desire.

New publications and theories, even nonliterary works, did not always find an easy hearing, however. Physician and sexologist Havelock Ellis would find his work censored; American birth control activist Margaret Sanger would be arrested and, after a hunger strike, forcibly fed. Many modernists had their texts banned, available only in foreign editions that were difficult to purchase. A partial list of those who found their work censored includes Radclyffe Hall, James Joyce, D. H. Lawrence, Wyndham Lewis, and Bernard Shaw, while other writers chose indirection (Nella Larsen, Amy Lowell, Gertrude Stein) or private and/or posthumous publication (Djuna Barnes, H. D., E. M. Forster).

If official censorship caused writers no end of frustration, then prevalent assumptions about who writers *were*, and what kinds of literature mattered, became perhaps even more pernicious. In 1855, Nathaniel Hawthorne had complained about the "damned mob of scribbling women" dominating American letters, and the generations who followed him were little more appreciative of work by female writers or writers of color. In the 1920s, James Joyce would joyfully opine that "T. S. Eliot ends [the] idea of poetry for ladies" (11). Even in the 1940s Edith Sitwell would write to a friend, "Women's poetry, with the exception of Sappho ... and a few deep, and concentrated, but frightfully incompetent poems of Emily Dickinson, are *simply awful*—incompetent, floppy, whining, arch, trivial, self-pitying" (116). It would be easy to compile pages of similarly nasty comments, but it is more difficult to assess the impact of a literary history that celebrated work by men. In her 1919 volume of *Pilgrimage*, "The Tunnel," Dorothy Richardson's aspiring writer Miriam Henderson searches for "woman" in the index of a book and discovers listed as subtopics, "*inferior*; mentally, morally, intellectually and physically ... her development arrested in her special functions"; she later reads in the same volume, "Woman is undeveloped man." Horrified, she contemplates, "If one could only burn all the volumes," reflecting, "But it was all the books, all the literature in the world, right back to Juvenal .... Education would always mean coming in contact with all that" (219–220). If education inculcated one into women's inferiority writ large, there was the equally daunting challenge of aspiring to write in a value system that celebrated men only. Women wrote in great numbers, but they had to battle overt discouragement as well as structural hindrances: Woolf, Sylvia Beach, Harriet Shaw Weaver, Margaret Anderson, Jane Heap, Charlotte Osgood Mason, and others started their own presses and little magazines and offered patronage to writers, but publishers, editors, and patrons were still often men looking for work that was recognizably masculine. While the modernist period is really the time that witnessed women's changing status in relation to literature, it would take decades until the range of women's contributions to modernism were recognized and even, in some cases, widely read. There is still work to be done.

Modernism, Sex, and Gender introduces readers to over a century of debate about modernism informed, then and now, by ideas on gender, sexuality, and the purpose of literature. Just as Woolf and her contemporaries wanted their readers to contemplate the roles and import of gender, sex, and sexuality when they read their work, so current critical studies of modernism insist on their importance. But this is a far cry from the way modernism was first introduced by scholars. In looking at the critical history of modernist studies, the difference between the current study of modernism from modernism as it was first introduced critically is striking.

If a student were to read modernist texts in a university in the 1940s or '50s, that student would have been influenced by two towering figures who advocated the idea of literary tradition in a recently established field of study known as English: T. S. Eliot and F. R. Leavis. Eliot's influential essay, "Tradition and the Individual Talent" (1919), argued for the importance of tradition in informing the true artist. In lines that make obvious the gendered and geographical biases of Eliot's notion of tradition, he writes, "the historical sense compels a man to write not merely with his own generation in his bones, but with a feeling that the whole of the literature of Europe from Homer and within it the whole of the literature of his own country has a simultaneous existence and composes a simultaneous order" (100). We are not surprised by the gendered or geographical biases inherent in Eliot's critique; they were widely shared. Even so, it is not difficult to discern the assumptions at work in "Tradition": men make up the tradition, and to continue it is the work of men who can come to terms with their European precursors. Virginia Woolf conceded such a tradition while she explained the psychological and material conditions that promoted it in *A Room of One's Own* (1928), noting that women writers "had no tradition behind them." Amy Lowell's poem "The Sisters" (1922) contemplates a mere three predecessors forming her "strange, isolated little family" of women poets: Sappho, "Mrs. Browning," and "Miss Dickinson." Women writers of the early twentieth century were very clear that there was but a sparse female literary tradition of the kind that men called great. The fact, however, that Eliot's sentence cannot be quoted today without comment about its biases points to a shift in the intellectual and academic landscape. Today's modernist canon and the traditions we choose to study are far more diverse and are approached from a broader range of critical stances.

One idea Eliot outlined in "Tradition and the Individual Talent" is that the introduction of a new artist or an important new idea has a ripple effect, not just in how we understand literature as we move into the future, but importantly in how we reread the literatures of the past:

> What happens when a new work of art is created is something that happens simultaneously to all the works of art which preceded it. The existing monuments form an ideal order among themselves, which is modified by the introduction of the new (the really new) work of art among them. The existing order is complete before the new work arrives; for order to persist after the supervention of novelty, the *whole* existing order must be, if ever so slightly, altered; and so the relations, proportions, values of each work of art toward the whole are readjusted; and this is conformity between the old and the new. (101)

Eliot's explanation of how a new work revises older work applies equally to how, in the last thirty years, literary criticism has undertaken a revision of the literature we preserve under the rubric of modernism. As the societies in which we live have come to value gender and sexuality differently, so we have come to value different aspects of modernist literature and to conceive modernism differently. We take as exemplary how a handful of landmark studies of the 1990s placed gender and sexuality at the center of modernist literary study. For instance, Bonnie Kime Scott's 1990 critical anthology, *The Gender of Modernism*, argues that "modernism is not the aesthetic, directed, monological sort of phenomenon sought in their own ways by authors of the now-famous manifestos ... and perpetuated in new critical-formalist criticism through the 1960s. Modernism as caught in the mesh of gender is polyphonic, mobile, interactive, sexually charged" (4). Scott made the case that the valuations of the great tradition had resulted in "lost and neglected textual treasures" and that in previous criticism the "inscriptions of mothers and women, and more broadly of sexuality and gender, were not adequately decoded, if detected at all" (2). Work like Scott's did not so much challenge Eliot's model of literary history as draw attention to the acts of forgetting and exclusion that had constructed "the existing monuments." Her anthology, and the work of many others, reintroduced multiple authors and works that could form a new "existing order."

In the same year that Scott was providing immersive reading by modernists about gender, Eve Kosofsky Sedgwick argued that what was truly new about the turn of the twentieth century was the "world-mapping by which every given person, just as he or she was necessarily assigned to a male or female gender, was considered necessarily assignable as well to a homo- or a hetero-sexuality, a binarized identity that was full of implications" (*Epistemology of the Closet* 2). Not only did gender take center stage, but sexuality and sexual orientation were historicized and thus denaturalized in ways that invigorated scholarly concern for modernist representations. Scholars identified homosocial desires in texts that had earlier seemed only to represent heterosexual couplings; moreover, critics began to posit a lesbian and gay literary history immersed within, but neglected by previous versions of, Eliot's ideal order.

While critics were dissecting the cultural workings of gender and sexuality, they began to highlight the ways that seemingly private and individual matters of identity and desire shaped the public sphere. The feminist rallying cry that "the personal is political" encouraged scholars to look for connections between institutions and experiences that had once seemed entirely separate. In her 1991 *Rich and Strange: Gender, History, Modernism*, Marianne DeKoven continued the evolution of modernist criticism when she argued that modernist form was a direct result of the radical movements of socialism and feminism, thus bridging a long-perceived gap between aesthetics and politics. In 1993, Edward de Grazia opened his book on obscenity and censorship by describing how lesbian feminist publishers Margaret Anderson and Jane Heap were advised by their lawyer not to appear in court to defend themselves for publishing *Ulysses* in their magazine, *The Little Review*, lest their presence offend the judge. His choice of vignette draws attention not just to the well-known modernist terrain of legal battles over the representation of sex in literature but also to the extralegal silencing of homosexuality even as so much of modernist literature was written and underwritten by those who loved people of the same gender. Studies of modernism, law, and politics were soon infused with examples of what a difference sex and gender made, not only to the treatment of specific individuals but to who could contribute to debates over issues of vital national and international importance.

Increasingly, too, scholars came to see modernism as one aspect of modernity; instead of applying their insights about sex and gender to literature alone, they began to read a range of texts to come to grips with how gender and sexuality colored the experience of being modern. Seeking to avoid "myths of modernity" in *The Gender of Modernity* (1995), Rita Felski chose instead to ask the following questions: "How would our understanding of modernity change if instead of taking male experience as paradigmatic, we were to look instead at texts written primarily by or about women? And what if feminine phenomena, often seen as having a secondary or marginal status, were given a central importance in the analysis of the culture of modernity?" (10). These books and so many others activated a tectonic shift in modernist scholarship and reading.

As *Modernism, Sex, and Gender* will show, the act of looking—who pays attention to what texts and why—has been at the crux of how we understand modernism, and more specifically, gender and sexuality in modernism. We propose that modernist literature, as considered through the lens of literary criticism and theory, might be understood as a palimpsest, a manuscript that has layers of writing, one on top of the other. From classical through medieval times, palimpsests were common as the parchment on which people wrote was costly and often hard to obtain. Scribes would scrape or wash off older inscriptions so that the parchment could be reused. Despite such efforts to efface the older text, however, contemporary scientists and scholars have succeeded in reading the long-vanished layers beneath the visible ink. In many cases, those buried layers preserve documents that *only* survive in this form. While modernist writers had plenty of paper at hand, the image of the palimpsest helps to capture much of the impact of work on modernism, sex, and gender. In our effort to know and understand modernism, we scrape away at the topmost layers—the Eliot and Leavis models of the great tradition—to search for the earlier inscriptions, and we find beneath the visible ink revelatory original print. At the same time, we can only focus on one layer of a palimpsest at a time, and as a result, we cover over, or even erase, other print to make our claims.

The story of this book begins with second-wave feminism, the period of feminist activity in the 1960s, '70s, and '80s that focused on inequality in the workplace, women's sexuality, abortion rights, and, more broadly, that raised consciousness among women about how they participated in their own unequal treatment, both at work and at home. One cannot overstate how profoundly the scholars of second-wave feminism altered the landscape of modernism in terms of what we read and study as well as what counts as art. As Chapter 1 demonstrates, feminist inquiry into modernism required a scraping off of top layers of early modernist criticism to find, just below, a body of work by women writers and early feminist thought. To be sure, feminist modernists such as Zora Neale Hurston, Mina Loy, Dorothy Richardson, May Sinclair, Rebecca West, and Virginia Woolf were fully cognizant of what second-wave feminists came to advocate: that men's and women's experiences were different and women were second-class citizens; that traditions of thought prized in Western culture rested on notions of women that were belittling; and that patriarchy was an ideological system from which women were excluded as full participants. These feminist modernists were, however, like Cassandra speaking truth that had little effect on those around them, in part because they spoke from a position of structural exclusion, as Woolf underscores when she asks, "since the daughters of educated men are not members of Cambridge University they have no say in that education, therefore how can they alter that education?" (*Three Guineas* 40). It was not until the 1960s and '70s that a broader shift in public consciousness occurred. Millions who had been trapped inside a system seemed suddenly able to step outside of that system and see it whole. Patriarchy was held up and slowly turned round in the hands of educated feminists of the 1960s, '70s, and '80s so that its many dimensions could be understood and critiqued from a position of relative detachment. And because this new wave of critics occupied positions of social authority as professors in universities, what they saw had stronger purchase on the truth and came to shape how we read.

The first effect of second-wave feminism in modernist studies, as Chapter 1 will illustrate, was to question the masculine canon, and to "recover," or in the language of palimpsest, uncover, the work of women whom the early modernist critics had covered over or marginalized because of the lesser value placed on women writers and their concerns. Although *readers* had not necessarily ignored these women in their own day—May Sinclair, for example, was widely read and respected—scholars needed to uncover the careers and works of authors whom a generation of critics had actively written out of the canon. After they began the process of recovering women, feminist critics began to uncover certain genres in which women's writing was more common, such as the middlebrow novel. By bringing critical attention not just to individual authors but to a broader field of literary production—the editing of little magazines, literary patronage, salons, or popular fiction—scholars not only incorporated women into our understanding of modernism but perhaps more importantly broadened conceptions of what modernism is or might be. To be sure, some of this work was deeply focused on femininity, coteries of women, and how women's and men's literary production was different; some excluded women of color, while some focused exclusively on women of color, and much of it ignored or excluded lesbians. With recovery work well established, however, a new generation of critics began to question the conceptual limits of woman-focused studies that seemed to privilege only certain classes of women, typically white and middle class. Thus began a shift away from women's studies toward the intersectional field of gender studies in the 1990s.

Methodologically, the shift from women's studies to gender studies replaced the emphasis on inequality and social subordination with exploration of the impact of multiple forms of difference. The shift toward gender studies also reflects an ever-widening intellectual base, including psychosocial as well as psychoanalytical theories, post-structuralist theory, postcolonial studies, critical studies of masculinity, lesbian and gay studies, queer studies, trans studies, critical race theory, critiques of whiteness, ecological feminism, and technoscience studies. Without gender studies, it is impossible to imagine that the renewed interest in sex and sexuality in modernism would have flourished as it has.

The study of sexuality as an object of social, scientific, and literary inquiry began in the modernist period, and modernist literature engaged in this inquiry in fascinating ways. If we were to dig down to early layers of the modernist palimpsest, we would find those who heralded the daringly modern sexual liberationists who based their representations of sexual desire on biological determinism, as H. G. Wells does in *Ann Veronica* (1909), or in protest against rational epistemology, as D. H. Lawrence's novels do, as well as those who mirrored and parodied mass cultural discourses of sexuality, as James Joyce does in *Ulysses* (1922). The narrative about why and how sex or sexual orientation might be represented has, since those first proclamations, undergone a number of critical shifts, first with second-wave feminism, then with Michel Foucault's paradigm-shifting *History of Sexuality, Vol. 1* (1976), and for a third time through the lens of queer theory. With these shifts, and a fairly radical, if not wholly realized, reassessment of sexuality as culturally constructed rather than biologically determined, critics have approached modernist writers with invigorated interest. For instance, critical attention to the work of Jean Rhys, who published four novels and a short story collection between 1927 and 1939, was nonexistent in early evaluations of modernism. Before 1970, only one article was published on her work, and before 1980, only thirty. However, by early 2018, there were approximately 700 journal articles, books, and dissertations written on Rhys's work. Critical attention to her fiction arose, at least in part, from interest in literature by women, representations of race and class, and female constructions of women's sexuality. But Rhys also rose to relative prominence because of her specific interest in representing the sexually transgressive figure of the good-time girl and thus challenging what she called "the grey disease of sex hatred" (qtd in Thomas 77), the British upper-class male misogyny directed toward eroticized working- or lower-class women. We needed new theories of sexuality to understand the importance of her fiction. Shifts in thinking about sexuality have also stimulated critical work on Djuna Barnes, whose writing was not engaged critically until 1975 and yet is now the subject of a mass of studies on gender, sexuality, and queer expression, whether on drag performance, queer temporality, or Sapphic modernism. Nella Larsen was similarly ignored until the 1970s and has enjoyed a parallel recovery with invigorated interest in how her novels frame women, sex, and sexuality. Following Deborah McDowell's introduction to a critical edition of *Quicksand* and *Passing* in 1986, representations of "that nameless ... shameful impulse," the representations of black female same- and hetero-sexuality in Larsen's work, have taken center stage. Modernist scholarship on these particular authors—Rhys was from the British West Indies, Barnes had same- and opposite-sex partners, and Larsen was African-American—also demonstrates new dimensions of feminist inquiry. Since the second wave, scholars have been attentive to how aspects of an individual's race, ethnicity, gender expression, sexuality, or class intersects with other factors to create discrete and shifting hierarchies of power.

New layers that make up the modernist palimpsest in the wake of feminist inquiry promoted a critical understanding of patriarchy as a system of thought and behaviors revolving around power. Scholars now look at both femininity *and* masculinity as social constructions, and, further, consider that within a system of power, there are hegemonic and subordinate forms of gender expression. Chapter 3 showcases how masculinity studies has, since the 1990s, played a role in the reevaluation of modernist literature as a field as well as how it has shaped the reception of individual works and authors. This reevaluation has homed in on the construction of early modernist canons in the early decades of the twentieth century through the political dynamics between men and women, not just because of the lower value put on women's work but also because so many male modernists made a concerted effort to excise specific kinds of writing associated with femininity, those that centered on the quotidian or domestic or those that demonstrated sentimentality. Masculinity and masculine writing, in other words, was an *effort*, a deliberately constructed effect largely aimed at appeasing other powerful men. Recent scholarship has also highlighted how subordinate masculinities, such as those of colonized subjects or African-Americans, created competing narrative formations of gender that challenged hegemonic masculinity. Taking a cue from queer theory, the move has been to refine and complicate simple binary understandings of masculinity, in whatever form. Scholarship on Wallace Thurman, for example, demonstrates that early Harlem Renaissance critics avoided discussing his work because he was neither gay enough nor black enough; his macho, queer, and decadent self-styling was perceived as a threat to the New Negro middle-class respectability, which was interested in modeling a form of urban black masculinity (see Ganter, Knadler, Pochmara). New work is now grappling with the contradictoriness of the masculinities represented in his fiction. When dealing with white writers in Europe and America, the dominant narrative of masculinity in the modernist period is of loss: a perceived loss of privilege and status that white, middle- and upper-class masculine subjects held in relation to women, colonized subjects, Jews and African-Americans.

The political and legal history of the ways that gender and sexuality feature in the production and reception of modernism has always been part of its story. As Chapter 4 shows, however, modernist scholars in the last twenty years in particular have refined their interest in the interaction of the political, legal, and aesthetic realms, and they have uncovered the role of gender and sexuality beneath the top story of the modernist palimpsest. If some of the early stories of modernism featured heroic males battling against narrow-minded censors, such stories excluded how those same writers portrayed sex precisely to avoid or court censorship, thus creating a unique formation out of a legal-aesthetic dialectic. Such stories also largely failed to acknowledge that an effort to police female sexuality was behind the bulk of political and legal action against modernist literature. In addition, critics have only recently turned their attention to this period as one that consolidated notions of same-sex desire as defining one's being. Recent scholarship has shown lawsuits and trials, whether Oscar Wilde's, Maud Allen's, or Radclyffe Hall's, as sites of silencing, whether shutting down talk of "the cult of the clitoris" lest a mass-reading public learn what lesbianism is, or demonstrating the power of the law literally to silence a literary lion. Where the political was long considered in opposition to art, modernist criticism has broken down that false barrier, and newer work on women's suffrage writing, for instance, uncovers yet another layer in the palimpsest of modernism and gender. As this and each chapter shows, there are many stories about gender and sexuality in modernism, and many left to be uncovered, written and rewritten.

We take as paradigmatic of the critical shifts and emphases foregrounded in this book the literary reception of Radclyffe Hall's *The Well of Loneliness* (1928). That reception touches upon new scholarship on women writers, sexualities, masculinities, *and* politics and the law. Throughout the twentieth century, *The Well* stood almost as a lone type: an infamous representation not just of lesbianism but of lesbian literature, a literature so dangerous as to have been removed from the public by courts of law. Ironically, if *The Well* had not been found obscene, it might not have been famous and would likely have suffered the fate of many other middlebrow novels written by women in the 1920s. It might have sunk into obscurity, perhaps to have been recovered by a feminist critic in the 1970s. Instead, the novel became the twentieth century's most famous lesbian novel in English. As Blanche Weisen Cook wrote in 1979, the novel's protagonist, Stephen Gordon, was *the* English language model of how to be a lesbian in the mid-twentieth century and, notably, that model was masculine-presenting or, as some recent critics have offered, transgender. Although *The Well* did not fit into the early modernist canon—it was not part of Eliot's nor Leavis's great tradition—it has enjoyed revitalized critical interest as a modernist text that has much to teach us about modernism, sex, gender, politics, and law. The chapters of this book will explain how and why.

1

Feminine Difference

Overview

It is difficult to discover who our mothers are, much less think through them, thanks to a long history of criticism [...] that veils them from us.
—ALICIA OSTRIKER

The year 1922 was an *annus mirabilis* of modernism. That year witnessed the publication of T. S. Eliot's *The Waste Land* and James Joyce's *Ulysses*, texts that still serve for many readers as exemplars of modernist poetry and fiction, respectively. It was also the publication year of Virginia Woolf's *Jacob's Room*. In that novel, which chronicles the coming of age of a middle-class British man who will die in the First World War, Woolf's narrator pays close attention to the educational and career opportunities offered to British men and women. At one point, the narrator focuses on the minor character Julia Hedge as she conducts research in the British Library:

> Miss Julia Hedge, the feminist, waited for her books. They did not come. She wetted her pen. She looked about her. Her eye was caught by the final letters in Lord Macaulay's name. And she read them all round the dome—the names of great men which remind us—"Oh damn," said Julia Hedge, "why didn't they leave room for an Eliot or a Brontë?" (107)

Hedge's observation—one Woolf's protagonist Jacob never makes himself—foreshadows a sentiment women modernists might have had about their own treatment could they have observed the historical trends of the twentieth century. While numerous women wrote modernist poetry, fiction, and plays, there seemingly wasn't "room" for them in the canon that consolidated in the middle of the century.

Many women writers were critically acclaimed and popular during their lifetimes, but as the Introduction to this book establishes, some of their most eminent male contemporaries sought to discredit specific female writers as well as women's writing and even women in general. Additional examples abound: Ezra Pound rudely dismissed Amy Lowell, his onetime fellow Imagist, as "Amy-just-selling-the-goods" (qtd in Bradshaw, *Diva Poet* 71), and he dubbed the Imagists Lowell championed "Amygism" as an attempt to carve her (and women) out of the "real" movement. And F. T. Marinetti, in his founding manifesto of Futurism, proclaimed: "We will glorify war—the world's only hygiene—militarism, patriotism, the destructive gesture of freedom-bringers, beautiful ideas worth dying for, and scorn for woman" (251). Even a comparatively supportive writer like E. M. Forster, who counted Woolf as among his friends, characterized his female contemporary as "stretching out from her enchanted tree and snatching bits from the flux of daily life as they float past" (17). Forster also blamed "Feminism" for "the worst of her books—the cantankerous *Three Guineas*—and for the less successful streaks in *Orlando*" (23). The latter would become, in time, one of Woolf's most widely read and critically examined novels.

When they were not writing explicitly about their female contemporaries, male modernists often cast their moment and movement in terms that excluded them. Eliot's 1921 essay "The Metaphysical Poets" speculated that

> We can only say that it appears likely that poets in our civilization, as it exists at present, must be *difficult*. Our civilization comprehends great variety and complexity, and this variety and complexity, playing upon a refined sensibility, must produce various and complex results. The poet must become more and more comprehensive, more allusive, more indirect, in order to force, to dislocate if necessary, language into his meaning. (232)

While Eliot's comments do not mention sex or gender, the allusivity and difficulty he prescribes were most easily achieved by writers who had a university education; in Eliot's generation, some women received such training, but the majority of university graduates were men. More baldly, Wyndham Lewis positioned himself among "the men of 1914," a claim that posited the importance of a small group of artists linked only by their sex. Privately and publicly, then, many male modernists worked to construct a vision of modernism in which there was little room for women.

A generation of critics later solidified a notably male canon of modernism. Between the 1920s and 1950s, the New Critics largely drew from earlier literary periods as they sought to develop a scientific approach to literary analysis, but contemporary male poets like Eliot and Hart Crane received attention. Modernist women were, in contrast, roundly mocked. Consider I. A. Richards's influential 1925 *Principles of Literary Criticism*, which uses H. D.'s "The Pool" as the first example in a chapter titled "Badness in Poetry" (199). Richards dismisses the short work as an example of "defective communication" albeit one "in which it is likely that the original experience had some value" (199). William Empson's 1930 *Seven Types of Ambiguity* states that some writers are "almost out of reach of analysis" (6), including Racine, Dryden, and "Miss Gertrude Stein, [who] implores the passing tribute of a sigh" (7). W. K. Wimsatt, Jr. would insult H. D. and Amy Lowell, quoting from their verse and then noting, "we may observe that this is the level of presentation at which we encounter not only the dismal schoolbook instance of particularity but such opaque pictorial fallacies as the slice of life and local color, the irrelevant reportage of amateur short-story writers, the meticulous chunking of coffee cups on counters in early sound movies" (139). And John Crowe Ransom faulted Edna St. Vincent Millay for "her lack of intellectual interest." Expanding on this criticism, he specified Millay's failing as a "deficiency in masculinity" even as he acknowledged that some male poets similarly "conceive poetry as a sentimental or feminine exercise" (98).

Such juicy put-downs and nasty asides are incredibly numerous; we have only touched lightly upon a few here to indicate that while some women writers ascended to visibility as modernists in the early twentieth century, many were singled out for ridicule and later sank below the horizon. Others never rose to visibility. In the struggle over who and what came to be seen as modernist—and as *valuable*, because modernism was for many decades a value judgment—more men than women came out victorious. But modernist literature is an expanded body of work that is read differently in the twenty-first century than it was in the early and mid-twentieth century, and this is due in part to the intellectual work of feminism that initiated a revaluation of the modernist canon. This chapter chronicles the work of recovery and rediscovery of female modernism carried out by feminist critics beginning in the 1970s but reaching a peak in the 1980s and 1990s; today, it remains an ongoing if less prevalent project.

Initially, critics focused their attention on individual writers, or groups of women, who had slipped from view or never had the audience they might have due to the period's rampant sexism. This type of work is often framed through the lens of biography (and autobiography, where available), with some authors (Woolf, H. D.) receiving earlier attention than others (Jessie Fauset, Amy Lowell, Hope Mirrlees). This strand of criticism aimed to expand the canon of modernism through an assertion of female difference. Briefly, critics argued that women's writing is fundamentally different from that of men. This difference was the reason women writers were discredited or left out of the modernist canon. In part, this line of thought was indebted to *écriture feminine*, a French feminist theory that posited language as embodied and thus necessarily rooted in biological sex. It was also indebted to modernist women writers themselves; consider *A Room of One's Own*, in which Woolf posits a woman's sentence and sequence before urging her readers to cultivate an androgynous mind. Female difference, whether grounded in theory or literary texts, was invoked as an explanation for women's exclusion from the canon and as a reason that the recovery project had intellectual and emotional merit. As Alicia Ostriker, riffing on another part of Woolf's *Room* in 1986, observed, "it is difficult to discover who our mothers are, much less think through them, thanks to a long history of criticism [...] that veils them from us" (478). Ostriker goes on to posit H. D. and Marianne Moore as "key ancestresses for the woman poet and the woman critic writing today" (479); this kind of argument continues to inform the recovery project, although it is often implied rather than explicitly asserted.

Another strand of criticism that takes up female difference departs from a literary or cultural quality associated with femininity if not women specifically. Critics take up the sentimental, the middlebrow, and even modernity itself to argue that modernism's most disparaged others ("poetry for ladies," progressive politics, consumer culture, and the middlebrow, among others) are actually central to an understanding of modernism. Like scholarship that departs from single or groups of modernist women, this second strand of recovery work introduces readers to writers they may have never read, but it does so in order to focus on a quality or idea associated with femininity. In this type of work, critics reframe how modernism *itself* should be understood, as at once more varied and complicated than a narrow masculine modernism had seemed. In a final twist, such scholarship begins to discover male writers who never made it into the modernist canon. This turn of events suggests that a move away from the sexed body of the writer to the gendered quality of literary work and culture expands critical modernist studies in a move that is an extension of feminist approaches even while it may not promote women writers.

In brief, then, the history of modernist studies reflects many of the intellectual moves that were characteristic of feminist scholarship, and women's studies, across the disciplines. If the top layer of the palimpsest that is modernism was initially inscribed with work by and about Joyce, Eliot, Pound, Faulkner, Hemingway, and other male modernists, the first layer feminist critics uncovered was the extensive body of modernist literature produced by women. These critics discovered that female writers were working in the territory modernist men thought they owned; this work had been forgotten because, for example, Zora Neale Hurston's approach to anthropology looked radically different than Pound's. Over time, as scholars worked on women, they began to uncover another layer of the palimpsest: the impact of gender, and specifically femininity, on women's lives and literature but also on the culture writ large. Some cultural practices, like domesticity, or registers, like popular or middlebrow writing, had been gendered feminine. As we tunnel beneath the top layers of the palimpsest, then, this chapter traces a shift from a focus on women to a focus on femininity. To a certain degree, this process operated in a linear fashion, but it's important to remember that work on the top layers remained and remains ongoing. As critics discovered H. D., others were still writing about male modernists; as scholars started to focus on the middlebrow, recovery of individual female authors was ongoing.

Regardless of whether they were uncovering the role of women or femininity in modernism, one challenge has dogged critics: the difficulty of keeping authors and ideas in the limelight. Many a scholar has discovered that the author she labored to get into the canon remains at the periphery or has fallen out of it. Miss Julia Hedge's desire for more women's names has thus been partially satisfied—Woolf and H. D. have room in our contemporary canon—but the only provisional success of other recovery projects remains alarming to many. Today, as the field has moved away from the idea that women write in a certain way, critics worry that the attention of the field has moved elsewhere, leaving the New Modernist Studies with an expanded—but still exclusionary—canon.

Finding modernist women

What a hopeless thing a man's consciousness was. How awful to have nothing but a man's consciousness.

—DOROTHY RICHARDSON, *The Tunnel*

There had always been a select number of critics who worked to draw attention to specific female modernists. A particularly early example is Ruth Gruber's doctoral thesis, *Virginia Woolf: A Study*, which was published by Tauchnitz Press in 1935. Gruber argued that "Virginia Woolf is determined to write as a woman. Through the eyes of her sex, she seeks to penetrate life and describe it. Her will to explore her femininity is bitterly opposed by the critics, who guard the traditions of men, who dictate to her or denounce her feminine reactions to art and life" (36). Gruber's argumentative moves, specifically her claim that Woolf "writes as a woman" and is opposed by a male critical establishment, would be repeated many decades later. Her uniquely early production of a feminist modernist study was enabled by her unusual position as a young American woman pursuing a doctorate at Cologne University, where a professor encouraged Gruber to write on Woolf because she was the only student whose English was up to the task (13). As Gruber herself explained when her dissertation was published in 2005, "after [Woolf's] suicide in 1941, with no new books or essays appearing, she receded in the minds" of readers and critics (9). It would take a political reawakening to focus attention back on Woolf and her female contemporaries.

The second-wave feminist movement of the 1960s, 1970s, and 1980s brought with it a renewed interest in, and attention to, work by women writers. Interestingly, some of the initial recovery work was not, however, feminist—scholars published studies on women writers but did not consider institutional sexism in their work. For example, in 1969, the journal *Contemporary Literature* devoted a whole issue (10.4) to a "reconsideration" of the poet H. D. Most of the essays were by male critics and none read the poet through a feminist lens. This volume, however, played an important role in inspiring an impassioned feminist response. In her powerful 1975 essay "Who Buried H. D.? A Poet, Her Critics, and Her Place in the Literary Tradition," Susan Stanford Friedman observed that "it was the hope of L. S. Dembo, *Contemporary Literature*'s editor, [...] that this special issue would spark renewed interest in her work. It did not" (804). Friedman attributes this critical silence to the first two articles in the 1969 issue, which examine the poet's relationship to Freud and treat H. D. as if she had a case of "penis envy" (804). After an extended denunciation of this approach, Friedman professed herself "far more concerned with the general issue of what impact the male-oriented criticism of modern scholarship has had on the literary reputations of women writers like H. D." (806). Using the rest of her essay to assess H. D.'s woman-centered view of the mythic tradition as well as sexual relationships, Friedman worked to establish a foundation for future criticism that would examine H. D. specifically, and female modernists generally, within the terms of her own artistic project and not through the lens of masculinist theories and assumptions (such as Freud's). Closing with the observation that "once excluded students are sitting in university classrooms" (813) and that area studies such as women's, Afro-American, and Chicano studies were prying open previously closed curricula, Friedman called for the integration of writers like H. D. into existing courses instead of teaching them in "separate niches" (814).

Friedman's essay is noteworthy not only for its early date but also for the argumentative moves that are paralleled by many other critics. She establishes how H. D.'s writing differs from that of canonical male modernists (H. D. "was a woman, she wrote about women, and all the ever-questing, artistic, intellectual heroes of her epic poetry and novels were women" [803]); she demonstrates previous instances of misreading based in conscious or unconscious misogyny; and she offers new interpretations that highlight the power of the poet's work in its own right as well as what said work brings to new readers. Friedman, who later published two monographs and one edited collection about H. D., thus demonstrates both the minefields confronting a generation of feminist critics (who might themselves be accused of "penis envy") and the opportunities to bring scores of writers to the attention of students and scholars. There is a heady quality to her prose that speaks to the urgency of early recovery work.

There is a great deal of recovery work like Friedman's essay (and later books) that aims to reintroduce a new generation of students and scholars to a single female author. Such work was partly facilitated, as the conclusion of "Who Buried H. D.?" indicates, by the increasing institutional leverage of feminist work as women's studies programs were founded in colleges and universities around the world. Whether these publications took the form of articles, book-length studies, essay collections, or new editions or collections of the authors' work, such efforts aimed to find writers who had fallen out of the canon and to position them as central to an understanding of both women's literature *and* modernism. Such scholarship is too extensive to survey in detail here, but noteworthy early examples include Jane Marcus's work on Virginia Woolf and on Rebecca West, Marianne DeKoven on Gertrude Stein, Virginia Kouidis on Mina Loy, Lillian Schlissel on Mae West, and Helen Nebeker on Jean Rhys. In addition, new biographies of women writers—some feminist and some not—provided information about lives that had faded from critical memory.[1] As we saw with the example of H. D., even criticism or biography that slighted a female writer or her work could have the productive result of inspiring a passionate defense. The 1960s, 1970s, and 1980s were decades in which the female modernist became a valid subject of academic study, even if some of those studies were dismissive of the person or work.

In addition to publications that sought to recover individual writers, the late 1970s, 1980s, and early 1990s would witness the publication of several tomes that aimed to recover a female modernist tradition. Sometimes, modernist women were addressed within the longer time frame of the literary tradition. Elaine Showalter's 1977 book, *A Literature of Their Own*, for example, placed writers like Woolf, Katherine Mansfield, and Dorothy Richardson within a lineage that is apparent in her subtitle: *British Women Novelists from Brontë to Lessing*. Showalter's aim was to advance the concept of a female literary tradition—specifically, a tradition of female fiction—that unfolded in three stages that she termed feminine, feminist, and female (13). Importantly, Showalter asserted the critical importance of including both so-called major and minor writers; "it is only by considering them all—Millicent Grogan as well as Virginia Woolf—that we can begin to record new choices in a new literary history, and to understand why, despite prejudice, despite guilt, despite inhibition, women began to write" (36). Grogan was a nineteenth-century author who wrote under a pseudonym, but Showalter's attention to Mansfield and Richardson *as well as* Woolf serves the same purpose of range when it came to chapters on modernism. A second significant aspect of her study is the critic's insistence on culture and history as constructing a female literary history:

> The theory of a female sensibility revealing itself in an imagery and form specific to women always runs dangerously close to reiterating the familiar stereotypes. It also suggests permanence, a deep, basic, and inevitable difference between male and female ways of perceiving the world. I think that, instead, the female literary tradition comes from the still-evolving relationships between women writers and their society. (12)

Showalter here encourages her readers not to base their arguments and assumptions on essentialism—the view that women are alike because they share one kind of sexed body—but on the claim that women experienced similar kinds of opportunities and limitations. In the case of female modernists, the opportunity was to create "a deliberate female aesthetic, which transformed the feminine code of self-sacrifice into an annihilation of the narrative self, and applied the cultural analysis of the feminists to words, sentences, and structures of language in the novel" (33). Finding a shared style as the outcome of parallel life experiences and their place in the tradition, Showalter offered an early example of how to recover neglected women and to link them without resorting to "the familiar stereotypes" or biology.

Similarly, Rachel Blau DuPlessis's *Writing beyond the Ending: Narrative Strategies of Twentieth-Century Women Writers* (1985) explores a slightly narrower historical period (roughly 1880s–1970) to argue that women writers "examine how social practices surrounding gender have entered narrative" and then "use narrative to make critical statements about the psychosexual and sociocultural construction of women" (4). Departing from the conventions of nineteenth-century fiction, which channeled women's *Bildung* into plots that ended in marriage or death, DuPlessis's archive ranges from Olive Schreiner to Muriel Rukeyser, Doris Lessing, and Adrienne Rich. Like Showalter, DuPlessis was careful to cast her attention to feminine difference as nonexclusive and nonessentialist: "even debased, ironized, and fetishistic couple-based romance remains at the center and is the privileged resolution of more significant narratives by men than by women. The point does not have to be exclusive to be studied: For reasons that can be linked to their gender position, women writers formulate a critique of heterosexual romance" (xi). Although a later generation of critics would insist that a "gender position" cannot be viewed as stable or unified, feminist literary studies in the 1980s was already quite careful when it positioned "women" as the object of inquiry.

As feminist work on women's literature came into its own, studies of narrower periods, and of modernism, began to illustrate the richness of a literature that had slipped from view in the middle of the twentieth century. One of the most notable, and still influential, examples of such scholarship is Shari Benstock's *Women of the Left Bank, Paris, 1900–1940* (1986). Weighing in at 518 pages, *Women* focuses on a group of writers who "discovered themselves as *women* and *writers* in Paris" (ix) and emphasizes the "primary significance [of] the experience of being a *woman* in this time and place" (3). Although Benstock was informed by deconstruction, which unsettled strict binaries like men and women, and her work is passingly attentive to "the difference *within* gender" (8), her argument is that "modernist writing by women is significantly unlike that of men" (32). In other words, Benstock's work insists on differences between the literature produced by men and women, and she posits a "common center of feminine consciousness" even as she acknowledges that individual women's backgrounds and experiences varied widely (89). Ranging across figures such as Edith Wharton, Natalie Barney, Colette, Gertrude Stein, H. D., and Bryher, Benstock establishes the biographical details of each woman's life in Paris, the other women artists with whom she had contact, and the kind of writing each produced. A 1996 documentary film grounded in Benstock's research, *Paris Was a Woman*, underlines the biographical impetus of *Women of the Left Bank* as well as the original's emphasis on "the radical *difference* of women's experience" from that of men (28).

While some of Benstock's primary case studies, including Wharton and Stein, had never been entirely absent from the modernist canon, her study importantly worked to recover neglected women writers and publishers without whom modernist work would not have been available to readers. Janet Flanner, for example, the author of one novel but best known as the Paris correspondent for *The New Yorker* magazine from 1925 to 1975, is the focus of an entire chapter in which Benstock unpacks the significance of Flanner's weekly "Letter from Paris." Tracing the arc of Flanner's career—she first wrote about art, fashion, and society, and only later devoted her "Letter" to politics—Benstock positions the Paris Letters as a "narrative chronicle through which an analysis of a woman's place in literary Paris can be focused" (101). In Benstock's terms, then, what matters about Flanner's work is that it provides an entrée to "the radical *difference* of women's experience" mentioned earlier. A subsequent chapter on the publishers Adrienne Monnier and Sylvia Beach, partners in life and work who brought out the first edition of James Joyce's *Ulysses* among other major titles, covers their business models, histories, relationship, and lovers, and extensively treats their relationship with Joyce. Here, Benstock is primarily interested in Beach's poor treatment by Joyce, although the critic notes that Beach was reluctant to criticize the author. As with the chapter on Flanner, *Women of the Left Bank* works to show what women accomplished in Paris and additionally provides insight into the ways in which canonical male modernists depended on efforts by women.[2] Where Friedman's essay "unburied" a single figure by arguing that male critics had misunderstood the author's corpus and then offered readings of her own, Benstock's sweeping study offered a panorama of writers who had spent time in Paris, a city that "offered a place to write, releasing [women] from the patriarchal cultural script of marriage and motherhood" (447–8).

A final highly influential aspect of Benstock's study is her attention to the "female-centered worlds" constructed by women who were evading those patriarchal scripts (448) and specifically to lesbian relationships and communities in Paris. In short, Benstock not only recovered a range of writers and publishers but also made the argument that lesbian sexual partnerships were *better* for women who sought to chart their own paths in Paris. As she writes in her conclusion,

> The individual circumstances of heterosexual women tended to confirm the normative pattern by which the interests of men took precedence over those of women. By choosing alternative erotic existences, homosexual women found it somewhat easier to redefine the emotional and psychological dynamics of their relationships with each other, often moving away from the standard of heterosexual behavior in which one partner assumed authority and control over the other. (451)

Part of what one sees in an emphasis on recovery work premised on feminine difference, then, is attention to sexual arrangements on which critics had generally been silent and an interest in discovering what a specifically *lesbian* difference might be. Although Benstock would focus her attention on the biographical differences between heterosexual and homosexual writers, and while she would argue that the latter experienced a personal and creative freedom the former did not, she did not trace this difference into the literary work.

As scholars continued to explore and reassemble a tradition of modernist women's writing, however, they increasingly identified not only differences between men's and women's *lives* but between the *work* they produced. Some critics generated what we might think of as macro accounts of modernism as a battle of the sexes. Sandra M. Gilbert and Susan Gubar's *No Man's Land* is a prime example. *No Man's Land* is a follow-up to Gilbert and Gubar's wildly influential *The Madwoman in the Attic: The Woman Writer and the Nineteenth-Century Literary Imagination*, which had been published in 1979. Like Benstock's *Women*, Gilbert and Gubar's study was expansive: *No Man's Land* was published in three volumes in 1988, 1989, and 1996. Although *No Man's Land* was not explicitly a recovery project, it included many lesser-known women authors in its analysis, such as Ellen Glasgow, Renée Vivien, Olive Schreiner, Kate Chopin, Marci Nardi, Sarah Orne Jewett, and Dorothy Richardson. Together with (by then) better-known writers including Woolf, Stein, Wharton, and Willa Cather, Gilbert and Gubar assembled what they called a "metastory" about "the place of the woman writer in the twentieth century," the subtitle of their series. As the Preface to the first volume explains,

> Once we reimagine the author as a gendered human being whose text reflects key cultural conditions, we can conflate and collate individual literary narratives, so that they constitute one possible metastory, a story of stories about gender strife in this period. In our view, the history of sexual battle that we shall relate here is one of the major tales that begins to emerge from the apparent chaos of history, and it is a tale told differently over time and formulated differently by men and women. (1: xiv)

Like Benstock, Gilbert and Gubar focus on the differences between women and men as they trace the evolution of a sexual conflict rooted in a "crisis of male dispossession and female self-possession" (1: 34). In common with other work premised upon sexual difference, their study examines the backlash against the increasing volume of fiction, poetry, and plays produced by women in the twentieth century, with the third chapter of their first volume hypothesizing "a reaction-formation against the rise of literary women [that] became not just a theme in modernist writing but a motive for modernism" (156). Their sweeping study positions modernism as a *product* of tensions between male and female writers who negotiated the First World War, the literary tradition, and conventional sex roles from opposing positions.

Gilbert and Gubar's work is rooted in biography but also in close reading of a variety of texts by women. They respond to a range of theorists, bookended by Sigmund Freud and Hélène Cixous, and examine the idea of an "anatomically determined body language" that results in different use of language by men and women (227–8). While they (like Showalter and DuPlessis) are cautious in their argument and stop short of endorsing a biological root to female difference, they advance the idea of a cultural difference—a difference of education, experience, and treatment—as the basis for their recovery work and a motive for their argument. Thus, for example, they suggest that the "woman's sentence" Woolf posits in *A Room of One's Own* was a *"fantasy* about a utopian linguistic structure"; this phrase served "to define (and perhaps disguise) her desire to revise not women's language but women's relation to language" (230). The kind of universalism this sentence rests upon (there is *a* women's relation to language, albeit one that is culturally and not biologically determined) reaches its apogee in their argument that there is a specific and identifiably collaborative lesbian aesthetic. According to Gilbert and Gubar, lesbian writers felt "estranged not only from the art produced by [...] men but also from a female literary tradition that could be just as biased against the female homosexual" (222). In a chapter that traverses by-then canonical (Stein) and less well-known (Richardson) authors, the two critics can be surprisingly dismissive of their subjects. Stein's work, for example, is judged "virtually unreadable and (for many years) unpublishable" (250). Despite such reservations, they find behind *The Autobiography of Alice B. Toklas* and other lesbian-authored texts a group of writers who "wrote for and as Sappho, their fantasy precursor, or for and as a lover" (256). This study, and others like it, demonstrates that an emphasis on female difference could move into ever more finely grained arguments that *particular* women adopted shared aesthetic strategies, making them different from not just men but also from their female contemporaries. Later work by Martha Vicinus (*Intimate Friends: Women Who Loved Women, 1778–1928* [2004]) and others would shift critical focus while maintaining the emphasis on lesbian community established in *No Man's Land*.

Gilbert and Gubar's study was not explicitly a recovery project; instead, it sought to supply an ur-narrative about twentieth-century literature by major and minor female writers. Other feminist critics worked to bring neglected writers' careers to public attention so that they could be considered in the new stories being told about literary history. Gloria T. Hull's *Color, Sex, & Poetry: Three Women Writers of the Harlem Renaissance* (1987) provides a terrific example. The position of the Harlem Renaissance vis-à-vis modernism had been unclear for much of the twentieth century, with some critics treating the two as overlapping projects while others viewed the movements as strictly separate. Addressing the relationship between the Renaissance and modernism was not, however, Hull's specific aim. "The absence of critical studies on black women artists is real," she laments, even as Hull notes that Zora Neale Hurston was beginning to enjoy "widespread interest" (4). Her book highlights Alice Dunbar-Nelson, Angelina Weld Grimké, and Georgia Douglas Johnson, three writers who had not to that date been the subjects of significant biographies or works of literary criticism (16). Hull's introduction clearly states why she felt that these authors, as well as other women of the Renaissance, had been excluded from the critical narrative: "male attitudes toward women impinged upon them" (7), pushing women writers out of the spotlight. Moreover, Hull characterized the Renaissance, "despite its veneer of equal opportunity," as "a time when not only Harlem and the Negro, but men as usual were 'in vogue'" (10). Hull closed by expressing hope for a "brand-new day" (216) for African-American women writers contemporary with her book as well as for the artistic legacies of her three case studies.

Shortly after *Color, Sex, & Poetry* arrived on bookstore shelves, Bonnie Kime Scott's critical anthology *The Gender of Modernism* (1990) was published. It is impossible to overstate the impact of this collection on the field of modernist studies: Scott's book offered readers a relatively compact introduction to twenty-six writers both increasingly famous (Woolf, H. D., Stein) and still obscure (Jessie Redmon Fauset, Charlotte Mew, May Sinclair, Antonia White, Anna Wickham), including Harlem Renaissance writers. Dedicated to the "the forgotten and silenced makers of modernism," the anthology included selections from featured writers (poems, plays, fiction, letters, journalism, essays, etc.) as well as introductions by critics to each writer's life and work. Unlike Benstock or Gilbert and Gubar, Scott's aim was not to make a specific argument about modernism or twentieth-century women writers, although Jane Marcus would notably use her introductions to two writers to challenge the "sex war" thesis of *No Man's Land* (535, 601). Generally, *The Gender of Modernism* instead offers readers a handy point of entry. It was and remains a text that many scholars study at the undergraduate or graduate level, and readers often come away from Scott's book with the desire to find their own female writer deserving of recovery.

The loose claim of the anthology is that "modernism was inflected, in ways we can only now begin to appreciate, by gender" (3). Scott's title—and claims like this one—is grounded in "gender" and not "women"; her collection includes chapters devoted to five men (Eliot, Joyce, D. H. Lawrence, Hugh MacDiarmid, and Pound) and the book's famous "Tangled Mesh of Modernists" (Figure 1)

A Tangled Mesh of Modernists

FIGURE 1 *From Bonnie Kime Scott,* The Gender of Modernism. *Courtesy of Indiana University Press. This illustration highlights the connections between male and female writers, among them the women anthologized in Scott's collection.*

includes men and women in its illustration of the personal and professional connections among writers. Scott writes that this strategy of inclusion of "male figures intricately involved in writing with women or on gender" enables the collection to "resist both determinism by sex and reversed neglect" (7). Scott's fears about "reversed neglect" seem groundless—of the male writers included in the collection, only MacDiarmid can be considered to approach that state—but the selections by writers of both sexes illustrate the ways in which ambivalence, fear, and anger characterize much modernist writing about the opposite sex.

Although Scott defines gender as only one of "many layers of identification" (3), and the anthology deliberately includes writing by African-American women, the point of her book is to establish "that the presence of women in modernism has been vastly underestimated. And the process of writing women into modernism must go on from here" (7). As Jane Garrity observed in a review of Scott's next anthology, *Gender in Modernism* (2007), the "conceptual limits" of *The Gender of Modernism* were many: "privileging gender at the expense of other categories of identity, such as race, ethnicity, class, nation, and sexuality; focusing primarily on white women and exclusively on white men" (803). And Lisa Rado's criticism of a particular strand of feminist criticism—"the tendency among some scholars to overidealize the women authors whom they study" (11)—has been directed at *The Gender of Modernism* by readers. Most introductions to women featured in the anthology tout the politically progressive nature of the writer's work, suggesting that writers particularly deserve recovery if they happen to hold views similar to those of critics working in the 1980s and 1990s. Despite its limits, however, Scott's work represents a moment when passionate scholarly interest in women writers produced some of the most exciting modernist scholarship. The way forward was seemingly to continue the recovery project without fetishizing female difference or insisting upon the political and social perfection of individual authors.

Over the next two decades, critics sought to meet these goals while bringing additional female writers to light. Work like Benstock's, Gilbert and Gubar's, and Scott's remained a touchstone for a new generation of critics; see, for example, Melissa Bradshaw's introduction to *Selected Poems of Amy Lowell*, which refers to a history of recovery work while bringing a new writer to the fore:

> Up until three decades ago few women held a secure place in the literary canon—now canonical female writers like Elizabeth Barrett Browning, Kate Chopin, H. D., and Virginia Woolf are read today only because of vigorous recovery efforts by feminist critics on their behalf. That the difficult and enigmatic Lowell— an imperious, politically conservative, physically imposing lesbian—has not yet made her way back into the spotlight should not surprise us. Thirty years ago we might not have known what to do with Amy Lowell. But today we are ready for her. (xxiv)

Bradshaw's comments nicely illustrate the ways in which recovery work gained momentum over time—recovering Chopin, H. D., and Woolf creates an audience Lowell and others. Her scholarship on Lowell also demonstrates that critics no longer feel the need to idealize their subjects. Bradshaw could write, here and elsewhere, about a neglected poet while acknowledging that her politics were no longer fashionable and without redressing Lowell's absence from the canon strictly in terms of her biological sex, gender identity, or sexual preference. As Bradshaw argues in *Amy Lowell, American Modern* (2004), Lowell's absence from the canon stems from many intertwined reasons: misogyny but also her "endless experiments, with a refusal to repeat herself" (xvii); homophobia but also fat shaming (xxiii); and even the loss of Lowell's performances as a reader. "Perhaps because of her charisma many of her detractors, and even some admirers, found her poetry deflated and faded after she was no longer around to read it" (xvi). This type of nuanced account of a woman writer's work and treatment illustrates the continued need for, and relevance of, the recovery project and also how said project could be advanced without claims of female difference.

Case study: May Sinclair (1863–1946)

May Sinclair provides a good example of the types of authors brought back through feminist recovery work even as she illuminates the unfinished nature of that project. Sinclair was a prolific and popular British writer of novels, poetry, and short stories. She was active in the suffrage movement, read psychoanalytic literature, and both practiced and defended modernism's experimental style. She is perhaps best known to modernist scholars today for her description of Dorothy Richardson's *Pilgrimage* as taking the form of "stream of consciousness" in an essay anthologized in *The Gender of Modernism*. Her 1914 *The Three Sisters* is an overtly feminist novel with dark wit, psychological acuity, and formal interest, while her 1919 novel, *Mary Olivier: A Life*, was first serialized in *The Little Review* in the same edition as *Ulysses*. *Mary Olivier* is like *A Portrait of the Artist as a Young Man* but written from a feminist stance; the novel is full of psychological interiority and employs a formally innovative second- and first-person interior narrative. Sinclair knew and had relationships with many of the authors we study or think about in connection to modernism, including H. D., Katherine Mansfield, Dorothy Richardson, Virginia Woolf, Arnold Bennett, and H. G. Wells. From about 1910 to 1920, Sinclair was considered *the* foremost British woman novelist, a mantle that was taken up by Woolf in the subsequent decade.

And yet, for decades Sinclair's books were out of print or only available in hardcovers. That fate began to change in 1973, when a biography and annotated bibliography of Sinclair's work were both published, and in the early 1980s, Virago reprinted three of Sinclair's novels in paperback, including *Mary Olivier* and *The Three Sisters* (Gillespie 436). In 1995, Bonnie Kime Scott asserted that "May Sinclair deserves to be much better known as a maker and connector of modernism" (*Refiguring* 58), and she included Sinclair in her 1990 *The Gender of Modernism*, with an insightful introduction by Diane Gillespie outlining the author's many contributions to the modernist canon and criticism. The field seemed ready for renewed attention to Sinclair's work. In fact, on the back jacket of the 2002 *New York Review of Books* reprint of *Mary Olivier*, the distinguished critic and biographer Hermione Lee declared, in *Gone with the Wind* fashion, "No one will be able to ignore May Sinclair again."

Sadly, a quick check of the MLA Bibliography indicates that Lee's enthusiasm was premature, if not misguided. From January 2003 to December 2017, there were 2,772 articles, chapters, or books published about Virginia Woolf and her literary corpus. This is eclipsed by the 3,414 articles, chapters, or books published in that period on James Joyce's works. During this same time, a mere fifty-five essays or books were written about May Sinclair, with thirteen of these included in *May Sinclair: Moving towards the Modern* (2006, edited by Andrew J. Kunka and Michele K. Troy) and eleven in the collection *May Sinclair: Re-thinking Bodies and Minds* (2017, edited by Rebecca Bowler and Claire Drewery). These new publications are noteworthy and exciting, as Sinclair studies appears to be gaining momentum. At the same time, the numbers speak for themselves: the major writers have remained major and most minor writers have remained minor in the New Modernist Studies.

Much of the early work on Sinclair did not put her squarely into the context of modernism, and when she is compared to other modernist writers, the juxtaposition is often historically framed through concerns that many writers of the time shared. Thus, you'll find Sinclair in work on spiritualism, on the Great War, on suffrage, and on mourning. Suzanne Raitt's literary biography of Sinclair (2000) is subtitled "A Modern Victorian," thus expressing one of the aspects of Sinclair's work that continues to marginalize her as the subject of modernist critique. As Kunka and Troy write in their collection's introduction, "Literary history has generally found her not-quite-modernist-enough for a place on the other side of the pearly gates with the likes of Ezra Pound, T. S. Eliot, Ford Madox Ford, and Virginia Woolf, although the case can be made that her contributions to the formation and dissemination of literary modernism rank with theirs" (2). Kunka and Troy suggest that Sinclair's "not-quite-modernist-enough" status may stem from her early work's popularity, the fact that she was from an earlier generation, or some critics' accusation that she mimicked the styles of Richardson and others. *May Sinclair: Moving towards the Modern*, they write, proposes that the author deserves renewed attention because "she eluded easy categorization" (3), and they are further interested in arguing that Sinclair paved the way for the writers who would make up a modernist canon that excluded her. While they present Sinclair as important to modernism because she championed the next generation of writers, she is, in their words, "a transitional writer" who moves *toward* the modern but never seems to have fully arrived (5).

More recently, writers have (re)claimed Sinclair directly for modernism. In *Modernism, Feminism, and the Culture of Boredom* (2012), for example, Allison Pease writes about female authors and their representation of boredom as a female complaint, including the work of Sinclair. Influenced by Lauren Berlant's 2008 book, *The Female Complaint*, which created a rich vocabulary for talking about affect as it creates and frays noninstitutionalized or minor publics of women, Pease compares the bored women in Sinclair's novels to those constructed by her male contemporaries (Wells and Bennett) to argue that her fiction diagnoses the "morbid inactivity" (61) women are forced to endure, which is only leavened by "moments of ecstatic vision" (72). Pease thus reads Sinclair's fiction as participating in modernism through her feminist and psychological investment in her female contemporaries' struggles to live meaningful lives *and* in her use of the psychological experience of boredom as impetus for her experimental style, which works to capture her characters' boredom. Pease's book, and the recent *May Sinclair: Re-thinking Bodies and Minds*, suggests that recovery work that aims to reshape the modernist canon is an ongoing process; scholars must continue to seek ways to challenge the standards that persistently devalue minor women writers, even as we acknowledge that there is no essential category called woman.

Finding femininity

While many critics in the 1970s, 1980s, and 1990s took their point of departure from individual female authors or selected groups of women, the next scholarly development organized itself around studies of literary and aesthetic qualities aligned with femininity. This type of scholarship often ended up recovering previously neglected figures, but it did so in the name of excavating culturally devalued categories like the sentimental, the melodramatic, the maternal, and the middlebrow. Scholars explicitly or implicitly argue that these conceptual markers have been denigrated—and written out of modernist studies—precisely because they were regarded as feminine. Their projects aim to alter how readers understand early twentieth-century literature while almost incidentally putting additional women (and even a few male) writers on the academic radar. This line of inquiry has many related strands but culminates in attention to popular and middlebrow literatures as well as to the gender not of writers but of modernity itself.

A good example of this approach is Suzanne Clark's *Sentimental Modernism: Women Writers and the Revolution of the Word* (1991). Clark argues that canonical modernism was consolidated as a response to "the increasing influence of women's writing"; scholars and critics achieved a narrow, largely male, canon by "discrediting the literary past and especially [...] sentimental history" (1). Quoting Cleanth Brooks, the influential New Critic, who advocated separating poetry (and canonical work generally) from "laundry lists and advertisements for face lotion" (10), Clark establishes the revulsion of writers and critics against the sentimental and claims that modernist literary history is skewed because it writes the quality out of the category of modernism. Recovering the sentimental, Clark asserts, can help to "make women's powerful role in modernism more visible" (13).

Clark's examples include literary women such as Edna St. Vincent Millay, long popular with readers but derided by critics, but also activists such as the anarchist Emma Goldman. Goldman often referred to literary works in her public speeches, and Clark reminds readers that Goldman was a "familiar figure among modernists" at the pre–First World War moment when radical politics and art were associated. Goldman "advocated a literature which would promote a progressive social philosophy" (51) and infused her work as a speaker, writer, and publisher with maternal and sentimental language. That she was written out of modernist literary history demonstrates not only the distaste with which her style was regarded but also "the legacy of resistance which artists and writers have represented" (58). By recovering the sentimental, a feminized category, Clark also recovered the relationship between anarchism and modernism as well as an individual woman.

Millay, in contrast, features in Clark's study as a poet working in a female literary tradition and "writing in a way that is easily understood, that invites the reader in, that makes community with the reader and tries to heal alienation" (69). Where canonical poets assume "an estrangement between the poem and the reader— difference, not familiarity" (71), Millay's verse instead communicates an unironic vision of passion and romantic love. The *pleasures* of her poetry made it suspect for a generation of academic readers who scoffed at Millay's stock in trade: the heart, the exclamations, the modesty, the relative paucity of allusion. *Sentimental Modernism* demonstrates that a popular poet trafficking in the sentimental could help highlight the different types of relationships writers forged with readers and how modernism might be understood more accurately if the field addressed "the difference that gender makes in literature" (96). The sentimental, in other words, brought back into view female authors who responded to modernity with later-devalued, but recovery-worthy, aesthetic strategies.

Projects parallel to Clark's abound.[3] In *Shadowed Dreams: Women's Poetry of the Harlem Renaissance* (1989), the first anthology "devoted exclusively to women poets of the Harlem Renaissance" (1), editor Maureen Honey used her introduction to squarely address the reason that the writers in her anthology had been so widely ignored. "Later critics [...] have tended to see women's verse as conventional and sentimental" (1), Honey writes, and the poets were regarded as "imitating European traditions and contributing little that was useful to the creation of a Black Aesthetic" (2). While she acknowledges the "seemingly anachronistic style and subject matter" of the writers in the collection, Honey situates the poets' conventional choices within a culture in which literary achievement helped to counter racist assumptions about the intellectual capacities of African-Americans (6–7). The collection thus serves as a compelling marker of the kind of work (and writers) left out when recovery efforts operated within the parameters of experimental modernism. Notably, when Honey (with coeditor Venetria K. Patton) later edited the anthology *Double-Take: A Revisionist Harlem Renaissance Anthology* (2001), which included many of the same writers anthologized in *Shadowed Dreams*, the introduction focused on the collection's "gender-balanced view of this remarkable literary awakening" (xxxix) and not on the style of the writers included. This strategy suggests that it remains easier to make the case for recovering women writers than for rethinking major modernist movements in terms of feminine qualities such as the conventional and sentimental.

Like *Shadowed Dreams*, critic Celeste Schenck unpacked what she called a "binary opposition between male Modernists and female poetesses" (227–228) to argue for the critical importance of addressing "the more traditional meters of Anna Wickham, Charlotte Mew, Sylvia Townsend Warner, Alice Meynell," and others (229). Many of Schenck's examples would be anthologized in Scott's *The Gender of Modernism* the following year, and it is instructive to contrast that project with Schenck's essay. While Scott's collection worked to recover female writers under the banner of a capacious modernism, Schenck faults feminist critics for privileging "those female poets who broke form with the boys" (230) and alleges a "feminist adherence to a politically suspect hierarchy of genre" (231). In other words, where Scott went looking for under-recognized women writers, Schenck argues that poetry—and specifically conventional twentieth-century verse—itself needs recovery, a labor that would incidentally highlight the work of many women. As these examples illustrate, efforts to recover women and to recover forms and styles that were gendered feminine often worked on similar ground—on the same writers. And yet, it took longer for the second approach to reshape the category of modernism proper because it was seemingly harder to rethink what modernism *is* than to include more women writers in the canon.

While Honey and Schenck dismantled a critical tradition that had diminished female poets who wrote in traditional forms, an increasing number of scholars similarly worked on fiction and reclaimed the category of the middlebrow. Although definitions of this term vary slightly, most scholars understand it as literature that was conventional as opposed to stylistically experimental, popular as opposed to critically acclaimed, and working within, as opposed to against, the literary tradition. As Nicola Humble writes in *The Feminine Middlebrow Novel, 1920s to 1950s: Class, Domesticity, and Bohemianism* (2001), the category "straddles the divide between the trashy romance or thriller on the one hand, and the philosophically or formally challenging novel on the other: offering narrative excitement without guilt, and intellectual stimulation without undue effort" (11). This register of literary work received little treatment until the turn of the twenty-first century; although Janice Radway's *Reading the Romance* (1984) and *A Feeling for Books* (1999) had demonstrated that the romance novel and Book-of-the-Month Club were deserving of scholarly attention, and although Nicola Beauman's *A Very Great Profession: The Woman's Novel 1914–39* (1983) and Alison Light's *Forever England: Femininity, Literature and Conservatism between the Wars* (1991) had focused on interwar fiction by women, their subjects were seemingly far removed from modernist studies. Beauman's introduction recalled an interview with a former supervisor at Cambridge ("the author of a classic work on Virginia Woolf") who was "almost too appalled to speak" about her former student's project (4). This anecdote indicates that even female scholars of modernist women like Woolf were not initially supportive of academic work on the middlebrow (4). And as Light writes, "a legacy of 'modernism' (and its domination of university English)" has been that "it turns the gaze elsewhere," away from the home and private sphere that is the focus of so much middlebrow women's writing (6). These examples indicate that Light and Beauman saw themselves as working in the trenches of middlebrow women's literature; however, they position their projects as *outside of* modernist studies albeit contemporaneous with it.

Humble's 2001 study, unlike the first generation of scholarship on the middlebrow, squarely addressed the relationship between modernism and the middlebrow, arguing that "our understanding of modernism is so limited" because most writing by women was considered middlebrow (15). Humble noted that the divisions between the two categories had already started to erode even as modernism and middlebrow continued to be framed as a binary:

> Any attempt to define the middlebrow novel in this period must inevitably run up against the monolith of modernism. In one sense middlebrow fiction is the "other" of the modernist or avant-garde novel, the bugbear continually reviled by highbrow critics and literary experimenters as corrupting public taste and devaluing the status of the novel. Yet the feminist middlebrow also provides the brimming bowl into which recent revisers of the modernist canon have dipped for new plums. (24)

Humble's project covered some such "plums"—Elizabeth Bowen, Agatha Christie, Stella Gibbons, Nancy Mitford—but also ambled across work by (at that point) obscure novelists such as Rachel Ferguson and Diane Tutton (4). Organizing her study thematically and not by individual author, Humble introduced readers to thirty writers many had not previously encountered while making a case for the significance of the middlebrow novel both as a source of pleasure and as a means of opening up the world of women who wrote and read them (6).

Middlebrow studies rapidly expanded, in part because of the increasing availability of new editions of earlier works published by Virago (established in 1973) and Persephone Press (founded 1998) and also in response to the invigoration of modernist studies in the early 2000s. Without claiming that modernist and middlebrow writers had the same aesthetic or cultural projects, scholars transvalued the middlebrow and argued that separating it from modernism had the effect of excluding women writers and writers of color from academic study. Lisa Botshon and Meredith Goldsmith's essay collection *Middlebrow Moderns: Popular American Women Writers of the 1920s* (2003), for example, introduced readers to many middlebrow American writers (Edna Ferber, Zona Gale, Winnifred Eaton, and others); their introduction argues that "attention to the popular women writers of the 1920s prompts a reconsideration of the way modernist literary studies have not only reinforced hierarchies of culture but also segregated and separated authors from different ethnic and racial groups" (5). Similarly, Faye Hammill's *Women, Celebrity, & Literary Culture between the Wars* (2007) observes that "the reinscription of the middlebrow into literary history is in part a feminist undertaking, since it involves attention to an undervalued literature which was, indeed, mainly produced by and for women" (6–7). On the face of it, *Middlebrow Moderns* and *Women* look a bit like the first generation of scholarship on feminine difference in their interest in reinscribing specific women into literary history. Both texts, however, work to make larger points about literary marketplaces and the effects of segregating the experimental from the popular. Hammill, for example, states that "the careers of these particular authors were selected as case studies because each illuminates a different aspect of the ways celebrities were constituted in interwar literary culture" (24). In other words, her interest in celebrity authorship motivates a study of middlebrow novels; the middlebrow's cultural alignment with femininity necessitates that her argument focus on (and in so doing, recover) specific women writers. Readers of her book thus learn about women they may never have encountered, but the larger project is to put a feminine mode of writing and public being on the map. Similar projects, such as Diana Wallace's *The Woman's Historical Novel: British Women Writers, 1900–2000* (2005) and Catherine Keyser's *Playing Smart: New York Women Writers and Modern Magazine Culture* (2010), abound.

It was, of course, possible to focus on feminized categories like the middlebrow and *not* draw one's examples from literature written by or for women. Robert Scholes's *Paradoxy of Modernism* (2006), which addresses the same tension between high and low Hammill navigates, provides one such instance through his attention to the "iridescent mediocrity" of Dornford Yates's middlebrow comic novels. Yates's fiction, Scholes argues, illustrates the "clash between the old values and the new world in which they were fighting a gallant but losing battle" (170). Gender only enters the study very briefly when the critic writes that readers can learn about modern culture "by examining the attitudes toward class and gender that are expressed in Yates's work" (174); notably, the examples Scholes provides all focus on relationships between men of different classes. *Paradoxy* thus demonstrates that there are other approaches to the middlebrow than one that explores the feminization of the cultural register, which a reader sees in most scholarship. It is important to note, however, that work like Humble's and Hammill's—criticism, that is, that takes as its point of departure the feminization of the middlebrow as well as the fact that many women were placed within it—has generated more traction in terms of conferences and symposia as well as publications.

If a focus on femininity and feminization could draw attention to women writers (and whole categories of literary production) who had been previously neglected, it could also shift attention *away* from literature proper—a shift from modernism to modernity. This sea change was initiated by Rita Felski's landmark 1995 study *The Gender of Modernity*, which explores "the question of the gendering of history, as well as the historicity of gender" (1). Where previous books by feminist modernist critics had reclaimed marginalized women artists along with feminized aesthetic qualities for the canon, Felski's book "aim[ed] to unravel the complexities of modernity's relationship to femininity" (7). Notably, she traces this relationship through an archive that is both literary and political and created by men and women: the sociological work of Georg Simmel, Emile Zola's *The Ladies Paradise*, Oscar Wilde's *A Picture of Dorian Gray*, Leopold von Sacher-Masoch's *Venus in Furs*, Marie Corelli's romance *The Sorrows of Satan*, tracts published in support of the suffrage movement, and the French decadent writer Rachilde's *Monsieur Venus*, among others. This wide range of examples provides a significant clue to Felski's unique contribution to our field's approach to sex and gender. The overarching claim of the book, that "gender [...] reveals itself to be a central organizing metaphor in the construction of historical time" (9–10), highlights not only the gender *of* modernist artists or the genders represented in their texts. Instead, Felski's work argues that to write about modernity is to write about "hierarchies of sexual difference" as well as a period with its own "tradition of questioning and contesting gender norms" (208). She thus positions "the figure of woman and the idea of the feminine" as key tropes for expressing ambivalences about the experience of the modern (210).

Readers of Felski's text might hear in her title an echo of Bonnie Kime Scott's *The Gender of Modernism* (1990), the groundbreaking anthology discussed earlier. Scott's collection, as we have noted, sought to recover women writers who had slipped into obscurity as well as to highlight the connections among, and debates about sex and gender carried out by, modernist writers of all stripes. In the change from "Modernism" to "Modernity," Felski signals both the author's indebtedness to Scott's project *and* her distance from it. She cites Scott's anthology as an example of work "at pains to acknowledge the subtleties and complexities of modernist writing through careful attention to its tropes, metaphors, wordplays, and textual rhythms" (24). While she more explicitly articulates a debt to Elaine Showalter, specifically to her 1990 study *Sexual Anarchy: Gender and Culture at the Fin de Siècle*, and to Gilbert and Gubar's *No Man's Land*, Felski's project takes its place in a conversation that had already begun to "reshape and redefine the contours of literary history" (24). Indeed, she acknowledges that "it is unlikely that an analysis of Rachilde would have appeared in a critical text of this kind ten years ago" (206). *The Gender of Modernity* thus positions itself as benefitting from, but a counterpart to, feminist work preoccupied with integrating women into the canon of literary modernism.

Felski refuses to construct an "overarching feminist myth of the modern" (7), but she unapologetically takes femininity—and "its varied and competing representations" (7)—as her subject. *The Gender of Modernity* is thus less interested in providing empowering models of femininity than in thinking through the ways in which gender helped those in the early twentieth century theorize their own historical moment. The myths and assumptions she takes up are not always gladdening for feminist scholars; they do, however, help to position modernity as preoccupied with gender in ambivalent and often reactionary ways. The experience of modernity, she argues, is navigated through a gender that was sometimes understood as primitive, and sometimes as modern, but always on the move.

The second major term of Felski's title positions her book as looking not at modernism per se but at the historical moment in which it emerged. And Felski is adamant that modernism is both a period *and* a particular style; she is emphatically not interested in modernism as a "catchall" category. In her words, to describe all cultural products of the early twentieth century as modernist "is to render an already vague term effectively useless by robbing it of any meaningful referent" (25). This does not mean, however, that feminist scholarship is limited to a small canon of "formally self-conscious, experimental, antimimetic" works. Instead, Felski asserts that "modernism is only one aspect of the culture of women's modernity" (25) and, in taking modernity as her key term, she radically expands her archive and encouraged others to do the same.

The Gender of Modernity works at the intersection of literary and cultural studies, and Felski praises the latter "for having irrevocably problematized the opposition between a 'high' literature assumed to be inherently ambiguous and self-critical and a mass culture equated with the reproduction of a monolithic ideological standpoint" (29). Her work on Simmel, analysis of popular fiction by Corelli, and analysis of the rhetoric of evolution and revolution in the suffrage movement are all part of her larger attempt not only to move away from modernism proper but to disentangle descriptive and normative discussions of modernity—to come to terms with a category that was and is often employed as a value judgment. Understanding the cultural workings of gender, her book suggests, requires a broad archive that moves outside the category of the literary and the high cultural.

The impact of Felski's book has been sweeping, inspiring a range of feminist work through her wide archive, her unsparing exploration of femininity as idealized and demonized in the discourses of modernity, and her argument that to be modern *was* to position oneself in relationship to femininity. Some studies that were released afterward, such as Ann Ardis and Leslie Lewis's edited collection *Women's Experience of Modernity: 1875–1945* (2003) and Martin Hipsky's *Modernism and the Women's Popular Romance in Britain, 1885–1925* (2011), explicitly work to extend Felski's arguments. Three brief examples illustrate the very different ways *Gender* shaped feminist criticism that followed it less overtly. First, Barbara Green's *Spectacular Confessions: Autobiography, Performance Activism, and the Sites of Suffrage 1904–1938* (1997) explores "the writings of militant suffragettes in relation to recent efforts to rethink the relations between gender, literary modernism, and modernity" (8). Focusing on work produced by and about suffragette militants, Green stresses that "underread feminist texts [...] confronted and shaped modernity" (8), illustrating (like Felski) that femininity was not only an identity but a tool to make claims for what was modern and for what was political.[4] Second, Liz Conor's *The Spectacular Modern Woman* (2004) deploys popular imagery to argue that "women's bodies became a place of action in modern visual culture" (2). Conor's argument that women learned to negotiate the uniquely *visual* culture of modernity through "appearing" has its roots in Felski's prioritizing of the experience of the modern and her argument that femininity was always yoked to modern temporality. Finally, Bonnie Kime Scott's *second* anthology, *Gender in Modernism: New Geographies, Complex Intersections* (2007), collects manifestos, essays on socialism and suffrage, documents of lesbian political history, and texts that take up mediumship and automatic writing, among many others. While the authors highlighted in Scott's first collection are peppered throughout this second anthology, Felski's assertion that "modernism is only one aspect of the culture of women's modernity" is everywhere evident in the expansive and non-hierarchical registers and discourses in *Gender in Modernism*. Scott chose to stick with "modernism" and not "modernity" in her title, but her introduction makes plain that many sections of her collection are linked to Felski's specific claims and archive. After citing Felski along with the foundation of the journal *Modernism/modernity* in 2003, Scott observes "a gradual turn toward modernity as a complement to, if not a substitute for, modernism as a field of study. The range of modernity is much wider than modernism" (13). These examples, different as they are, underline the impact of *The Gender of Modernity*, as well as the increasing interest in femininity (gender) instead of in women (biological sex).

Case study: Jessie Redmon Fauset (1882–1961)

Jessie Redmon Fauset provides a clear example of an author recovered in large part because of the transvaluation of qualities long gendered feminine (such as the middlebrow, the domestic, and fashion) that this chapter traces. Fauset, a highly educated African-American who began her career as a teacher, was the author of four novels as well as of poetry, reviews, essays, and journalism. Notably, she served as the editor of *The Crisis*, founded by W. E. B. Du Bois as the official magazine of the National Association for the Advancement of Colored People (NAACP) from 1919 to 1926. Under Fauset's guidance, *The Crisis* became a major outlet for the literary productions of the Harlem Renaissance, and Fauset supported or published writers ranging from Countee Cullen to Langston Hughes. Famously dubbed by Hughes as one of the individuals who "midwifed" the Renaissance, Fauset was, in Cheryl A. Wall's 1995 assessment, "one of the most prolific writers of the Renaissance, male or female." Sadly, Wall continues, Fauset became "among the least respected" (38). In part, Fauset's reputation declined because Robert Bone declared her among the "Rear Guard" of the Renaissance in his influential 1958 study *The Negro Novel in America* (102). Her novels went out of print, and her work was largely forgotten.

In the 1980s and 1990s, Fauset's reputation began to be resuscitated through feminist recovery work. Carolyn Wedin Sylvander published a combined biography and critical study in 1981; Fauset's poems were anthologized in Maureen Honey's 1989 *Shadowed Dreams*, and she was also included in Scott's 1990 *Gender of Modernism* anthology. What is striking about some of this early work, however, is the criticism directed at Fauset's fiction and poetry. Deborah McDowell, who viewed the content of Fauset's novels as groundbreaking, described *There is Confusion* (1924) as suffering from "multiple stylistic weaknesses" (93). Wall, who introduced Fauset in *Gender* and later devoted a chapter to the writer in *Women of the Harlem Renaissance* (1995), asserted that "Fauset's critics are correct when they identify such weaknesses in her novels as melodramatic plots, flat characterizations, and stilted prose" (36). She concludes her chapter on Fauset by calling her fiction "cripple[d]" by "the privileging of the private over the public, the retreat into domesticity, and the denial of difference" (84). Although Ann duCille's *The Coupling Convention: Sex, Text, and Tradition in Black Women's Fiction* (1993) helped to challenge the perception that Fauset's attention to bourgeois values and particularly to marriage was politically retrograde or simplistic, Fauset's reputation was far outpaced by Nella Larsen and Zora Neale Hurston, whose work was more formally innovative.

When feminized categories like the sentimental and the middlebrow were recuperated, scholars began to offer appreciative readings of Fauset. Attention to the "little" (and big) modernist magazines similarly shone a spotlight on her significant work as a contributor and as an editor. Fauset's reputation was additionally enhanced by the global and transnational turn in modernist studies; the author spent time in Paris and Africa and wrote about her experiences, and some of the characters in her novels travel abroad. These multiple lenses helped to recuperate a writer whose star is now rising.

In 2007, an influential reading by Cherene Sherrard-Johnson, *Portraits of the New Negro Woman: Visual and Literary Culture in the Harlem Renaissance*, positioned Fauset alongside Larsen, Jean Toomer, and others in a study of the mulatta "as an icon of visual and literary Afro-modernism" as well as "an ambiguous symbol of racial uplift" (xx). Reading Fauset's *Plum Bun* (1929) alongside advertisements and illustrations in *The Crisis*, Sherrard-Johnson's work illustrates how a cultural studies approach, which is not invested in hierarchies of presumed literary quality, benefited the author. Fauset is also read in the context of *The Crisis* in Ann Ardis's 2011 article "Making Middlebrow Culture, Making Middlebrow Literary Texts *Matter: The Crisis*, Easter 1912." Placing Fauset squarely in the frame of middlebrow culture, Ardis makes an impassioned case for studying periodicals in that register and offers an account "of how the *Crisis* engaged an aspirational black middle class audience in 1912" (22). Ardis reads Fauset's poem "Rondeau," which appeared in the Easter issue, alongside the other texts that surround it in the magazine. Concluding that readers must "recognize the magazine's interest in having its readers find beauty in [...] literary forms" that were not formally experimental, Ardis reconstructs a cultural moment in which "modernism simply did not define the coordinates of modernity" (35). Sherrard-Johnson's and Ardis's productive new approaches to Fauset demonstrate that scholars have stopped apologizing for the author's traditional style; whether they regard Fauset as modernist (Sherrard-Johnson) or middlebrow (Ardis), they position her as a significant Harlem Renaissance voice.

More recently, Elizabeth Sheehan has written about Fauset's internationalism in a chapter in *A Companion to the Harlem Renaissance* (2015). Comparing the author's 1921 essay "Impressions of the Second Pan-African Congress" to her first novel *There Is Confusion* (1924) as well as to *Plum Bun* (1929), Sheehan examines Fauset's vision of internationalism as refracted through feminized discourses and practices such as fashion. Building on studies of Fauset's internationalism and its relationship to domesticity by Carol Allen and Valerie Popp, Sheehan argues, "Just as Fauset's heroines manipulate textiles, so does Fauset take up, trim, and refit current and established narrative genres, including the marriage plot, the passing narrative, the fairy tale, the *Bildungsroman*, and the *Kunstlerroman*" (137). This approach casts Fauset as not slavishly copying the tradition but rather remaking it. Sheehan also demonstrates that Fauset investigates "the gendered relationship between domesticity and internationalism" (138), perhaps most notably in *Plum Bun*'s representation of "the romance between an African American fashion illustrator turned painter, Angela Murray, and a black Brazilian artist, Anthony Cross" (146). This kind of approach does not deny that Fauset relied on the conventional romance plot; instead, it argues that such a plot enabled Fauset to meditate on the black diaspora and internationalism. Scholars like Sherrard-Johnson, Sheehan, Ardis, and others have provided readers with new reasons to read Fauset unapologetically.

Beyond binaries?

Scott's *Gender in Modernism* points to additional shifts in approaches to the study of gender, sexuality, and modernism. As she writes, "today, sex [...] is less regularly discussed as a simple binary. The transsexual and the intersex condition now routinely enter considerations of sexuality and the body." Gender, she also observes, "is less often seen as a division between oppositional feminine and masculine traits or traditions" (2). In addition to challenging the founding assumption of a female difference—of a modernist binary of men versus women or masculinity versus femininity—Scott's book highlights "the vast array of identity constructions that have become apparent through the burgeoning of cultural theory" (15). In place of her first anthology's "Tangled Mesh of Modernists," which represented connections between specific writers, the second collection's "Intersections with the Gender Complex" (see Figure 2) offers a Venn diagram of overlapping categories, including not only the Gender Complex but also Race & Ethnicity, Global Situation, and Class (11). As a visual representation of intersectional feminism, this latest image points toward a profound shift in orientation. Scott professes the hope that *Gender in Modernism* will encourage publishers to reprint modernist authors anthologized in the book, but recovery (and discovery) of individual writers is not her primary aim.

It is illustrative to similarly contrast a recent book by Susan Stanford Friedman with her essay "Who Buried H. D.?" As we

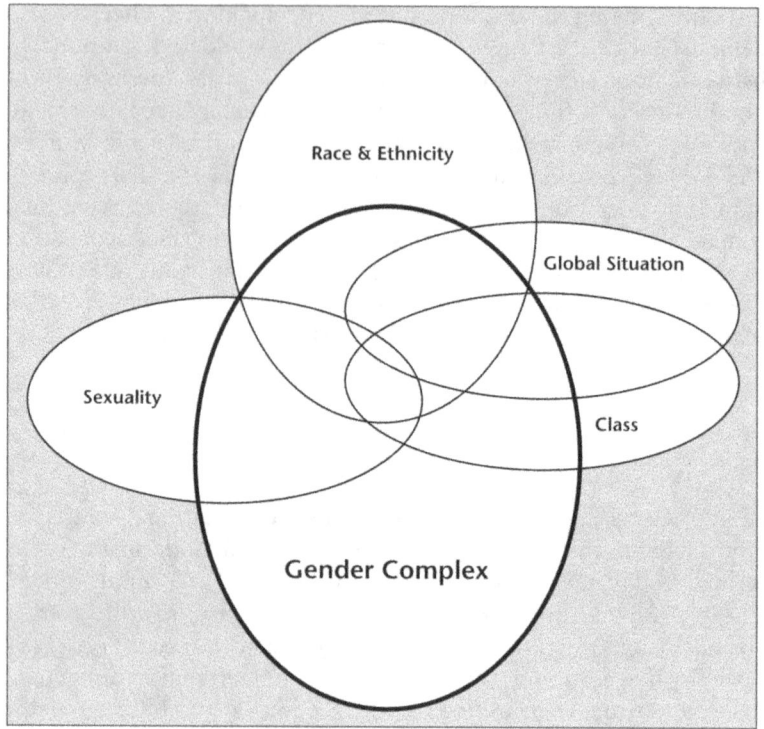

FIGURE 2 *Intersections with the Gender Complex. From* Gender in Modernism: New Geographies, Complex Intersections. *Copyright 2007 by the Board of Trustees of the University of Illinois. Used with permission of the University of Illinois Press. This illustration reflects the shift away from sex and gender as the sole focus of feminist modernist criticism.*

have noted, the 1975 article exemplifies argumentative strategies of early recovery work. In *Planetary Modernisms: Provocations on Modernity across Time* (2015), the critic makes the argument that a "planetary turn" necessitates rethinking modernism and modernity beyond their usual framing within the nineteenth and twentieth centuries (7). At the end of her sweeping study, Friedman pauses to meditate: "Why doesn't *Planetary Modernisms* systematically theorize gender's centrality to a rethinking of *modernism/ modernity*?" (338). This self-reflection points toward the fact that a major scholar, once deeply invested in thinking about the careers of neglected female modernists, has shifted focus. Although a few chapters of her book place gender "front and center," in others she acknowledges that it is "hardly anywhere" (339). The critic's answer to her own question hinges on her claim that many of the book's theoretical inquiries "represent an expansion of the familiar feminist critique of androcentrism and phallogocentrism" while its keywords come "explicitly out of feminist theory" (339). *Planetary Modernisms* demonstrates that even critics deeply committed to feminist work have found themselves asking other kinds of questions—in this case, about the place and temporality of modernism and modernity—that are informed by feminism but address gender (and sex) indirectly. Feminist inquiry, in other words, becomes less about women and femininity than about the kinds of questions asked and the language used to answer those questions. Instead of focusing on work by or about women, many feminist scholars now see their task as analyzing structures of dominance writ large, including European and American dominance in the canon and theorization of modernism.

This shift in attention, one that might be crudely characterized as a redirection of some critical energy from sex and gender to the global, has not gone unnoticed or unchallenged. Jane Garrity lamented in a 2013 essay, "the passionate interest in women's writing that exploded in the 1970s is no longer pervasive" (16). The critic marshals a range of evidence in support of her claim that "women modernists have not been faring very well in recent years" (17), including the absence of women (other than Woolf) in tables of contents in recent monographs, the small number of women writers in new anthologies, and the unexplored archives of women writers. Garrity's concern is that "the labor of seemingly old-fashioned feminist recovery work is far from done" (21) and that the women writers who have critical traction today—Woolf but also Mansfield and Rhys—are only in the spotlight because they fit into a transnational frame (17–8). Writers who do not fit the "critical trends of the moment" are, in contrast, neglected (20). Garrity's essay closes with a call to develop new conferences and resources that focus on women modernists, and the effects of that call have already been felt in the formation of a new journal, *Feminist Modernist Studies*, which published its first issue in January 2018, as well as conferences such as the 25th annual

Woolf conference on the theme of "Virginia Woolf and Her Female Contemporaries." These developments help to temper what Garrity called the "marginalization of women's writing within modernist studies today" (23), but critics invested in recovery work often express the opinion that the larger field regards such scholarship as passé.

Additional efforts to buck the critical tide against explicitly feminist studies of modernist women continue to appear. In 2013, the journal *Modern Fiction Studies* devoted a special issue to "Women's Fiction, New Modernist Studies, and Feminism." In her introduction, Anne Fernald, the issue's editor, diagnosed the same malady as Garrity: "one hallmark of the new modernist studies has been its lack of serious interest in women writers" (229). The special issue, which included essays on Olive Moore, Muriel Rukeyser, Marghanita Laski, and others, presented "new work on women writers from the first half of the twentieth century" but also aimed to demonstrate:

> the theoretical energy, historical importance, and intellectual weight of current feminist work on women writers. In doing so, it makes the case that no new work on modernism should go forward without serious engagement with women and feminist theory. To understand the uneven, surprising, and profound impact of modernity, we must remember, despite our theoretical, practical, and somatic sophistication, that gender played and continues to play an enormous role in defining social roles and economic opportunities. (229)

Along with other special issues and edited collections produced this decade,[5] it seems clear that the dedication of scholars to the study of sex and gender, and specifically of women, non-binary sex and gender identity, and femininity, will continue to produce prominent new criticism.

On a final note, scholars have recently demonstrated that feminist approaches to women and to gender can be advanced through new theoretical frameworks such as affect theory and cognitive approaches to literature. These studies highlight not simply the representation of particular emotions in modernist texts but how readers experience the same feelings through their interaction with style and content. Jane F. Thrailkill's *Mind, Body, and Emotion in American Literary Realism* (2007), for example, illustrates the feminist consequences of reading a text like *The Yellow Wallpaper*, which takes the reader through an experience that is at once physical and intellectual. Laura Frost's *The Problem with Pleasure: Modernism and Its Discontents* (2013) dissects high modernism's suspicion of easy, bodily pleasures and "valorization of that which requires effort and training" (9). Analyzing both male and female writers, Frost's book highlights how we might read Gertrude Stein, in one instance, as "tickling" readers through texts that are both "delight-inducing and irritating" (30). And Allison Pease's *Modernism, Feminism, and the Culture of Boredom* (2012) traces the modern problem of women's boredom that pervades texts as diverse as Dorothy Richardson's *Pilgrimage* and D. H. Lawrence's *Lady Chatterley's Lover*. Pease's argument illustrates the evolution of the treatment of feminine difference particularly well. Although she argues that male and female writers engage bored women differently—the former prescribe sexual desire as a "cure" for boredom while the latter expose boredom as inherent to the gendering of modern individuality and agency—she also observes that earlier generations of feminist critics sought to write a *positive* account of gender differences. In a conclusion that engages Benstock, Scott, Gilbert and Gubar, and Showalter, Pease diagnoses "a strong note of anxiety in feminist criticism that women's writing not be interpreted as simply a response to patriarchy, that its own narrative be 'vital'" (121). As a result, boredom was ignored by scholars until affect studies offered a means of connecting "the so-called private emotions to a role in public life" (122). Together, this type of work suggests that we can read not only modernist literature but the history of feminist modernist studies for emotions and experiences that "still make us anxious" (121) and uncomfortable and then trust those responses to lead scholarship toward additional gendered experiences that have yet to be addressed.

Notes

1 For example, Quentin Bell on Woolf; Anne Chisholm on Nancy Cunard; Lovat Dickson on Radclyffe Hall; Douglas Messerli on Djuna Barnes.

2 This project was furthered by Jayne Marek's 1995 *Women Editing Modernism: "Little" Magazines & Literary History* and later Dean Irvine's *Editing Modernity: Women and Little-Magazine Cultures in Canada, 1916–1956* (2008).
3 See, as an additional example, Nina Miller's *Making Love Modern: The Intimate Public Worlds of New York's Literary Women* (1998), which focuses on love poetry by women. As Miller writes, "we may see even love poetry, that most 'feminine' and quietist of genres, as actively invested in the sphere of public value, shaping and responding to public debate, and defining identity in relation to the terms of a public ethos" (7). Although Miller does not position the women about whom she writes as modernist, she focuses on their "public embodiment of femininity" (7) and frames their work as distinctively *modern*.
4 In a parallel move, scholars focused their attention on the representation of the feminine subject in work by men and women. Tamar Katz's *Impressionist Subjects: Gender, Interiority, and Modernist Fiction in England* (2000), for instance, argues that the modern woman "as an enigma that cannot be pinned down or conclusively placed [...] provided a figure for modernism's experiments and its privileging of ambiguity" (12). While Katz's examples are all literary—writers who were categorized as literary impressionists—she, like Felski and Green, figures femininity as specifically modern (and modernist).
5 A partial list would include Maren Tova Linett's *The Cambridge Companion to Modernist Women Writers* (2010); Cambridge Companions to individual modernist women (such as H. D., published in 2012) or works by women (e.g., *To the Lighthouse*, published in 2014); Allan Pero and Gyllian Phillips's collection *The Many Facades of Edith Sitwell*; the 2012 anthology *Plays and Performance Texts by Women, 1880–1930*, edited by Maggie Gale and Gilli Bush-Bailey; Tori Young and Jeff Wallace's issue of *Literature Compass*, "The Future of Women in Modernism"; and the forthcoming *Edinburgh Companions to Women's Print Media in Britain* (volume 3 will cover "The Modernist Period" and volume 4 the interwar years).

2

Sexuality

> *Many of the major nodes of thought and knowledge in twentieth-century Western culture as a whole are structured—indeed, fractured—by a chronic, now endemic crisis of homo/heterosexual definition.*
> —EVE KOSOFSKY SEDGWICK, *EPISTEMOLOGY OF THE CLOSET*

Overview

Overt interest in sexuality is one of the defining features of the modernist period. From burgeoning medical and psychological interest in declaring sex and sexual desire as fundamental to human experience and identity, to tabloid and court scandals that exposed same-sex behaviors to a mass-reading public, to obscenity trials of modernist magazines and novels that represented explicit sex acts and same-sex desire, sexuality moved to the foreground of concern. Marking new aesthetic territory, bodies in sexual contact made their way into texts with literary pretentions. For example, James Joyce's *Ulysses* (1922) makes the reader witness to Leopold Bloom's beachside masturbation, his sadomasochistic transgender reveries in a brothel, and the explicit details of Molly Bloom's nighttime musings: "I wished he was here or somebody to let myself go with and come again like that I feel all fire inside me or if I could dream it when he made me spend the 2nd time tickling me behind with his fingers I was coming for about 5 minutes with my legs round him" (754). Published from 1911 to 1930, D. H. Lawrence's novels feature masturbation, same-sex attractions, anal sex, and, most insistently, heterosexual coupling that celebrates the phallus and vaginal climax. In other modernist texts, sexual behavior is the object of representation, but presented with less medical or pornographic detail, as in e.e. cummings's "I like my body when it is with your" (1925):

> i like kissing this and that of you,
> like, slowly stroking the, shocking fuzz
> of your electric furr, and what-is-it comes
> over parting flesh.

Or, in the metaphorically veiled lesbian sexuality of Amy Lowell's poems in which the speaker's hands search, strip, and part the vegetal bits of a lover, as in "Aubade" (1914):

> As I would free the white almond from the green husk
> So I would strip your trappings off,
> Beloved.
> And fingering the smooth polished kernel
> I should see that in my hands glittered a gem beyond counting.

To read modernist literature is to encounter sexuality, and to read modernist criticism is to understand that our perception of the role and meaning of sexuality continues to shift.

While erotic literature has always existed, there are unique qualities to sexuality as represented in modernism. This chapter will take on sex and sexuality as a range of desires and body-based actions, thoughts, and sensibilities, while being mindful that those meanings changed during the modernist period itself. Sexuality in the modernist period can mean physical expressions or interactions with or without genital contact that promote feelings of genital pleasure; it can also mean copulation for the purposes of procreation in which pleasure is not privileged. Equally important and epoch defining, sexuality in the modernist period began to designate an orientation of sexual desire toward a particular sex that became synonymous with a personal identity, as in he or she is "a homosexual," or, as would have been more common in the early twentieth century, an invert, a sapphist, a bugger, a uranist, or a tribad. While non-heterocentric self-identification is new in the modernist period, it is not universal. If some authors such as Radclyffe Hall self-identified as inverts, others, such as Virginia Woolf, Djuna Barnes, or Wallace Thurman, each of whom had sexual partners of both sexes as did many modernist authors, evaded identifying with any particular sexual identity, and this was equally important to their self-image. The political and social territory of sexual self-identification was far less defined in the early twentieth century than it became in the final thirty years of the twentieth century, and thus what it would have meant to assume such an identity was interpreted differently by, and presented different risks for, modernist authors around the globe. Representations of sexuality in modernism, therefore, encompass both identity formation and sexual acts, which themselves became broadly conceived and catalogued.

How sexuality has been conceived and interpreted in modernist criticism has been very much a matter of visibility. Sex acts were framed by modernists as those things that had not been seen in generations prior but should be. But to make one thing visible is to obscure another, and this chapter will show how various strands of modernist criticism have competed to make visible one aspect of sexuality, only to be shadowed by another. The first two sections, "Liberation narratives, sexology and psychoanalytic readings" and "Sexuality as discourse: critiquing the liberatory narrative, politicizing sex," will trace modernist authors' own views on the role of sexuality in literature as well as the first challenges to this view in the 1970s from critics who framed sexuality not as natural but as constructed culturally. "Sexuality and discourses of otherness" will show how a new paradigm of sexuality as constructed by cultures to fulfill sociopolitical needs allowed for fresh readings of modernist works that demonstrated how nonnormative sexuality is often projected onto nondominant groups for political purposes. The fourth section of this chapter will identify an important strand in modernist criticism that was particularly dominant from the 1970s to 1990s, making visible "Modernist lesbian and gay histories and identities." This work formed part of the feminist recovery work discussed in Chapter 1 but supplemented it and often critiqued mainstream feminism for its omission of gay and lesbian histories. The very notion of sexual visibility, making legible that which is strange to dominant culture, comes under attack, however, in the 1990s, as will be explicated in the section "Queer theory and challenges to queer theory," which continues to feed approaches to modernist sexuality. The final section of the chapter "Sexology and perversion, beyond power" will discuss recent critical approaches to modernist sexuality that appear to draw from the modernist well of sexual understanding in order to challenge current dominant thinking about sexuality, identity, and narrative.

If, then, the top layer of the palimpsest that is modernism was initially preoccupied with detailed representations of sex—and mainly *heterosexual* sex—as natural and antibourgeois, this chapter highlights the layers of inscription beneath what had seemed modernism's straightforward tale of heterosexual liberation. The treatment of sex as discourse, the diagnosis of sexuality as constructing regimes of political power, and the finding in modernism of precursors to gay and lesbian identities are all layers that scholars initially uncovered. The anti-normative provocations of queer theory, and a rethinking of sexuality beyond power, are the most recent layers of the palimpsest to be detected. In all cases, scholars have found modernist writers who were seemingly ahead of their own times in constructing representations of sexuality, and living lives, that anticipate later ways of sexual being.

Liberation narratives, sexology, and psychoanalytic readings

Suddenly the door opened and the long and sinister figure of Mr. Lytton Strachey stood on the threshold. He pointed his finger at a stain on Vanessa's white dress.

"Semen?" he said.

Can one really say it? I thought and we burst out laughing. With that one word all barriers of reticence and reserve went down. A flood of the sacred fluid seemed to overwhelm us. Sex permeated our conversation. The word bugger was never far from our lips. We discussed copulation with the same excitement and openness that we had discussed the nature of good. It is strange to think how reticent, how reserved we had been and for how long. It seems a marvel now that so late as the year 1908 or 9 Clive had blushed and I had blushed too when I asked him to let me pass to go to the lavatory on the French Express. I never dreamt of asking Vanessa to tell me what happened on her wedding night. Thoby and Adrian [her brothers] would have died rather than discuss the affairs of undergraduates. When all intellectual questions had been debated so freely, sex was ignored. Now a flood of light poured in upon that department too. We had known everything but we had never talked. Now we talked of nothing else. [...] All this had the result that the old sentimental views of marriage in which we were brought up were revolutionized. —Virginia Woolf, "Old Bloomsbury" (from *Moments of Being,* pp. 195–196)

Virginia Woolf's Bloomsbury reminiscence is archetypal of the dominant modernist narrative about the emergence of sexuality into liberatory discourse after a repressive silence. Many modernist authors perceived representing sexuality as freeing them from a rigid bourgeois morality that had associated sexuality with shame and privacy. To speak of sex aloud, to write about it, to render it visible as Lytton Strachey's words do in the excerpt given earlier, was in and of itself, revolutionary. During the first half of the twentieth century, representing sex was understood not just as liberatory and healthy, but importantly, modern. In his 1985 book *James Joyce and Sexuality*, Richard Brown argues that though Joyce did not have a moral program for sexuality in the ways that, for instance, Henrik Ibsen and George Bernard Shaw did in protesting women's role as sexual chattel in marriage, "Joyce's fiction ... would have less stature, less of a sense of centrality to the intellectual life of our century, less 'modernity' in our estimation, did it not respond to this felt importance of sexuality and sexual change" (4). D. H. Lawrence's stated purpose in writing sex is the need to "clean" it from its shameful associations and to insist on its central role in human existence. In the essay "A Propos of *Lady Chatterly's Lover*" (1929) Lawrence argues, "This is the real point of the book. I want men and women to be able to think sex, fully, completely, honestly and cleanly. Even if we can't act sexually to our own satisfaction, let us at least think sexually, complete and clear" (92). Sexual modernity was not just a reaction against Victorian prohibitions but an "epistemological transformation, an individualization and psychologization of sexuality" (Oosterhuis 9). If writers were not showing sex on the page, they were still centering plots around it and demonstrating its centrality in the lines of poetry and the lives of characters.

Modernist studies have increasingly included literatures from outside of North America and Western Europe, yet there are aspects of literary modernism's preoccupation with sexuality that are specific to these regions. Changes in the perception and practices of sexuality occurred as Judeo-Christian traditions, which had long dictated sexual mores, lost their hold on public opinion while science, as a competing explanation and foundation of truth, became increasingly influential. England's and America's relationship to sexuality is more puritanical than other countries of Europe, Russia, and Latin America, and this is reflected in the relatively happy endings afforded to same- or queerly-sexed protagonists in the early twentieth-century literatures of non-Anglophone regions. In nations open to, or colonized by, Western powers, such as India and Japan, sexual emancipation movements accompanied women's emancipation movements and made the case that women were sexually autonomous and their role was not simply as a receptacle of men's pleasure. The poems of Japanese writer Yosano Akiko's 1901 *Midaregami*, for instance, give voice to sexually assertive women and represent lips, breasts, and sexual desire. As such they were a direct challenge to aesthetic and cultural conventions in Meiji Japan. Muslim Indian author Ismat Chughtai's short story "Lihaaf" (The Quilt), published in an Urdu literary journal in 1942, led to an obscenity trial and is a literary landmark for its depiction of sex and its suggestion of lesbianism.

Where in the years leading to modernism Naturalist narratives by Émile Zola, Frank Norris, Kate Chopin, Thomas Hardy, and Theodore Dreiser had taken their cue from scientific and Darwinian narratives of sexual selection to chronicle heterosexual sexual instincts as largely shaping (mostly tragic) experience, modernist narratives continued Naturalism's propensity to decouple sexuality from religious constraints while further complicating and playing with notions of sexuality as enmeshed in a nexus of biological, psychological, and cultural factors. In the late nineteenth and early twentieth centuries, the new interdisciplinary field of sexology attempted to catalogue and explain human sexual behavior using scientific methods that aimed for detachment from moral or religious judgment. The belief that the modernist period experienced a sexual liberation arises from the idea that treating sexuality scientifically rather than religiously can free one to pursue sexual interests and desires without social costs. German psychiatrist Richard von Krafft-Ebing's *Psychopathia Sexualis* (1886), written for psychiatrists, physicians, and judges, was the foundational sexological text containing detailed psychiatric classifications and analyses of sexual disorders. In *Modernism and Perversion* (2012), Anna Katharina Schaffner describes the preoccupation with perversion as a specifically modern phenomenon (*Introduction*). Originally, Krafft-Ebing labeled a perversion any kind of sexual activity or desire not directed toward procreation. Despite its intended audience, *Psychopathia Sexualis* was widely read by general readers and, in response to its claim that same-sex desire was caused by hereditary degeneracy and was comorbid with mental disease and moral corruption, many homosexuals volunteered to be subjects of his case studies, eventually convincing him that most of his subjects were physically, mentally, and morally healthy and that homosexuality was not a mental or physical illness. English sexologist Havelock Ellis differed from Krafft-Ebing in that he believed one's sexuality was congenitally and biologically grounded. In their 1897 *Sexual Inversion*, just as German sexologist Magnus Hirschfeld did in *Die Transvestiten* (1910) and *De Homosexualität des Mannes und des Weibes* (1914), Ellis and co-author John Addington Symonds argued that homosexuality was a natural and innate characteristic, an identity that defined an individual's self-concept. This notion was furthered by the literary and mystical treatment given to homosexuals by Edward Carpenter in his 1896 book *Love's Coming of Age* and his 1908 book *The Intermediate Sex: A Study of Some Transitional Types of Men and Women*, which was the first generally available text in English to frame homosexuality positively, rather than as a moral or medical problem. Those sexological accounts in turn influenced literary modernism, and critical studies continue to examine the relationships between individual texts and sexological tracts. Brown, for instance, makes much of Joyce's original desire to be a doctor. In finding a number of sexological books in Joyce's library, he argues there are

> several aspects of the transition from nineteenth- to twentieth-century attitudes to sexuality that seem particularly relevant to Joyce's fiction: this sense of new interest in sexuality; the growth of a sexual science; and the development of a new concept of sexuality worked out in distinction from traditional associations between sexuality and reproduction and in relation to new enquiries into sexual perversity. (52)

Similarly, Laura Doan notes in *Fashioning Sapphism* (2001) that the period's self-identified lesbian writers—Bryher, Radclyffe Hall, and Vita Sackville-West—kept sexological books in their homes (133). Among the many British and American authors acquainted with sexology were Djuna Barnes, Bryher, H. D., T. S. Eliot, William Faulkner, F. Scott Fitzgerald, E. M. Forster, Radclyffe Hall, Ernest Hemingway, Langston Hughes, Christopher Isherwood, James Joyce, D. H. Lawrence, Claude McKay, Wallace Thurman, and Virginia Woolf.

Even more influential than sexologists on modernist literature, however, was the work of Austrian neurologist and psychoanalyst Sigmund Freud, whose late nineteenth- and early twentieth-century studies were translated by Bloomsbury psychoanalyst James Strachey and published by Virginia and Leonard Woolf's Hogarth Press, thus ensuring that his ideas were in circulation among many modernist authors writing in English. Freud found in sexuality a series of hidden truths to be uncovered and made visible. Built on and in dialogue with a well-advanced sexological discourse, Freud's studies positioned the sex drive (*libido*) as the primary human instinct, developed a theory of repression that explained how unpleasurable thoughts and desires could be hidden from the conscious mind, and proposed in 1905's *Three Essays on the Theory of Sexuality* that infantile sexuality determined the formation of adult sexuality. Demonstrating the normative hold Freud's ideas had on mid-twentieth-century modernist criticism, critic Graham Hough's 1957 approval of *Lady Chatterley's Lover* is explicated in by-then manifest Freudian grounds: "It is obvious that the nature and quality of sexual experience has a powerful influence on character and development. We cannot therefore deny that Lawrence has opened up a wide new territory to the novel by presenting openly what everyone knows in private and what everybody knows to be important" (159). Equally influential, Freud demonstrated a method of interpretation that became of a model of reading "below the surface" for masked motivations and truths found in symbols that communicated the mysterious workings of the unconscious.

Although Freud built on the insights of sexologists and was in correspondence with Magnus Hirschfeld and Havelock Ellis as well as many other European sexologists, the distinct differences in style and approach, and Freud's framing of sexuality as an overall drama of mental life, separated the fields, especially in public awareness. Rita Felski explains,

One of the effects of the Freudian revolution was to erect a seemingly impenetrable barrier between the modern view of sexuality as an enigmatic and often labile psychic field rooted in unconscious desires, from the work of nineteenth-century sexologists such as Richard von Krafft-Ebing and Havelock Ellis, with its emphasis on the physiological and congenital roots of human erotic preferences. ("Introduction" 1)

Pushing past medical and scientific explanations, Freud created the myth of sexuality as that which is invisible—unconscious—but through the right processes—talk and analysis—could be made visible. In doing so, he influenced both modernist writers and decades of literary criticism that adapted his hermeneutic approach, ascribing to texts, authors, or characters, various pathological, repressed, or unconscious conditions. Many scholars of modernism continue to use Freudian ideas to interpret modernist works, but his influence was particularly strong from the 1960s through the 1990s. In Freud's time, writers who were aware of and incorporated his theories into their works include W. H. Auden, H. D. (who was also his patient), Ralph Ellison, E. M. Forster, Zora Neale Hurston, James Joyce, D. H. Lawrence, Mina Loy, Thomas Mann, Henry Miller, Anaïs Nin, Jean Rhys, Dorothy Richardson, May Sinclair, and Virginia Woolf. Even for those who had not read Freud, there was a great deal of "Freudianism without Freud" in popular as well as elite literature and these, combined, influenced social attitudes about sexuality. The widespread belief in sexual liberation through accepting the naturalness and centrality of sex to life heavily influenced the early reception of modernism; in the 1970s, the narrative of sexuality as a biological and psychological imperative was challenged.

Sexuality as discourse: Critiquing the liberatory narrative, politicizing sex

If the literary output between 1870 and 1970 was largely dominated by a scientifically based narrative that articulated sexuality as a biological imperative and thus natural, the 1970s witnessed a series of challenges to that narrative as well as the rise of the idea that has dominated understanding about sexuality since: that sexuality is socially constructed. The first challenge to modernist representations of sexuality came from Kate Millett, whose 1970 *Sexual Politics* catalogued the patriarchal violence of many of the most admired male writers of the twentieth century. Put simply, Millett argued that all sex is political, including sexual representations:

> Coitus can scarcely be said to take place in a vacuum; although of itself it appears a biological and physical activity, it is set so deeply within the larger context of human affairs that it serves as a charged microcosm of the variety of attitudes and values to which culture subscribes. Among other things, it may serve as a model of sexual politics on an individual or personal plane. (22)

Fiercely feminist, *Sexual Politics* provides readings of Henry Miller, Jean Genet, Norman Mailer, and D. H. Lawrence, which show the sexism and unbalanced power dynamics inherent in seemingly small sexual details. For instance, looking at a passage from Henry Miller's *Sexus* (1949), Millett argues that the use of the word "muff" "carries the tone, implicit in the whole passage, of one male relating an exploit to another male in the masculine vocabulary and with its point of view" (5). She directly contradicts Lawrence's own claims about the healthiness of his sexual representations: "While insisting his mission is the noble and necessary task of freeing sexual behavior of perverse inhibition, purging the fiction which describes it of prurient or prudish euphemism, Lawrence is really the evangelist of quite another cause 'phallic consciousness.' ... This is sexual politics in its most overpowering form" (238). Millet notes Lawrence's dislike of New Women, feminists, women who achieved climax through clitoral stimulation, and lesbians, and concludes, "The scenes of sexual intercourse in the novel are written according to the 'female is passive, male is active' directions laid down by Sigmund Freud. The phallus is all; Connie is 'cunt,' the thing acted upon, gratefully accepting each manifestation of the will of her master" (240). Joining a burgeoning school of feminist critique of Freud, Millet also proffers that his ideas about women and women's sexuality are not scientific facts but mere validation of traditional roles that pathologize some of the basic truths of female anatomy, such as her lack of a penis. Of Freud's influence on sexual behavior in the twentieth century, Millett declares, "Although generally accepted as a prototype of the liberal urge toward sexual freedom, and a signal contributor toward softening traditional puritanical inhibitions upon sexuality, the effect of Freud's work, that of his followers, and still more that of his popularizers, was to rationalize the invidious relationship between the sexes, to ratify traditional roles, and to validate temperamental differences" (178). Millet's *Sexual Politics* was a jarring first crack at revealing the role that culture plays in modernist sexuality; a few years later, Michel Foucault would follow with even greater effect.

In the last fifty years, no critical theorist has had a more profound effect on the interpretation of sexuality than Foucault, and thus his influence on modernist criticism is inescapable and profound. Where Freud described sexuality as interior to the subject, arising out of instinctive drives that are transfigured through familial and social constraints, Michel Foucault in *The History of Sexuality* (1976) redefined sexuality not as internal to the subject but as an effect of multiplying discourses that exercised control over subjects. *Volume 1* of *The History of Sexuality* criticizes the "repressive hypothesis," the widely held belief popularized by Freud that Western societies had suppressed sexuality from the seventeenth to the twentieth centuries and that the early twentieth century initiated a sexual liberation. Instead, Foucault argued, "All these negative elements—defenses, censorships, denials—which the repressive hypothesis groups together in one great central mechanism destined to say no, are doubtless only component parts that have a local and tactical role to play in a transformation into discourse, a technology of power, and a will to knowledge that are far from being reducible to the former" (12). Foucault's most-cited claim from *The History of Sexuality* is that "Western man has been drawn for three centuries to the task of telling everything concerning his sex ... since the classical age there has been a constant optimization and an increasing valorization of the discourse on sex; and that this carefully analytical discourse was meant to yield multiple effects of displacement, intensification, reorientation, and modification of desire itself" (23). To make the case that sexuality had not been repressed but had been expanded through discourse, Foucault pointed to the proliferation of institutions since the seventeenth century that had induced individuals to speak about their sex, from confession to medical sciences to pornography. "What is peculiar to modern societies," Foucault argues, "is not that they consigned sex to a shadow existence, but that they dedicated themselves to speaking of it *ad infinitum*, while exploiting it as *the* secret" (35). He attributes this discursive explosion of sexuality to the need to reproduce labor and to perpetuate social relations (37) and, importantly, to do so extralegally. Where Freud and Havelock Ellis had identified understanding one's own relation to sexuality as a key to self-knowledge, Foucault suggested that those who listen to the sexual confessions, the interlocutors and interpreters, become the masters of truth, not the sexual subjects themselves (*History of Sexuality, Vol. 1* 66–67). Thus, while the notion of sexual liberation is undergirded by the belief that in saying yes to sex, one is saying no to power, Foucault argued that sex and the proliferation of sexual discourse demonstrated a modern form of power whose origin lay not in law or the monarch but in multiple competing spheres, making power an endless contest without origin, exercised from the bottom, the middle, and the top all at once. In looking at the sexual liberation in which many writers of the early twentieth century believed themselves to take part, Foucault argued it "was really less a rupture than an inflexion of the curve: this was the moment when the mechanisms of repression were seen as beginning to loosen their grip; one passed from insistent sexual taboos to a relative tolerance with regard to prenuptial or extramarital relations; the disqualification of 'perverts' diminished, their condemnation by the law was in part eliminated; a good many of the taboos that weighed on the sexuality of children were lifted" (115) but that "Broadly speaking, at the juncture of the 'body' and the 'population,' sex became a crucial target of a power organized around the management of life rather than the menace of death" (147). Foucault claims that power over sexuality is not enacted through repression but through regulated articulation; one's sexuality is encroached upon by an ever-expanding number of institutions that, through a discursive ferment, inserted sexuality into systems of social utility and made it function according to an optimum, changing the nature of desire itself. Although his views have been challenged, as we will see later in this chapter, the Foucauldian paradigm continues to feed a rich vein of scholarship on modernist sexuality that links sexual discourse to social control.

By 1990, the idea that sexuality was constructed by, and subject to, an array of sociopolitical influences was firmly established and became the norm of modernist critique. Evidence of this shift in thinking can be found in the July 1990 "Note from the Editor" for the inaugural issue of *The Journal of the History of Sexuality*, which explains, "Traditionally the study of human sexuality has been dominated by scholars who, since the late nineteenth century, have characterized themselves as sexologists .... Now the study of human sexuality is being addressed by social historians, sociologists, anthropologists, philosophers, psychologists, literary scholars, classicists, art and film historians, and scholars in other fields from a variety of disciplinary and cross-disciplinary perspectives" (1). The year 1990 was also the year that critical theorist Judith Butler published *Gender Trouble: Feminism and the Subversion of Identity*, a book seen as foundational to queer theory. Butler built on Foucault's framework to claim that there is no essence or foundation to one's sex or gender (and that sex does not signify without gender) but rather no identity exists prior to acts. According to Butler, even genital pleasure is culturally constructed:

> "Becoming" a gender is a laborious process of becoming *naturalized*, which requires a differentiation of bodily pleasures and parts on the basis of gendered meanings. Pleasures are said to reside in the penis, the vagina, and the breasts or to emanate from them, but such descriptions correspond to a body which has already been constructed or naturalized as gender-specific. In other words, some parts of the body become conceivable foci of pleasure precisely because they correspond to a normative ideal of a gender specific body. (70)

Butler's argument expands on Foucault by arguing that there is no subject that exists prior to the doing of gender and sexuality; gender and sexuality are themselves acts that are repeated as reflections of phantasies about gender and sexuality available in discourse. Butler's central focus is on gender as a perpetual becoming, a repeated series of actions that gain meaning through a variety of discourses but have no ontological status apart from them. As an extension of this concept of gender, she conceives of sex and sexuality as likewise an internalized fantasy enacted on and produced by the body. Butler writes, "acts and gestures, articulated and enacted desires create the illusion of an interior and organizing gender core, an illusion discursively maintained for the purposes of the regulation of sexuality within the obligatory frame of reproductive heterosexuality" (136). In claiming that "the notion of an original or primary gender identity is often parodied within the cultural practices of drag, cross-dressing, and the sexual stylization of butch/femme identities" (137), Butler influenced modernist scholarship that gave weight to sexuality as discourse and performance, and as such, to sexual fluidity, nonnormative queerness, and play as part of that relationship.

Sexuality and discourses of otherness

Representation of groups within any given society is controlled by the group or groups that have greater political power. Building on Foucault's argument about the expansion of sexuality as discourse, many critics have written about how modernists contributed to or worked against an othering of the sexuality of those not in power. Edward Said's 1979 *Orientalism*, for instance, found an "almost uniform association between the Orient and sex" (188) in Western writing. Said explains Orientalism as the distorted thoughts and fantasies of the West that turned cultural representations of the Orient into an exotic and reviled caricature based on the self-affirming needs of the cultures that inscribed them. He identifies the works of André Gide, Joseph Conrad, and W. Somerset Maugham as participating in making "Oriental sex"—any type of sexuality deviating from what the West considered normative at the time—a standard commodity in mass culture (190). Said's seminal book continues to generate critical discussion about representations of sexuality by Westerners in non-Western settings in which they are granted license to transgressive sexual expressions if they adopt a non-Western persona or engage with non-Westerners sexually. For instance, critics have frequently pointed out the fecund sexuality of Kurtz's African lover in Conrad's *Heart of Darkness* (1899) as positioned in opposition to his virginal "Intended" in Belgium. Joseph Allen Boone's *The Homoerotics of Orientalism* (2014) updates Said's project by maintaining that Orientalism is not the result of one culture's unidirectional projection onto another culture but an ongoing exchange, and Boone further explores how European writers in the early twentieth century appropriated Middle Eastern forms to author homoerotic poems that they pretended were "found" manuscripts from the "Orient." A 1909 French translation of Ottoman Turk Enderûnlu Fâzil's *Hubanname* (1792–93; "Book of Beautiful Boys"), for instance, is found to have many passages that cannot be attributed to the original. The French text creates new portraits of boys of nationalities not in the master text, including the *beaux* of Ceylon, Java, Malaysia, and China, omits all European boys presumably because they aren't exotic enough to titillate, and modernizes the sentiments and story of "The Beauty of Baghdad" who "wins more money with his idle buttocks than a miller can produce of flour turning his grist-stone always" (267). Early twentieth-century writers joined the modernist rebellion against sexual censorship most easily if they attributed sexual activities to any kind of exotic other.

Just as Said showed how modernist representations of sexuality participated in cultural constructions of those from the Orient as sexual others, so critics have found that US literature worked with and against white stereotypes of blacks as, in the negative vein, sexually ungoverned or, in a particular strain of modernist romanticism, primitive and therefore more in touch with their sensuality/sexuality. Hazel Carby, in *Reconstructing Womanhood: The Emergence of the Afro-American Woman Novelist* (1987), showed how writers in the United States worked with "two very different but interdependent codes of sexuality" for white and black women. Carby explains, "Racist sexual ideologies proclaimed the black woman to be a rampant sexual being, and in response black women writers either focused on defending their morality or displaced sexuality onto another terrain" (174). Carby presents Nella Larsen's *Quicksand* (1928) as embodying the dilemma for black women writers:

> Larsen recognized that the repression of the sensual in Afro-American fiction in response to the long history of the exploitation of black sexuality led to the repression of passion and the repression or denial of female sexuality and desire. But, of course, the representation of black female sexuality meant risking its definition as primitive and exotic within a racist society. Larsen attempted to embody but could not hope to resolve these contradictions in her representation of Helga as a sexual being, making Helga the first truly sexual black female protagonist in Afro-American fiction. (174)

Larsen's work has received ongoing critical attention for its negotiation of sexual boundaries (Blackmer, duCille, McDowell), while other critics have focused on those who aimed to stifle sexual expression in favor of middle-class black respectability. In *Cruising Modernism*, Michael Trask explains how Carl Van Vechten's 1926 novel, *Nigger Heaven*, infuriated W. E. B. Du Bois, Countee Cullen, Jessie Fauset, and Sterling Brown because of its "exotic" sexuality that promoted sexual stereotypes based on "the cult of primitivism" (105). In *Celibacies: American Modernism and Sexual Life* (2013), Benjamin Kahan argues that in response to the racist eroticization of black bodies, celibacy became a tool of black activism during the Harlem Renaissance.

Writing about the ways that in-groups attribute extreme or negatively perceived sex acts, orientations, and inclinations to others in modernist scholarship has not been restricted to race or nationality but extends to classes and types. Laura Frost's *Sex Drives: Fantasies of Fascism in Literary Modernism* (2002), for example, traces the literary genealogy of eroticized images of fascism in British and French modernist literature and beyond. Frost finds "women pining for tyrants, men craving the hand of a master, and soldiers whose uniforms serve as arousing aphrodisiacs" as evidence that "political and national identities are constructed around and shored up by particular sexual identities" (3). In *Modernism, Mass Culture, and the Aesthetics of Obscenity* (2000), Allison Pease argues that British modernists incorporated mass cultural pornographic tropes and images into their works in the name of high art and, in doing so, moved lower-class bodies and sexuality into *haute bourgeois* literary practices. Given that modernist literature was produced during a period steeped in eugenic thinking, it is not surprising that a lack of self-control was almost always imputed to those groups considered ill-fit to breed.

Modernist lesbian and gay histories and identities

Simultaneous to, and in keeping with, critical theory that promulgated a view of sexuality as socially constructed, self-identified gay and lesbian literary critics and historians of the 1970s, 1980s, and 1990s wrote new literary histories and revised the modernist canon. Lesbian feminist historians played an important role in making visible modernist lesbian networks that had been obscured in the middle of the twentieth century. Blanche Wiesen Cook expanded the understanding of lesbian representation in modernism by talking about what had *not* been talked about. In "'Women Alone Stir My Imagination': Lesbianism and the Cultural Tradition" (1979), Cook identified 1928 as a banner year for lesbian publishing, touting Woolf's *Orlando*, Barnes's *Ladies Almanack*, and Hall's *Well of Loneliness* as three novels about lesbians published in the same year (she did not cite Elizabeth Bowen's *The Hotel* or Compton Mackenzie's *Extraordinary Women*, as Susan Lanser did in her 2016 essay, "1928: Sapphic Modernity and the Sexuality of History"). She registered surprise at the variety of lesbian representations and argued that "most of us lesbians in the 1950s grew up knowing nothing about lesbianism except Stephen Gordon's swagger, Stephen Gordon's breeches, and Stephen Gordon's wonderful way with horses" (719). Cook's point is that the obscenity trial had made *The Well of Loneliness* famous but modernist lesbian literature was invisible, in part because of the court's negative response to the novel that reflected an increasingly homophobic public climate from the 1930s to '60s. As a result, Cook argued, lesbianism in the 1950s was shaped in ways it might not otherwise have been. What would it have been like to be a lesbian in the 1950s if one had known about Virginia Woolf's affair with Vita Sackville-West or that there had been a Parisian social circle of lesbian writers and artists with the glamorous, polyamorous Natalie Barney at its center?

Lillian Faderman's influential 1981 history, *Surpassing the Love of Men: Romantic Friendship and Love between Women from the Renaissance to the Present*, uses literature as a primary source to argue that romantic friendship between women from the sixteenth to the nineteenth centuries was normative until the turn of the twentieth century when sexology declared love between people of the same sex a medical problem; Faderman claims that "openly expressed love between women for the most part ceased to be possible after World War I" (19). Faderman is among many historians and critics to observe that the twentieth century has a distinct relationship to sexuality dissimilar from previous centuries; "it is in our century that love has come to be perceived as a refinement of the sexual impulse, but in many other centuries romantic love and the sexual impulse were often considered unrelated" (19). One effect of the perceived linkage between sex and love in the twentieth century is that women's romantic friendships were no longer understood or probable. Loving relationships between women were reframed as necessarily sexual and therefore lesbian. Because some sexologists such as Richard von Krafft-Ebing had declared women who had sex with women diseased and Freud had described them as suffering from arrested sexual development, women who loved other women achieved subaltern status. The effect of the pathological/outlaw status of the lesbian in the twentieth century, Faderman claims, is that "not only did twentieth-century lesbian literature by heterosexuals usually show love between women to be a disease, but that women who were professedly lesbian generally internalized those views. This was reflected in their own literature, which was full of self-doubts and self-loathing until the 1960s" (20). As a result of Freudian and sexological views of lesbianism as a perversion of normal instincts, Faderman presents one example of what she sees as "flagrant misreadings" by twentieth-century critics of Henry James's pre-sexological novel, *The Bostonians*. Where twentieth-century critics see the relationship between Verena Tarrant and Olive Chancellor as "a study of a disease," she counters that James presented Verena's heterosexual marriage as destructive (191–192): "Twentieth-century critics have overlooked such an apparent reading of this novel because in our label-prone post-Freudian society, 'lesbian' is 'sick,' and if Olive can be called a 'lesbian,' then her love for Verena is certainly 'perverse' .... James, however, believed that a romantic relationship between two women was not of itself sick" (195).

Faderman detects a dramatic shift in literary representations of women-loving women between 1900 and 1918, from celebrated to reviled, from platonic to sexual, and explains this shift as a response to sexological literature, itself based on images of lesbians created by French aestheticism of the nineteenth century that were in part reactions to women's increasing independence. Several chapters of the book recount the anti-lesbian plots of popular fiction in the first half of the twentieth century, but Faderman also admits that the rhetoric could not have been overwhelming, as there are multiple examples of lesbian couples central to the literary production of modernism, among them Sylvia Beach and Adrienne Monnier, Margaret Anderson and Georgette LeBlanc, and H. D. and Bryher (373).

Faderman's extensive overview of the changing nature of women's relationships and the writing by and about lesbians was part of a larger critical movement in the 1980s to recognize gay and lesbian literature and history. In a 1981 essay, Bonnie Zimmerman critiqued the absence of lesbian material in women's studies journals, at Modern Language Association panels, and in important feminist studies, taking aim at Elaine Showalter for not integrating lesbian issues into her discussion of the "crucial generation of early twentieth-century writers (Virginia Woolf, Vita Sackville-West, Dorothy Richardson, and Rosamond Lehmann)" and adding that "Sandra Gilbert and Susan Gubar's *The Madwoman in the Attic* does not even index lesbianism" (454). *Hidden from History: Reclaiming the Gay and Lesbian Past* (1989) is another example of the recovery work of the 1980s in that Eric Garber was among the first to identify the Harlem Renaissance with gay and lesbian literature, writing:

> At the beginning of the twentieth century, a homosexual subculture, uniquely Afro-American in substance, began to take shape in New York's Harlem. Throughout the so-called Harlem Renaissance period, roughly 1920 to 1935, black lesbians and gay men were meeting each other [on] street corners, socializing in cabarets and rent parties, and worshiping in church on Sundays, creating a language, a social structure, and a complex network of institutions. (318)

Mark Lilly echoes this claim for gay men's writing in his 1993 book, *Gay Men's Literature in the Twentieth Century*, which makes it clear that up until and through the 1980s, criticism dealt with the homosexuality of modernist authors and texts through elision or marginalization (1–6).

In her study *The Apparitional Lesbian: Female Homosexuality and Modern Culture* (1993), Terry Castle picks up on Faderman's argument that lesbians only become a threat when women gain their independence from men and claims that "Western civilization has for centuries been haunted by a fear of 'women without men'" and the lesbian is a "haunting figure" in literature. Castle uses Sylvia Townsend Warner's little-studied 1936 novel, *Summer Will Show*, as a paradigm of the lesbian fiction that has what she describes as a ghostly presence in traditional literary studies. In answer to the question, "What then is a lesbian fiction?" Castle explains that *Summer Will Show* functions as "typical lesbian fiction" in that it "is likely to be an underread, even unknown, text—and certainly an underappreciated one. It is likely to stand in a satirical, inverted or parodic relationship to more famous novels of the past ... as if to infiltrate her own fiction among them as a kind of subversive, inflammatory, pseudo-canonical substitute" (90).

Laura Doan's *Fashioning Sapphism: The Origins of a Modern English Lesbian Culture* (2001) does not identify the typical lesbian text but rather how markers of "typical lesbian" self-presentation emerged out of *The Well of Loneliness* obscenity trial in 1928 (see Chapter 4 for more on this trial). Although short hair and masculine dress were the height of fashion for the modern woman in the 1920s, Doan demonstrates how this style, which Radclyffe Hall adopted, became inextricably linked with lesbianism after Hall's novel was tried, and her identity received media attention. Until this time, Doan contends, there was no such thing as lesbian identity:

> In the early 1920s lesbianism was not a "fact" marked on the body, nor was it commonly understood as a particular sexual object choice or sexual practice between women, nor was it (as yet) a modern identity or subjectivity—instead lesbianism was ... unintelligible to many people. Nameless or not, the entering of the "vice between women" into legal discourse and public consciousness marked an important step in the formation of a subcultural identity because, as Weeks so aptly explains, "social regulation provides the conditions within which those defined can begin to develop their own consciousness and identity." (63)

Thus, Doan likens the 1928 obscenity trial of *The Well of Loneliness* to the 1895 prosecution of Oscar Wilde for gross indecency in that each trial marked the arrival of the male or female homosexual as a knowable type in public culture (see Figure 3) (27). For men and women of means who chose same-sex partners, Doan indicates that sexological literature was an important resource. She found sexological works by Havelock Ellis, Karl Heinrich Ulrichs, Richard von Krafft-Ebing, and Edward Carpenter in the personal libraries of three lesbian writers—Bryher, Sackville-West, and Hall—and argues that for those engaged in same-sex relationships, such books would have been as important and influential as Marie Stopes's *Married Love* (1918) was to heterosexuals.[1]

FIGURE 3 *Marguerite Radclyffe Hall and Lady Una Troubridge, August 1927. Getty Images. Fashionable and modern, Hall's masculine dress and self-presentation would become associated with lesbianism in the twentieth century.*

Although Doan's account is persuasive, Esther Newton had claimed in "The Mythic Mannish Lesbian" (1984) that from 1900 the "mannish lesbian" was already a known type, emerging from the pages of sexology to break the nineteenth-century models of romantic friendship. Newton maintains that Radclyffe Hall, like Gertrude Stein and Vita Sackville-West, associated herself with the congenital "third sex" figure articulated first in Krafft-Ebing and later by Havelock Ellis; this was a woman who expressed lust for other women and had a distinct trace of masculinity (568). Newton's critique is typical of pre-Judith Butler and -1990s criticism in that she embraces gender and sexual identity essentialism, maintaining, "cross-dressing for Hall is not a masquerade. It stands for the New Woman's rebellion against the male order and, at the same time, for the lesbian's desperate struggle to be and express her true self" (570). It was important to Hall, Newton notes, that the New Woman lay claim to her full sexuality outside of the male discourses of pornography, literature, and medicine and to do so she had to "enter the male world, either as a heterosexual on male terms (a flapper) or as—or with—a lesbian in male body drag (a butch)" (573).

Of note, the term "lesbian" does not enter the English language until the 1890s when sexological texts use it to describe sexual behavior between women. However, by the 1920s, the term "lesbian" is used to describe a sexual identity. Women who loved women in the first three decades of the twentieth century would more likely have identified themselves as inverts or sapphists than lesbians, if they identified themselves at all, but many recent studies take the term "lesbian" as the subject of their investigation with the understanding that the modernist period is when the *term* became culturally operative through a field of social and political representations. Exemplars of these studies include books by Laura Doan, Deborah Cohler, Heather Love, Jane Garrity, and Gay Wachman. Jodie Medd's *Lesbian Scandal and the Culture of Modernism* (2012) reads the allegation of lesbianism as a tool for creating scandal that extended past sexuality. Deborah Cohler's *Citizen, Invert, Queer: Lesbianism and War in Early Twentieth-Century Britain* (2010) explores the ways that lesbianism emerged out of sexology-defined "inversion" through the nationalist transformations of the First World War. Medical descriptions of inversion focused on the body, whereas lesbianism, like modernism, was described by its relationship to consciousness. Cohler argues that "once we understand citizenship, empire, and nation to be just as constative of sexual and gendered identities as legal prohibitions and medical discourse, the representational politics of homosexual men and women become far more intertwined than separated" (xvii). In fact, she claims that *The Well of Loneliness*, *Orlando* and Compton Mackenzie's *Extraordinary Women* (all of which appeared in the second half of 1928) "struggle to represent a relatively new cultural phenomenon—homosexuality in women—through an oblique, direct, or metaphoric leverage of Britain's decreasing global dominance as referents for their representations of female homosexuality. 'England' becomes the almost invisible signifier of sexual and cultural normativity" (Cohler 153). Susan Lanser (2016) builds on this argument regarding the lesbian texts of 1928 to argue that modernist lesbian narrative takes the form of picaresque:

> The Sapphic narratives of 1928 re-gender the adventure story: *Orlando* and *Ladies Almanack* are overtly picaresque fantasies, the former spanning several countries and four centuries, the latter figuring a lifespan through movements charted in monthly episodes. *The Well of Loneliness* is more conventionally plotted, yet it "exiles" Stephen Gordon from her English country house to London, then to Paris, to the battlefields of France, to the Canary Islands, and back to Paris with sojourns to Italy and Switzerland, in what one could argue is a marriage plot thwarted by the picaresque.

Lanser argues that modernist lesbian novels forged a particularly modern way of being in the world that does nothing less than renew subjectivity. The absence of home spaces in these novels extricates them from domestic ties, and in doing so, Lanser contends, "relocates and thereby reinvents the individual subject."

Modernist scholarship on gay male authors was slower to take root than lesbian scholarship, and there is less of it. There are possible legal reasons why this is so. Where lesbianism was not a crime and was perceived as illegible to most readers who thought it impossible, sodomy was a crime in the UK until 1957, and in the United States, it was a crime in some states until 2003. In the UK, "gross indecency"—any sexual activity between men short of anal penetration or sodomy—was criminalized from 1885 to 1967. As a result, representations of gay male sexuality are oblique in modernism. Although John Fletcher has called E. M. Forster's *Maurice* "the one explicitly homosexual *Bildungsroman* produced within the mainstream English literary tradition by a canonical author," Forster wrote the novel in 1913–1914 and did not allow for its publication until after his death in 1971. The history of lesbian and gay self-censorship is an important aspect of the production and reception of modernism in the twentieth century. In a 1992 essay on textual and critical silences in twentieth-century gay and lesbian literature, Diana Collecott noted, for example, that W. H. Auden's love poems were written for a male lover but escaped notice because they were addressed to "you." In *Epistemology of the Closet*, Eve Kosofsky Sedgwick argues that modernism's commitment to abstraction is motivated by a need to make illegible a desire too dangerous to make clear; what is abstract, silent, or coded can always be universalized or read otherwise. Brian Glavey argues that this is what Gertrude Stein's writing does in first inciting and then frustrating the reader's desire to discover the truth of identity (17). Where authors did not self-suppress, others did it for them. Collecot notes that when H. D.'s poems written for Bryher were published in 1983, the editor moved the inscriptions to the poems, "for W.B." (Winifred Bryher), to a note in the back of the book, enacting a kind of censorship of the poems' context and, arguably, composition.

Most modernist scholars who discuss twentieth-century gay male identity begin with the three trials in the spring of 1895 that ended in convicting Oscar Wilde to two years' hard labor for acts of gross indecency. The trials outed Wilde's sexual trysts with young men and his imprisonment made an object lesson of his behavior. His imprisonment, however, created a ripple of homophobia in its wake, silencing male-male sexuality in modernist literature. The legal circumstances for same-sex sexuality were different in the United States, but its own racist legacy has made scholars slow to recognize the queer black writers of the Harlem Renaissance as part of modernism. Sedgwick's 1985 *Between Men: English Literature and Male Homosocial Desire* charted a homoerotic literary tradition that comes to a halt at the turn of the twentieth century and, in doing so, created a surge of interest in tracking gay male literary culture in the early twentieth century. Ed Cohen's *Talk on the Wilde Side: Toward a Genealogy of a Discourse on Male Sexualities* (1993) localized Foucault's claim that homosexuality was an invention of the nineteenth century by arguing that Wilde's trials shaped the sexual imagination of an international news-reading audience and created a paradigmatic example of a "new 'type' of sexual actor: 'the homosexual'" (2). Where prior to the trials aesthetic effeminacy was a counter-hegemonic positioning Wilde and other dandies took up to challenge middle-class values, Cohen argues, as does Alan Sinfield in the 1994 *The Wilde Century: Effeminacy, Oscar Wilde and the Queer Moment*, one of the consequences of the wide press coverage of Wilde's trials is that those things for which he stood, aestheticism, effeminacy and wit, come to be perceived as synonymous with male sexual inversion (ch. 5). In the press, Cohen argues,

Wilde's person(a) had been publicly redefined so that both in the court and in the press he came to exemplify the "kind" of man who had a "tendency" toward the commission of "certain" (sexual) acts with other men. Indeed, the representational practices through which Wilde's "exemplary" status was widely disseminated produced "Oscar Wilde" as an iconic (sexual) "character" whose particular attributes could then be read off as evidence of a more general type. (174)

In Wilde's case, the arguments made against him in charging him with the relatively new and vague "acts of gross indecency," rather than sodomy, blurred the distinction between criminal charges and a range of nonsexual behaviors and attributes, shifting the "locus of the new legal definition from the particularity of a sexual practice to the generality of a gender identity" (181). At root in Cohen's explanation is defining the gay male as in opposition to middle-class respectability in England. Looking at US examples, historian George Chauncey sees a similar class dynamic at play in the naming and not naming of gay men.

Chauncey's *Gay New York* (1994) details late nineteenth- and early twentieth-century gay culture in New York. As do most critics in the wake of Foucault, Chauncey argues that the hetero-homosexual binary is a recent creation, but Chauncey provides historical nuance in identifying that in the early twentieth century, gender expression was a more important marker of "inversion" than sexual behavior:

Particularly in working-class culture, homosexual behavior per se became the primary basis for the labeling and self-identification of men as "queer" only around the middle of the twentieth century; before then, most men were so labeled only if they displayed a much broader inversion of their ascribed gender status by assuming the sexual and other cultural roles ascribed to women. The abnormality (or "queerness") of the "fairy," that is, was defined as much by his "woman-like" character or "effeminacy" as his solicitation of male sexual partners; the "man" who responded to his solicitations—no matter how often—was not considered abnormal, a "homosexual," as long as he abided by masculine gender conventions. Indeed, the centrality of effeminacy to the representations of the "fairy" allowed many conventionally masculine men, especially unmarried men living in sex-segregated immigrant communities, to engage in extensive sexual activity with other men without risking stigmatization and the loss of their status as "normal men." (13)

As one example of the currency of inversion of gender as a way of explaining same-sex relations, Chauncey points to Harvard literary historian and critic, F. O. Mathiessen, who, as a graduate student at Oxford in 1925, wrote to his lover, the painter Russell Cheney, and described them as "neither wholly man, woman, or child" but that their love was a "female" love, as explained in the treatises on inversion by Havelock Ellis (104). Chauncey also points out that the Harlem Renaissance was fostered by networks of men who were either gay-identified or sexually active with both men and women, including Alain Locke, Carl Van Vechten, Countee Cullen, Wallace Thurman, Bruce Nugent, Claude McKay, and "possibly" Langston Hughes (264) (this "possibly" will become a critical game of "was he or wasn't he?" that queer theorist Robert Reid-Pharr critiques as beyond the point in *Archives of the Flesh*, 2016). Chauncey claims that in the 1920s, homosexuality was so much a part of the cultural landscape of New York that several Broadway plays addressed the topic. In 1926, Edouard Bournet's lesbian drama *The Captive*, and Mae West's *Sex*, attracted large audiences. It was only when Mae West promised to bring to Broadway from its New Jersey production *The Drag*, a play defending the rights of homosexuals to live as they saw fit, that police raided *The Captive* and *The Drag* on the same night in January 1927 and charged the productions with obscenity. As Chauncey sees it, this marked the beginning of the "closeting" of gays and lesbians in New York and of gay-positive narratives. He notes that though the early 1930s produced a "flurry of gay-themed novels—*Strange Brother* by Blair Niles (1931), *Twilight Men* by Andre Tellier (1931), *A Scarlet Pansy* by Robert Scully (1932), *Goldie* by Kennilworth Bruce (1933), *Better Angel* by Richard Meeker (1933), and *Butterfly Man* by Lew Levenson (1934)—most ended with the death or suicide of the gay protagonist as a sop to public morality" (324).

Michael Lucey's *Never Say I: Sexuality and the First Person in Colette, Gide, and Proust* (2006) demonstrates a parallel but different history in France where Gide, Proust, and Colette, along with minor writers such as Jean Lorrain and Catulle Mendès, engaged in a "kind of extended conversation or debate with each other" in which they sought to rid themselves of the ideological baggage of naturalism that equated homosexuality with degeneration and instead contribute to a "social dynamic in which manners for speaking about same-sex sexual relations ... were evolving" (82). Whether in continental Europe, Great Britain, or North America, those who engaged in same-sex sexual relations could not help but be aware of widespread social disapprobation of such behavior and the labels that might or might not attach to them as a result.

Queer theory and challenges to queer theory

Growing out of, but theoretically distinct from, gay and lesbian studies, queer theory emerged in the early 1990s as a refusal to define sexuality in relation to heterosexuality, so-called normative desires, or any kind of identity that necessarily participated in a hierarchy of significance. Like many modernist texts do, queer theory questions normative desires and challenges the ways that language, meaning, and identity solidify the status quo. Identities and labeled behaviors are understood as reifying and restricting by queer theory, which is anti-normativity and anti-foundationalist. Where Foucault identifies the construction of a homosexual identity as a twentieth-century problem, and Butler provides a model for deconstructing it, Eve Kosofsky Sedgwick, in *Epistemology of the Closet* (1990), identifies the binary structure of sexual identities as a crisis: "many of the major nodes of thought and knowledge in twentieth-century Western culture as a whole are structured—indeed, fractured—by a chronic, now endemic crisis of homo/heterosexual definition" (1). Sedgwick points to the modernist period as enacting a new male homosexual identity arising out of medical, legal, literary, and psychological discourses. This identity, she argues, is pernicious in that it robs a person of their humanity in defining them solely under the rubric of the homosexual:

> What *was* new from the turn of the century was the world-mapping by which every given person, just as he or she was necessarily assignable to a male or female gender, was now

considered necessarily assignable as well to a homo- or a heterosexuality, a binarized identity that was full of implications, however confusing, for even the ostensibly least sexual aspects of personal experience. (2)

The formation of this identity occurred during the period between the Oscar Wilde trials in 1895 and Proust's 1913 publication of *À la recherche du temps perdu (In Search of Lost Time)*, Sedgwick claims. Although certainly others concerned with the representation of women have extended this period to the 1928 obscenity trial of *The Well of Loneliness*, Sedgwick frames these two decades as a time of naming, explaining, and defining the homosexual as the keeper of sexual secrets that had to remain in an imaginary space called the closet. She reads *Billy Budd* and *The Picture of Dorian Gray* as 1891 parallel texts featuring beautiful young men who must die because they represent vacant, "epistemologically arousing" keepers of secrets (95). In terms of modernism's formalist experiments, Sedgwick argues that the "rhetoric of male modernism serves a purpose of universalizing, naturalizing, and thus substantially voiding—depriving of content—elements of a specifically and historically male homosexual rhetoric," and thus to read formally significant high modernism is to see the erasure of sex as knowledge at its core (165).

A persistent theme of critique in US modernist scholarship is the way that American culture has associated blackness with sexuality. Siobhan B. Sommerville's *Queering the Color Line: Race and the Invention of Homosexuality in America* (2000) uses post-structuralist binary logic and Butler's explanation of gender and sexuality as an effect of discourse to show "that questions of race—in particular the formation of notions of 'whiteness' and 'blackness'—must be understood as a crucial part of the history and representation of sexual formations, including lesbian and gay identity and compulsory heterosexuality in the United States" (5). Sommerville makes the case that the legal system classified black and white bodies as distinct in the 1896 legal case *Plessy v. Ferguson* at the same time that sexological discourse, informed by eugenics, was creating a distinction between heterosexuals and homosexuals. Queerness, Sommerville posits, was defined by racial and sexual alterity, "the not named thing" that could "pass" as either white or heterosexual or both. Through readings of Pauline Hopkins, James Weldon Johnson, and Jean Toomer, *Queering the Color Line* argues that constructions of racial identity at the turn of the century were foundational in constructing homosexuality as a distinct category of identity; in the United States, racial and sexual identity must be understood as mutually constitutive.

Working within the field of queer theory that seeks to undo the binary distinction between hetero- and homosexual, Scott Herring's *Queering the Underworld: Slumming, Literature, and the Undoing of Lesbian and Gay History* (2007) aims to produce a queer history of American modernism that champions writers who frustrated modernist-era attempts to classify and know, attempts he finds that parody the middle-class slum-narrative genre. Herring provides readings of Willa Cather, Carl Van Vechten, Wallace Thurman, Richard Bruce Nugent, and Djuna Barnes to show how their writing frustrated the era's sexological classification systems and emphasized the unknowable, the idiosyncratic, and the antisystemic. What he sees in these authors' works is:

> They just don't fit into conventional narratives of modern U.S. lesbian and gay underworlds that often guide queer American studies .... [They use] antirevelatory strategies, they also do not defer to a logic of the closet, a predominant mode of reading that is still intrinsic to many understandings of U.S. sexuality. They instead give a distinctive resistance to sexual exposure since what they expose, finally, is that there was nothing to hide. (23)

In this way, Herring directly challenges the work of Chauncey and Faderman, among others, for charting what he characterizes as "the insular, in-the-know nature of early twentieth-century U.S. gay and lesbian subcultures and their complex relation to middle-class notions of sexual identity" (26). What he writes he studies have in common, he claims, is their ability to frustrate the reader who seeks definitive sexual knowledge. Their works are characterized by modernism's ambiguity and impossible resolution.

Providing another challenge to gay and lesbian history is Heather Love's *Feeling Backward: Loss and the Politics of Queer History* (2007), which critiques gay and lesbian history of the 1970s and 1980s, not for reifying gay identity, but for excluding the difficult and depressing hardships of the gay and lesbian past out of the progressive need to promote a more just present. Participating in queer theory's turn to affect and temporality, Love argues that "for groups constituted by historical injury, the challenge is to engage with the past without being destroyed by it" (1). Thus, Love explores texts she says are marked by queer suffering she identifies with backwardness: "Backwardness means many things here: shyness, ambivalence, failure, melancholia, loneliness, regression, victimhood, heartbreak, antimodernism, immaturity, self-hatred, despair, shame. I describe backwardness as both a queer historical structure and as a model for queer historiography" (146). Backwardness, she argues, is intimately bound to the idea of modernity, with its suggestion of progress, rationality, and technological advance; backwardness is the other side of the binary that affords modernity its definition. Looking at "the saddest texts in the queer canon" (3) by Walter Pater, Sylvia Townsend Warner, Willa Cather, and Radclyffe Hall, Love finds they turn toward the past, toward isolation, and they disconnect from any larger historical continuum. She aligns this turn with Freud's psychoanalytic framework that positions homosexuality as a failure to mature or overcome primary cathexes. While Willa Cather's work is championed by queer theorists Judith Butler, Eve Kosofsky Sedgwick, and Scott Herring for "her powerful disidentifications, her ambivalence, and her refusal of community" (25), Love chooses instead to focus on *The Well of Loneliness* as a "crucial account of what it felt like to bear a newly public and newly stigmatized identity in the 1920s" (26). Love notes that *Well* has undergone its own share of interpretations and identifications:

> *The Well* has repeatedly come into conflict with contemporary understandings of the meaning and shape of gay identity. During the 1970s, the novel was attacked primarily for its equation of lesbianism with masculine identification; in the years of the 'woman-loving-woman,' it was anathema with its mannish heroine, its derogation of femininity, and its glorification of normative heterosexuality. Although recent recuperation of butch-femme practices and the growth of transgender studies have sparked a renewed interest in the book, Hall's embrace of the discourse of congenital inversion is still at odds with the antiessentialism of contemporary theories of sexuality. (101)

Critics have come to align the disruptive elements of modernist literary practices with the disruptive work of queer theory. The works of certain authors are more frequently described as queer, largely because of their resistance to heterosexuality at the same time that they defy naming, political order, and identities. For instance, the work and to some degree the personas of Jamaican writer and poet Claude McKay and the German performance artist/poet Baroness Elsa von Freytag-Loringhoven—both of whom lived and wrote in New York (see Figure 4)—have each been labeled queer in modernist scholarship due to their anti-capitalist, sexually charged work; equally, neither self-identified sexually

FIGURE 4 *Claude McKay and Baroness Elsa von Freytag-Loringhoven, 1922. Library of Congress, Prints & Photographs Division. The fancy dress was considered part of the Baroness's performance art; McKay's outfit has received differing interpretations.*

despite having partners of both sexes. Other writers frequently discussed as queer are Djuna Barnes (Azzarello, DeLauretis, Herring, Galvin, Glavey, Salvato), Willa Cather (Azzarello, Butler, Haralson, Herring, Lindemann, Love, Sedgwick), and many of the writers associated with the Harlem Renaissance (Holcomb, Vogel). Because of the sexual fluidity and the emphasis on multiplicity and disidentification of the works published in Wallace Thurman's 1926 Harlem Renaissance single-issue magazine *Fire!!*, for instance, Matthew N. Hannah argues that it was a "manifesto that made visible the dynamically queer sexualities operative in Harlem through a modernist politics of aesthetic representation in direct opposition to racial uplift and sociological analysis" (163). Richard Bruce Nugent's "Smoke, Lillies, and Jade," published in *Fire!!*, is often called the first piece of openly gay fiction by a black writer, but its polymorphous sexuality may equally be called queer.

In a 2009 *PMLA* essay "Modernism at Night," Heather Love asks the question, "Is queer modernism simply another name for modernism?" (744). Love notes that "since the term queer is so closely linked to the concept of the margin, the prominence of exile and alienation in even dominant modernism resonates with the outsider glamour of *queer*" (745). She identifies Oscar Wilde, Djuna Barnes, and Jean Genet as champions of the unnatural, the perverse, and the artificial, those who pushed against the normative and the natural, but also avers that "what makes *queer* and *modernism* such a good fit is that the indeterminacy of *queer* seems to match the indeterminacy, expansiveness, and drift of the literary—particularly the experimental, oblique version most closely associated with modernist textual production" (745). In his 2011 essay "Queer Modernism," Robert L. Caserio identifies several hearty strands of queer modernism but importantly critiques the by-now standard narrative of the medicalization of homosexuality: "The modernist construction of homosexuality evolves from an alliance of plural erotic dispositions that are united in antagonism to opposite-sex love, bourgeois marriage, and family. To emphasize homosexuality as a product of medical and juridical innovations is to overlook the alliance" (201). Caserio sees homosexuality in the modernist period as one of several of modernism's revolutionary challenges to cultural repertoires. Caserio argues that the subversive power of eros, its disorientations, and disruptions that do not seek to name but rather to defy the impulse to order that demands names can be found in the works of Federico García Lorca, Dorothy Richardson, James Joyce, G. B. Shaw, Joseph Conrad, Ronald Firbank, Willa Cather, and Djuna Barnes.

Benjamin Kahan's *Celibacies* uses the queer theoretical apparatus to make celibacy visible as a historical sexual formation invoked by modernists from the political left. Not a failure or a renunciation of pleasure, Kahan historicizes the discourse of celibacy as one that finds pleasure, power, and the organization of identity to subvert the regimes of the normal. Kahan claims many authors who, for at least long periods of time if not continuously, organized their identity and behavior around celibacy. Among them are Baron Corvo, Marcel Proust, E. M. Forster, Franz Kafka, Edna Ferber, Edith Sitwell, T. E. Lawrence, Langston Hughes, and Eudora Welty. Although celibacy had a robust life in the late nineteenth and early twentieth century, Kahan explains that by the late 1920s, sexual happiness rather than spiritual union was an expectation of married life, and celibacy was then vilified as unhealthy and unnatural (21–22).

Sexology and perversion, beyond power

Not all modernist critics have worked within the Foucauldian framework without critiquing it, or suggesting systems to compete with social power. In modernist scholarship, there are critics who have challenged Foucault's central claim in *The History of Sexuality, Volume 1*. Turning to psychoanalysis and the power of eros as perceived within a queer theoretical framework as boundary-dissolving, they provide an alternative model to Foucault's vision of an all-encompassing social power. Claiming that modern fictions of sexuality have produced a poetics and politics of the perverse in *Libidinal Currents: Sexuality and the Shaping of Modernism* (1998), Joseph Allen Boone frames sexuality as not necessarily or only shaped by relations of power:

> Difficult as our disciplinary culture makes it to conceptualize acts of surrender that are not acts of submission, I want to suggest that the longing to yield to a space in which subject meets subject in terms other than those accruing to the rhetoric of power— whether expressed in the interchanges that form the substance of

sexual fantasy or fictional narrative—is not an exercise in self-deluded mysticism or nostalgic transcendentalism. Rather, as soon as intersubjective desires enter the imagination, they take on a phenomenological reality, becoming a materially embodied (which is to say real) component of the individual's emotional, psychic, and somatic life. And this reality belies the myth of power's hegemony as, in fact, a myth. (2)

This Foucauldian/Butler-enabled understanding of psychic interiority as an enabling fiction relies, seemingly without contradiction, on Freud's hydraulic model of the libido. The polymorphous perverse exceeds the structure of disciplinarity and power à la Foucault and affirms Freud's original repressive hypothesis; modernist narrative mirrored this. Boone defends Freud's ideas on the grounds that the conceptual shift of sexuality from the periphery to the center of human identity was pivotal to twentieth-century epistemology and identity formations, informing the plot of sexual awakening quintessential to twentieth-century literature. Boone argues that "to the extent that sex has come to signify the central but hidden *essence* of one's nature, it follows that the instinctual drives, the pent-up floods of libidinal desire, are forces which must be *released*, as it were, from their interior and anterior captivity before any *awakening* can occur as a conscious event" (69). Ultimately, Boone's sprawling readings of Kate Chopin's *The Awakening*, D. H. Lawrence's *The Virgin and the Gypsy*, Freud's *Dora*, Joyce's *Ulysses*, Woolf's *Mrs. Dalloway*, Bruce Nugent's "Smoke, Lilies, and Jade," Djuna Barnes's *Nightwood*, Charles Henri Ford and Parker Tyler's *The Young and Evil*, Blair Niles's *Strange Brother*, William Faulkner's *Absolom, Absolom!*, and Christina Stead's *The Man Who Loved Children* do not point to a coherent theory of modernist sexuality but rather to "the breakdown of unitary modes of representation" (71). The perversity to which Boone points is not sexology's catalogued list of nonnormative sexual behaviors but rather the errant nature of modernist narrative itself, which he frames as a reflection of the libido. Robert L. Caserio's "Queer Modernism" closely mirrors this approach, arguing that "art shows us what eros perceives beyond the social order, hence 'beyond sexuality.' Art is not sublimation of eros, however. Art ... manifests the queer character of eros" (216). Notably, Kahan, in

Celibacies, critiques Boone's approach as one in which "sexual transgression is naturalized and fetishized as the quintessential modernist modality" (7). There are other modernisms besides the queer, polymorphous perverse one, but it is difficult to deny the "willful derangement of established order" that occurs in so many modernist texts (Caserio 203).

Just as Joseph Allen Boone's critique privileges desire and perversity in modernism as irregular, polymorphous, and fruitfully disruptive, so Michael Trask in *Cruising Modernism: Class and Sexuality in American Literature and Social Thought* (2003) seeks to show how social class in the United States becomes "stipulated in the idiom of the new psychology of sex, so mobility and desire in this period stipulate each other through the irregular bodies of the underclass" (2). Similar to Boone, Trask critiques Foucault's narrative of sexuality as overly determined rather than based on "the contingency or fragmentariness of power/knowledge systems" (36). Instead, Trask looks to sexology for a different model:

> As a form of taxonomy, a function of categories and nomenclature, sexuality in the Foucauldian scheme emerges as the means to singularize and to place each individual with a specific identity. It provides a safe ontological harbor for an ever more efficacious epistemological governance. Yet for social theorists around 1900, neither ontology nor epistemology was particularly stable, and the focus on sexual desire rather than on sexual identity was indicative of the conceptual crisis these thinkers faced .... perversion was not a categorical niche populated by distinct species of sexual deviants so much as synonymous with the breakdown, the vexing precariousness, of categorization itself. (36)

Ironically, although Foucault sought to critique the order created in and through sexuality in the modernist period, he has increasingly become the cited target for creating that order. Trask finds in literary and social scientific texts of the early twentieth century profound interest in and anxiety about desire, mobility, and flux. Observing that in the United States sex was a franker subject of public discourse than class, he claims that "the concept of sexual perversion regulated the discourse of social thought in the first decades of the twentieth century, permeating knowledge systems well beyond the domain of sexology as the explanation of a host of social effects and behaviors" (25). With this, desire became an important category of social theory as middle-class and elite Americans increasingly encountered lower-class "others" whose lives represented disturbing mobility and erotic deviance. Trask looks at figures of immigrants and the underclass in Henry James, Hart Crane, Willa Cather, and Gertrude Stein to make the case that "it is literary modernism that makes the unstable and restless eros of the class outsider most apprehensible" (15). Both Trask and Boone thus appear to be returning to the modernist notion of the sexual/libidinal as disruptive potential, a question more than an answer.

Case study: Willa Cather's "Paul's Case: A Study in Temperament"

American writer Willa Cather and her short story "Paul's Case: A Study in Temperament" provides a clear example of how attitudes about and critical approaches to sexuality have affected how we read modernist texts. Published in 1905, "Paul's Case" was Willa Cather's favorite short story, the only one she allowed to be reprinted and anthologized. Both the story and Willa Cather have received marked critical attention since the emergence of feminist, lesbian, and queer theories.

First there is the case of Cather's sexuality. Cather was notoriously private, and despite having two female live-in companions for the duration of her adult life and no erotic attachments to men, she was not identified as a lesbian until 1975 when Jane Rule's book, *Lesbian Images*, simply included her in its roster of lesbian writers. Rule argues, as did Deborah Lambert in 1982, that Cather wrote from a heterosexual position, or guise, despite her erotic preferences. Writing from a man's point of view, they claim, allowed her to eroticize the women her male characters loved. In a 1984 article "'The Thing Not Named': Willa Cather as a Lesbian Writer," Sharon O'Brien used what is now understood as a common trope of lesbian and gay modernist writing, absence or silence, to explain how Cather's writing is emblematic of lesbian writing of the period. O'Brien writes:

> Certainly the most prominent absence and the most unspoken love in her work are the emotional bonds between women that were central to her life. From one perspective, Cather in "The Novel Démeublé" is the modernist writer endorsing allusive, suggestive art and inviting the reader's participation in the creation of literary meaning. But from another, she is the lesbian writer forced to disguise or to conceal the emotional source of her fiction, reassuring herself that the reader fills the absence in the text by intuiting the subterranean, unwritten subtext. (577)

O'Brien's work, along with other feminist and queer theoretical work on Cather, was the target of a critical take-down by Joan Acocella in "Cather and the Academy," published in the *New Yorker* in 1995. Criticizing what she characterized as literary criticism's attempt to politicize Cather and her work, Acocella questions, "If we now argue that those subjects of hers were just covers, and what she was really writing about was the very things she chose not to write about, sex and gender, is this a vote for the rights of women and homosexuals?" (71). The debate as to whether and how a person's sexual desires/behaviors/identifications affect their art persists.

"Paul's Case: A Study in Temperament" is a particular favorite of queer theorists, in part because it defies easy definition and labeling. The story has been read as one about the difference between art and life or as a medical case of "hypersensitivity." It was not until 1975 that the story was identified as having a "homosexual motif" by Larry Rubin. The fact that Paul's is a "case" renders Paul the subject of inquiry from some official body, whether medical, legal, literary, or psychological, which would, as Acocella intimated earlier, appear to want to render a final judgment in order to advance a political or ideological agenda. As if anticipating Acocella's critique, Judith Butler wrote in her 1993 *Bodies That Matter*:

> It is not easy to know how to read gender or sexuality in Willa Cather's fiction. Cather has appeared not to place herself in a legible relation to women or lesbianism. For her reader, then, to place or affirm her with a name engages a certain violence against her texts, texts which have as one of their persistent features the destabilization of gender and sexuality through the name. (143)

Butler reads "Paul's Case" as working in and through the structuring prohibition against homosexuality by thwarting all ideals and in particular the integrity of the body. Butler describes Paul's body as refusing to cohere or make itself legible in terms of gender or sexuality (163–164). But Butler is not the first queer theorist to have attended to "Paul's Case."

In a 1989 essay, "Across Gender, across Sexuality: Willa Cather and Others," Eve Kosofsky Sedgwick observes that Cather wrote two essays in 1895, condemning Oscar Wilde for his then-publicized "sins" and further for creating insincere art. Sedgwick reads "Paul's Case" as a softening of that stance and a reckoning with "a feminized or homosexualized culture and artifice" (55). She says,

> In what I am reading as Cather's move in 'Paul's Case,' the mannish lesbian author's coming together with the effeminate boy on the ground of a certain distinctive position of gender liminality is also a move toward a minority gay identity whose more effectual cleavage, whose more determining separatism, would be that of homo/hetero*sexual* choice rather than that of male/female *gender*. (70)

In distinguishing between sexual orientation and gender expression, Sedgwick attends to the ways that the language of the story points toward a false gender for Paul, much like the artifice to which Paul is attracted throughout the story, as Cather's elision of his sexual orientation. Both Butler and Sedgwick read "Paul's Case" as the loci of queer or perverse desire, but they do so by reading the story as working through a set of complicated cross-identifications.

In 2007, Scott Herring argued that these readings of "Paul's Case" equate Cather the author with her fictional subjects, assuming that her sexual orientation underlies her fictional constructs. Herring contended that

> through this project of 'claiming' Cather for a postmodern queer audience, we perhaps repeat the inquisition that Pittsburgh High undertakes against one of its own, a pedagogical diagnosis mirroring, in turn, a sexological one. We attempt to make Cather's desires (and, with them, her sexuality) intelligible by cracking the semiotic code that she herself so flippantly tosses off in the opening paragraphs. (71)

In Herring's reading, the story dislocates the sexual self and moves it past subcultural affiliations.

Whether looked at through the lens of affiliation or disaffiliation, the question of sex and sexual identity has occupied a substantial thread of Cather criticism in the past fifty years, just as it has with other modernist authors and modernist texts. We now turn to the question of how gender and gender expression of masculinity has contributed to the shape of modernist studies.

Note

1 *Married Love* advocated egalitarian sexual partnership in marriage and sold more than 400,000 copies in the 1920s.

3

Masculinities

Overview

To be modern is to assert the masculine self paradoxically as lost, dying, anachronistic.
—SARAH COLE, *MODERNISM, MALE FRIENDSHIP, AND THE FIRST WORLD WAR,* 2003

We have thus far suggested that women were finding new powers and public recognition during the modernist period. It may, therefore, seem contradictory to assert that the period also produced extreme forms of masculinity and male homosocial behavior that the literature of the period manifests. And yet these two facts coexist. Women's increasing social power was in taut dialectical tension with masculinity and male power. Those who felt the push of women's demands for participation in public life reacted with a sense that masculinity was somehow in crisis. Modernist critics agree that masculinity in the modernist period expresses and mourns its own losses. In the epigraph to this chapter and throughout her book on *Modernism, Male Friendship, and the First World War* (2003), Sarah Cole cites as a central modernist motif the idea that the male or masculine self is expressed as having already passed, locked out of the present time (137). Ariela Freedman, in *Death, Men, and Modernism: Trauma and Narrative in British Fiction from Hardy to Woolf* (2003), makes a similar claim, if with shifted emphasis, writing that the "paradigm of male modernism [is] not the dead body but the impotent friend, the male onlooker, spectator and complicit contributor to the death itself" (22). Although one might understand the death of masculinity as tied to the First World War, as Cole and Freedman do, the motif of masculinity in peril, if not lost, was articulated as early as 1886 when Basil Ransom in Henry James's *The Bostonians* agonizes that "the whole generation is womanized; the masculine tone is passing out of the world." The womanization of the world Basil Ransom decries originates from male doubt about the ability to assume world-shaping powers. If the first challenge to hegemonic masculinity's ability to shape the world arose from the advent of the New Woman and imperialist clashes that took place around the *fin de siècle*, the second challenge arose after the First World War with the unraveling of imperial masculine authority, the traumatic losses of the war, and the increased presence of women in the public sphere. Masculine doubt could be said to define the poetry of T. S. Eliot. From "The Love Song of J. Alfred Prufrock" (1915) to the fragmented voices of *The Waste Land* (1922) to "The Hollow Men" (1925), Eliot's poetic narrators are insecure, impotent, empty, and paralyzed. Seemingly different in tone, the male characters in Ernest Hemingway's novels and short stories are, as Robert Penn Warren put it in 1947, "tough men, experienced in the hard worlds they inhabit, and not obviously given to emotional display or sensitive thinking" (1), but they are also living in a world of blurred gender boundaries in which, for instance in *The Sun Also Rises* (1926), war veteran Jake Barnes is impotent and in love with Lady Brett Ashley, a short-haired, twice-divorced woman who expropriates masculine traits not just in dress but in sexual behavior. Hemingway's self-deluded men are not the self-doubting thinkers of Eliot, but as inhabitants of violent worlds, neither are they potent, capable, or able to affect the world satisfactorily. Masculinity in modernism is largely ambivalent or, as Greg Forter has said of American authors Eliot, Cather, Fitzgerald, Faulkner, and Hemingway, melancholic in response to the loss of authentic manhood (23). From *Ulysses*'s cuckolded Leopold Bloom, to *Sons and Lovers*'s oedipally anguished Paul Morel, to the writers of the Harlem Renaissance who contended over whether to conform to W. E. B. Du Bois's demand to represent normative middle-class masculinity in the form of self-restrained "race men" who would adhere to heteronormative reproductive futurity or the Claude McKay and Wallace Thurman school of decadence, which embraced and ironized so-called primitive masculinity in all of its pleasure-soaked ambisexual vigor, modernist texts contested what masculinity was or should be.

Literary criticism from the modernist period through the 1960s assumed a masculine point of view, taking for granted a universal "I" that was male. F. R. Leavis, for example, was one of the first proponents of modernism, and his essays in *Scrutiny* and lectures at Cambridge were highly influential in composing a modernist canon from the works of Henry James, Joseph Conrad, T. S. Eliot, Ezra Pound, D. H. Lawrence, and James Joyce. His was the modernism of masculine difficulty and masculine despair. Notably he did not champion any living female writers during the modernist period, and yet Leavis never discussed masculinity or manhood in his criticism. It was an assumed point of view. With a few exceptions, Leavis's male modernists describe a relatively impotent and infertile, complex masculinity at war with itself and its imperatives. Like Leavis, Frank Kermode, another formidable critic of modernism in the mid-twentieth century, neglected female writers, championing the work of W. B. Yeats, T. S. Eliot, James Joyce, D. H. Lawrence, E. M. Forster, and Samuel Beckett. As noted in Chapter 1, in the United States, the New Critics such as John Crowe Ransom and Cleanth Brooks, while largely espousing a method of reading, reinforced a male canon through anthologizing and explicating the works of primarily male American writers such as T. S. Eliot, Robert Frost, and William Faulkner. Early critical concern as the modernist canon was formed in the twentieth century was unselfconsciously masculine.

Masculinity studies that would work to expose the presumptions of earlier criticism's implicit bias emerged subsequent to, and as an outgrowth of, feminist and women's studies. While in the 1980s Eve Kosofsky Sedgewick's *Between Men* (1985), Klaus Theweleit's *Male Fantasies* (1987), and Sandra M. Gilbert and Susan Gubar's *No Man's Land: Sexchanges* (1989) ushered in new frameworks for considering male relationships and masculinity during the modernist period, studies of masculinity up until the 1990s were rare and generally took as their subject singular, monolithic masculinity. With the production of much of the critical thought to be discussed in this chapter, masculinity studies, alongside queer studies in and after the 1990s, began to flourish and to differentiate between masculinities, casting gender as a plural phenomenon.

In what is now the most-cited work on this topic, R. W. Connell's *Masculinities* (1995) identifies a critical break between early masculinity studies of men or male behavior and later masculinities studies as exploring "the *idea* of masculinity" as constructed through interactions, enmeshed in the history of institutions, and produced within "relations of alliance, dominance and subordination" (28, 37). The critical works this chapter links together approach gender, and by extension masculinities, as sets of practices by which individuals locate themselves in relation to others and in reference to power, the entirety of which they do not control because of time, place, the production of gendered effects by others, and semiotic systems that preexist and supersede them. In the introduction to his book *Masculinities, Modernist Fiction and the Urban Public Sphere* (2007), Scott McCracken identifies the located and relational nature of masculinity as it pertains to modernism: "Masculinity as lived process is always part of an intersubjective formation rather than an individualized subjectivity. Café masculinities, in other words, always depend on who is in the café" (8). The relative nature of masculinities will be important both because we are taking a historical approach to them and because literary criticism's position has changed, but also because modernist scholars have chosen to highlight only certain aspects of masculinity at any given time. Masculinities are multiple and shifting but are always the sites of contest around social power, which has historically been the purview of biological men.

R. W. Connell makes the case that "our concept of masculinity seems to be a fairly recent historical product, a few hundred years old at most" (68) and that its study began in the modernist period when Sigmund Freud created the "first sustained attempt to build a scientific account of masculinity" through his depth psychology. Freud explained sexuality and gender not as fixed by nature but as constructed over time through parental and social conflict that transmitted "the patriarchal organization of culture between generations" (8, 10). Connell defines "hegemonic masculinity" as "the configuration of gender practice which embodies the currently accepted answer to the legitimacy of patriarchy, which guarantees (or is taken to guarantee) the dominant position of men and the subordinate position of women" (77). Men are rewarded for their participation in patriarchy through "honor, prestige, and the right to command" (82).

In the modernist period, European and American formations of hegemonic masculinity were confronted with an array of challenges. New sexological and legal taxonomies of sexuality contributed to a panic around homosexual males whom some medical professionals defined as inverted women, "inverts," and thus not authentic masculine subjects according to the logic of the time. National and local governments created new laws to further criminalize homosexual male behavior to add clarity to patriarchal order. At the same time, women asked men to share power by allowing them to become voting citizens of their countries with a range of legal rights. The increased visibility and power of those who were racially other to white Europeans or their descendants, whether in the form of free black men in the United States, Jews in Europe, or imperial subjects throughout the colonized world, simultaneously bolstered and weakened white patriarchal constellations of power and occasioned the development of extreme forms of masculinity. Meanwhile, new forms of mass culture contributed to a perceived feminization of modernity against which artists needed to make their work more "hard" and abstruse, in other words, more masculine. Finally, the First World War altered women's social and economic roles such that men began to have to compete publicly and privately with women. With women, the lower-classes, non-European subjects, and homosexuals taking a share of power, new forms of hegemonic and subordinate masculinities were created.

The first part of this chapter will trace the major theoretical interventions that called attention to the ways we interpret modernist masculinities, looking at key works from the 1980s to the present. The remainder of the chapter will look at the central and recurring tropes of masculinity in modernist literature to understand how critics have interpreted them within the field of modernism. One way to understand the developments we describe here is to think of them in tandem with the work described in Chapter 1. As we argue there, what started as an effort to recover women writers developed into a focus on gender and specifically femininity. This interest in gendered experiences and categories often overlapped with female authors, but it did not do so exclusively. When femininity became the object of analysis, it was only natural that scholars would then turn their attention to masculinities. If the palimpsest of modernist studies had a male modernist canon as its manifest content, the New Modernist Studies would uncover complicated inscriptions of gender underneath. Masculinities, such scholars would argue, were always more complicated and nuanced than the topmost narrative had suggested.

Major theoretical interventions

Three formative works of the 1980s—Eve Kosofsky Sedgwick's *Between Men: English Literature and Homosocial Desire* (1985), Klaus Theweleit's *Male Fantasies* (translated into English in 1987), and Andreas Huyssen's *After the Great Divide: Modernism, Mass Culture, Postmodernism* (1987)—underscored the structural importance of hegemonic masculinity to modernist literature and, in doing so, started a critical investigation into masculinities in modernism that has flourished since the 1990s. Each text identifies how the desire to support and uphold hegemonic masculinity undergirds plotlines, establishes new genre hierarchies, and quite literally, starts era-defining wars. Sedgwick, Theweleit, and Huyssen each position masculinity as a hegemonic force that acts to exclude women and femininity in order to sustain and assert its own dominant power.

Eve Kosofsky Sedgwick's *Between Men: English Literature and Homosocial Desire* invites readers to identify how male homosocial bonds function in the Western social structure as evidenced through the love-triangle plot of eighteenth- and nineteenth-century European literature. Sedgwick famously explained that "in any male-dominated society, there is a special relationship between male homosocial (*including* homosexual) desire and the structures for maintaining and transmitting patriarchal power" (25). She identifies the manifestation of male homosocial desire in the repeated literary trope of the love triangle between two men and a woman in which the woman is a merely competed for/bartered/undesired item that solidifies bonds between men and thus maintains or exchanges power between them. The paradigm of the male traffic in women, Sedgwick shows, underlies not just the Western canon but also the homosocial institutions that shape social relations such as public schools, the Church, the Army, Parliament, the civil service, and the legal and medical professions. Sedgwick's monograph makes clear that the bonds of patriarchy preclude women and necessitate that power circulate from man to man. Male homosocial desire refers to the structuring impulse of all male bonds; it is not a sexual desire but a social force, a consistent stimulus that shapes choices, plots, and lives. Although Sedgwick did not expound on modernist literature in *Between Men,* had she done so, she would have found an archetype in Wyndham Lewis's novel *Tarr,* first serialized in *The Egoist* in 1916 and published in final version in 1928. In the novel, set in prewar Paris, the English painter Frederick Tarr and the failed German artist Otto Kreisler tangle over "a beautiful woman" and duel, after which Kreisler hangs himself. Although Tarr is involved in love relationships with women, it is his competition with Kreisler that structures the novel. Sedgwick's point that the woman in a love triangle functions as a necessary, if undesired, structural prohibition against homosexuality is made transparent when Kreisler thinks of his desire to kill Tarr in the duel using language that is barely concealed sexual metaphor: "He *loved* that man! Na ja! It was certainly a sort of passion he had for him! But—mystery of mysteries!—because he loved him he wished to plunge a sword into him, to plunge it in and out and up and down! Oh why had pistols been chosen?" (Lewis 236). Once Tarr has dispensed with Kreisler and gained Anastasya, the woman over whom they dueled, the plot is complicated because he realizes that the intelligent and urbane Anastasya is not a "true" woman as was his former lover, the pretty and unintelligent Bertha. According to Tarr, the true woman is the "lower form of life," who displays "a lack of energy, [inhabits a] permanently mesmeric state, [and is] almost purely emotional." Because he finds that Anastasya is not "an empty vessel to flood with his vitality" but instead a person of intelligence, "an equal and foreign vitality" (278), he resolves he cannot live with her. He marries Bertha and carries on his affair with Anastasya, limiting the influence of and his reliance on either woman. *Tarr* thus illustrates Sedgwick's claim that literary love-triangle plots reinforce the homosocial bonds between men and uphold hegemonic masculinity.

In a similar, if alarming, fashion, Klaus Theweleit's *Male Fantasies* compiles excerpts from the novels and autobiographies of soldiers of the German Freikorps Movement between 1918 and 1923 to lay bare the misogyny and fear of sexuality undergirding the masculinity on which Nazi Germany was built. Theweleit's selections make obvious that, to the men of the Freikorps, women were the embodied symbols of the porous and disintegrating boundaries of their own bodies and the failed German state with which they identified after the First World War. The men of the Freikorps, the very men who laid the foundation for Nazi behavior, were not just afraid of women but wanted to murder them. According to Theweleit, the men "construct an image of a high-born woman ('white countess'). They then worship that image, which must be asexual. They persecute the sexuality of the 'low-born' woman—proletarian, communist, Jew (=whore)—by first making her a prostitute, then murdering her .... All these forms of oppression—adoration, murder, exploitation—are related" (367). The soldierly men faced women with annihilating violence, Theweleit reckons, but in accord with Sedgwick's claims, they did so without any regard for the women. In fact, they fought for dominance within their own stratum to maintain hegemonic masculinity.

Andreas Huyssen's *After the Great Divide: Modernism, Mass Culture, Postmodernism* argues that those who defended against mass culture and created the high versus low culture binary did so in support of hegemonic masculinity. Huyssen asserts that certain authors tried to separate modernist writing from the feminine in order to maintain the status of their work:

> In the age of nascent socialism *and* the first major woman's movement in Europe, the masses knocking at the gate were also women, knocking at the gate of male-dominated culture. It is indeed striking to observe how the political, psychological, and aesthetic discourse around the turn of the century consistently and obsessively genders mass culture and the masses as feminine, while high culture, whether traditional or modern, clearly remains the privileged realm of male activities. (47)

In identifying "the persistent gendering as feminine of that which is devalued" (53), Huyssen underscored the defensive, anxious masculinity that contributed to the building of so-called high modernism, as the select, predominantly male modernist canon was referred to in the second half of the twentieth century.

Together, Sedgwick, Theweleit, and Huyssen's work describes a historical arc of gynophobia that reaches a fever pitch during the modernist period. Several studies in the 1990s take this idea a step further to identify the mother as the female target of such murderous rage and jealousy. Ann Douglas's 1995 book, *Terrible*

Honesty: Mongrel Manhattan in the 1920s, contends that the spirit of American modernism can be found in its animus to the matriarchal figure that had dominated American culture in the nineteenth century. American writers of the 1920s revolted against sentimentality, falseness, and unattainable moral standards, Douglas explains, and many found justification for attacking the matriarch—the symbol of these standards—via Freud. Douglas observes that modernist attempts to expunge femininity often contain cultural elements associated with the feminine. For instance, T. S. Eliot's *The Waste Land* (1922), one of the "central masculinizing documents of the era," was hailed by James Joyce as the poem that ended "the idea of poetry for ladies." Yet Eliot described it as a "nerves monologue," thereby associating it with effeminate men and female maladies (7). Douglas also maintains that the New Negro strategy of self-empowerment through cultural ascendancy rather than through economic or political power was taken straight out of the playbook of white women of the late nineteenth and early twentieth centuries as they used their religious and cultural authority to alter the political landscape. Douglas traces examples of the desire to stamp out feminine influence, that is to commit metaphorical matricide, in the works of Sidney Howard, Ernest Hemingway, Hart Crane, Sophie Treadwell, and Sigmund Freud. She opines that "in an era of open lawbreaking, symbolic matricide was the crime of choice, and it affected American culture in crucial ways" (8).

Interestingly similar in tackling the problematic figure of the mother is Christine Froula's 1996 *Modernism's Body: Sex, Culture and Joyce*, which takes a psychoanalytic approach to show how James Joyce's "masculinized psyche projects his forbidden mother/self into fetishized, feminized figures" (27). Froula positions Joyce as surpassing Freud and Lacan in his critique of psychohistory and analysis of masculinity by making "a distinction between the oedipal Law of the Father, which subsumes identificatory desire within sexual desire, and what I am calling the law of gender: the social and cultural taboo against the son's *identificatory* desire for his mother, the maternal body, and those attributes his culture categorizes as 'feminine'" (12; italics in original). The "law of gender" originates in the infant's early identification with its mother, a oneness with the biological source that the male child must later renounce as the price of adult malehood and masculine privilege. The unconscious, however, knows no negations and the early mother-child union "makes the masculine unconscious a repository of all the desires it marks as feminine" (13). In Joyce's work, Froula finds a progression leading to freedom and critique in *Finnegans Wake*, which displays "a versatile strategy for obviating, parodying, and defying with impunity the cultural law of gender around which Joyce structures both *Portrait*'s auto-initiation narrative and *Ulysses*'s perverse quest-romance" (202). Douglas's and Froula's critical works take masculinity as the foundation of modernism and distinguish within its impulses a need to *either* murder or internalize for oneself the metaphorical—or literal—mother, the symbol of femininity.

At the same time that literary critics were taking on the mother-murdering impulses of modernists in the 1990s, a wave of critical work on gender and masculinities emerged, which is essential to understanding contemporary critical approaches to modernist masculinities from the 1990s onward. Although not all address masculinities in literature, their ideas have been absorbed into literary criticism. As discussed in Chapter 2, Judith Butler's *Gender Trouble* (1990) shifted the theoretical landscape in arguing that gender is a repeated performance of interiorized discourse; one is constantly in the process of becoming or moving toward a gender through acts, gestures, and desire, but one can never achieve what is essentially a platonic ideal. In so arguing, Butler disrupted the presumed unitary subject of masculinity as well as the link between sex and gender and, within literary criticism, popularized a constructionist understanding of gender. In her 1992 *Male Subjectivity at the Margins*, Kaja Silverman took on Freud's version of phallic masculinity and identified structures of masculinity predicated on lack, masochism, or other forms of identification with femininity. Grounded in psychoanalytic theory, Silverman articulates how desire and identification do not always aim toward or result in identification with the father, or phallic ideal, thus resulting in marginalized but no less operative masculinities. R.W. Connell's *Masculinities* offered a historical paradigm that places the modernist period at the chronological center of a reorganization of available masculinities:

> The history of European/American masculinity over the last two hundred years can be broadly understood as the splitting of gentry masculinity, its gradual displacement by the new hegemonic forms, and the emergence of an array of subordinated and marginalized masculinities. The reasons for these changes are

immensely complex, but I would suggest that three are central: challenges to the gender order by women, the logic of gendered accumulation processes in industrial capitalism, and the power relations of empire. (191)

Similarly, Michael Kimmel's *Manhood in America: A Cultural History* (1996) tracks changing expressions of masculinities over time in the United States. He argues that the women's suffrage movement, for instance, contributed to the cult of the outdoorsman, as exemplified in literature by Owen Wister or Jack London. Following Sedgwick's logic, Kimmel's central observation about masculinity is that it is "other men who are important to American men; American men define their masculinity, not as much in relation to women, but in relation to each other" (5). Furthermore, Kimmel identifies homophobia as central to policing the boundaries of masculinity as homophobia is, simply, the fear of other men unmasking one, revealing to the world that one does not measure up as a real man (6). He offers as one example John Steinbeck's *Of Mice and Men* (1937), which reveals this masculine performance in a passage in which Curley's wife says,

> "Funny thing ... If I catch any one man, and he's alone, I get along fine with him. But just let two of the guys get together an' you won't talk. Jus' nothin' but mad." She dropped her fingers and put her hands on her hips. "You're all scared of each other, that's what. Ever'one of you's scared the rest is goin' to get something on you."

Kimmel identifies self-control, exclusion, and escape as the ways that American men have historically attempted to secure their sense of themselves as men (6).

An important contribution to diversifying understanding of masculinities in modernism is Judith Halberstam's 1998 *Female Masculinity*, which further distanced gender expression from biological sex. Halberstam argues that amid turn-of-the-century upheaval regarding gender roles, specific iterations of gender expression arose that "clearly showed that femininity was not wed to femaleness and masculinity was certainly not bound to maleness" (48). More specifically, *Female Masculinity* makes the case that "female masculinity is a specific gender with its own cultural history rather than a derivative of male masculinity" (77). Halberstam observes this gender expression as visible during the "transition from affiliation marriages to romantic marriages" and further considers that "the development of the women's rights movement, the trials of Oscar Wilde, the social upheaval caused by World War I, and the development of sexological models of sexual definition all played a part in untangling once and for all the knots that appeared to bind gender to sex and sexuality in some mysterious and organic way" (48). The period between 1900 and 1940, Halberstam claims, was a unique moment in gender expression before sex reassignment surgery became possible in the 1940s. During this time, some expressions of homosexuality and transsexuality shared a history. For instance, in the narratives of Radclyffe Hall's "Miss Ogilvy Finds Herself" (1934) and *The Well of Loneliness* (1928), the reader finds that "Miss Ogilvy quite distinctly desires to be a man, whereas Stephen Gordon desires masculinity and female companionship" (86). Halberstam suggests that Stephen Gordon may well be an account of transgender subjectivity, a masculine subject in a female body. Importantly, Halberstam differentiates transgender subjectivity from same-sex desire:

> In the 1920s women were living their lives as, if not men, wholly masculine beings. Many women in the 1920s did effectively change sex inasmuch as they passed as men, took wives as men, and lived lives as men. It is inadequate to call such women lesbians, and in fact to do so is to ignore the specificity of their lives. (87)

The masculine women Halberstam studies were not identically masculine; they represent unique and historically located forms of masculinity available to women in the early twentieth century. In showing a nondominant form of masculinity, Halberstam launches exploration of masculinities that occur outside of white, middle-class maleness, noting that excessive masculinity is typically ascribed to black bodies, Latino/a bodies, or working-class bodies, just as insufficient masculinity is ascribed to Asian or upper-class bodies. Halberstam's exploration has enabled other scholars to identify various forms of female masculinity in modernist literature. Scott McCracken in *Masculinities, Modernist Fiction and the Urban Public Sphere* (2007), for instance, has used Halberstam's argument to reread Miriam Henderson from Dorothy Richardson's multivolume novel *Pilgrimage* (1915–1938) as an urban flaneur who appropriates aspects of available masculinities in response to the limited options available for women.

The theoretical account given earlier is not exhaustive, but it represents the major strands of thought that have shaped current understanding of masculinities as they pertain at least to European and American modernist literature. Many other critics have written about individual authors or aspects of modernist masculinity, and their ideas will be touched on later. Before we get there, however, it will be useful to summarize the historical mapping of another critical text, Michael Kane's 1999 *Modern Men: Mapping Masculinity in English and German Literature, 1880–1930*, which argues for three stages of masculine crisis in European literature at the turn of the twentieth century. Kane's argument largely maps on to the consensus view of the evolution of European masculinities in modernism. The first stage is a crisis of upper-class European men who overidentify exclusively with themselves. Kane sees this stage manifesting in the trope of the literary double that proliferates in the final decades of the nineteenth century in such works as Robert Louis Stevenson's *The Strange Case of Dr. Jekyll and Mr. Hyde* (1886) and Oscar Wilde's *The Picture of Dorian Gray* (1890). The double illustrates both the repression of those qualities excluded from hegemonic masculinity at the time and a preoccupation with narcissism and homosexuality that are the logical extensions of patriarchy. Echoing Sedgwick's *Between Men*, Kane argues that,

> far from being pure of any "taint of homosexuality," patriarchal thinking is so saturated with it that it institutionalizes the love of men for men, the admiration of the male body and the masculine intellect and loves nothing more than to express this either sexually or symbolically or both .... One should therefore not be surprised if a crisis of that patriarchal culture should bring to light not only male fantasies of giving birth but also suggestions of male narcissism and homosexuality for, as the foregoing suggests, such ideas were always situated at the *core* of patriarchal thinking, loath though it might have been at times to admit this to itself. (6)

In response to the troubled masculine identity expressed in the literature at the *fin de siècle*, Kane shows how male authors employed strategies to shore up masculine identities by scapegoating others and reemphasizing the boundary of selves and/as nation. If Max Nordau's *Degeneration* (1892) is a nonfiction text that shows the hegemonic male fear that non-Europeans, women, homosexuals, and art were contributing to the decay of men and traditional masculinity, Joseph Conrad's *The Nigger of Narcissus* (1897) and Bram Stoker's *Dracula* (1897), Kane argues, represent those same fears. In the second phase, Kane shows, literature produced during the First World War focuses on intense male relationships as a way of reclaiming traditional masculinity, with works by D. H. Lawrence, Jack London, Robert Walser, Franz Kafka, and Bertolt Brecht supporting this motif. Kane describes the final phase, the 1920s–1930s, as "after patriarchy," a time in which the rise of fascism represents a "paranoid attempt to restore homosocial patriarchy and exorcise it of its own fears and confusions by projecting these onto others who could be isolated and exterminated" (viii). Kane identifies a timeline of almost-incestuous upper-class masculine triumph in the 1880s–1890s, threat and crisis from 1900 to1920, and finally a post-patriarchal breakdown in the 1920s–1930s.

Case study: Ernest Hemingway and *The Sun Also Rises*

It is of course a commonplace that Hemingway lacks the serene confidence that he is a full-sized man. Most of us too delicately organized babies who grow up to be artists suffer at times from that small inward doubt. But some circumstance seems to have laid upon Hemingway a continual sense of the obligation to put forth evidences of red-blooded masculinity. It must be made obvious not only in the swing of the big shoulders and the clothes he puts on, but in the stride of his prose style and the emotions he permits to come to the surface there. This trait of his character has been strong enough to form the nucleus of a new flavor in English literature, and it has moreover begotten a veritable school of fiction-writers—a literary style, you might say, of wearing false hair on the chest.

—Max Eastman, *The New Republic*, June 7, 1933

Max Eastman's review of Ernest Hemingway's 1932 nonfiction book, *Death in the Afternoon*, spurred a now-famous incident of masculine bravado a full four years later. Hemingway, encountering Eastman in his editor's office, ripped open his shirt to reveal his chest hair and proceeded to rip open Eastman's shirt and mock his hairlessness before asking, "What did you say I was sexually impotent for?" Hemingway, nicknamed "Papa," has long enjoyed a reputation as the he-man of American letters, and this story, which was printed in news accounts and has become part of the writer's legend, reinforces not only that Hemingway cared deeply about the appearance of his masculinity, but that readers and critics have been invested in it as well. Hemingway's works have enjoyed a critical resurgence alongside the growth of masculinity studies in modernism (Figure 5).

Critics have read Hemingway's relationship to gender as either enforcing rigid gender boundaries, and thus homophobia, or

FIGURE 5 *This 1933 illustration of Ernest Hemingway by Mexican artist Miguel Covarrubias, though never published, may have been intended for the* Vanity Fair *series "Private Lives of the Great"; herpicide in hand, the image clearly references Hemingway's dispute with Eastman.* © María Elena Rico Covarrubias.

exploring how the cultural constraints of gendered behavior operate to limit human potential. Mark Spilka's *Hemingway's Quarrel with Androgyny* (1990) argues that he enforced rigid gender boundaries with the claim that Hemingway's progressive parents had raised their children with no sex roles, or reversed ones, and that the writer's career was an attempt to deny and explore what Spilka calls "the wound of androgyny" through a particularly rigid masculine pose. Robert Scholes and Nancy Comley see more flexibility and subtlety in terms of gender, arguing that Hemingway's work explores the constraints of culturally engendered behavior and provides a more complex and sensitive presentation of gender than Hemingway's public personae has allowed (*Hemingway's Genders* 1994).

The Sun Also Rises offers an archetype of literary postwar masculine crisis. A wounded and now-impotent former soldier is made to look on as the woman he loves enacts a series of love affairs in front of him. His impotence, voyeurism, and lost manhood are right on the surface of the story. The status and meaning of masculinity in the novel has provoked rich debate. Debra Moddelmog claims Hemingway critiques sexual and gender binaries whereas Ira Elliott argues that Jake Barnes is unable to accept the potentialities of gender and sexual mutability. David Blackmore sees in Jake's war wound, and the lost masculine potency it represents, a metaphor for social anxiety about masculinity and sexuality. Greg Forter positions Jake's loss as symbolizing the loss of two different and incompatible forms of manhood, the sentimental and the hard, and writes, "masculinity is not simply mourned as a lost illusion of the past. Nor is it openly celebrated as an authentic content for modern man—a move forbidden by the modernist redefinition of manhood in relation to lack and loss. Instead, phallic manhood is melancholically idealized *as lost*" (30). Although more has been written about masculinity in *The Sun Also Rises*, this brief synopsis shows both how masculinity studies have opened up new interests in modernist texts and continues to redefine how we understand canonical works with fresh readings.

Reactionary masculinities

There are repeated tropes and motifs in the scholarship of modernist masculinities. The following section of this chapter will explore three overriding themes in modernist literature and criticism as they have occupied the bulk of critical work about masculinities in modernism to date: (a) reactionary masculinities, (b) soldiers, imperialists, and cowboys, and, finally (c) the others who define European and American masculinities: Jews, blacks, and imperial subjects.

As Huyssen and Theweleit established in their work, a foundational aspect of modernist masculinities is fear: fear of women, fear of the masses, fear of decadence, fear of sexuality, fear of loss of identity and stable ego boundaries, and as Kimmel argues fear is foundational to hegemonic masculinity itself, fear of other men unmasking one as inauthentically masculine. Futurist manifestos are among the earliest and most blatant modernist texts to articulate misogyny and fear of femininity. Filippo Marinetti goes so far as to suggest segregated child rearing in "Against *Amore* and Parliamentarism" (1911–15) in order to preserve masculinity in its purest form:

> We will finally do away with the mixture of males and females that—during the earliest years—produces a damnable effeminizing of the males. The male babies should—according to us—develop far away from the little girl so that their first games can be entirely masculine, that is, free of every emotional morbidity, every womanly delicacy, so that they can be lively, pugnacious, muscular and violently dynamic. When little boys and girls live together, the formation of the male character is always retarded. They are always attracted by the charm and willful seductiveness of the little woman, like little cicisbei or stupid little slaves. (in Scott, *Gender in Modernism* 86)

As the Futurists see it, effeminacy is a threat to modernity from which men must be saved. Terry Smith argues in *In Visible Touch: Modernism and Masculinity* (1998) that for Marinetti, Umberto Boccioni and Wyndham Lewis—artists whose manifestos of the first two decades of the twentieth century champion the destruction of bourgeois traditions and the assertion of virility—"domination of society by those with the most masculine of energies was essential not only to their world picture but to modernity itself" (14). In her essay on "Manifestos from the Sex War," Janet Lyon connects the sense of masculine crisis in modernist-era manifestos to women's unstable relation to the state (68). Rachel Blau DuPlessis argues that manifestos are a way, in an uncertain context, to elevate literary and artistic acts to high seriousness. In an era of capitalist imperialism, men used manifestos to reject art and poetry as limited, decorative, or genteel activities of the overcivilized and instead to assert their authority and power ("Virile Thought" 21).

A host of critics have identified Wyndham Lewis, T. S. Eliot, Ezra Pound, Marcel Proust, Filippo Marinetti, and D. H. Lawrence as exemplars of those who shared what Colleen Lamos has called "the modern problem of a loss of confidence in the status and meaning of masculinity" (9). Although Wyndham Lewis and Ezra Pound's Vorticist "Manifesto I" in the first issue of BLAST (6–20, 1914) critiqued the entirety of the Victorian era—the manifesto entreats the reader to "BLAST years 1837 to 1900" (20)—many critics agree that much of the phallic modernism of the manifesto era arose in response not just to women's increasing power but to a confluence of events and influences from the 1880s and '90s that seemed to call for vigilant masculinity, including British struggles in the Boer War, eugenic thinking that promoted gender essentialism in claiming that only "manly" men and "womanly" women could properly regenerate the population, the jostling of European powers over their empires, the military buildup of modern nations, sexological tracts that identified perverted or deviant masculinities, and an active and public persecution of male homosexuality across Europe through new laws and trials. While women who had sex with women remained largely invisible to the public until the 1920s, any kind of sexual contact between men came under increasing scrutiny. In 1885, in the UK, the Labouchere Amendment of the Criminal Law Amendment Act expanded on the centuries-old sodomy laws to define as illegal "gross indecency," which included any sexual act between men, not just anal intercourse. This made sexual behavior between men easier to prove and convict. Oscar Wilde's trial for gross indecency in 1895 not only publicized such acts broadly via media coverage of the case but further compounded the association between artistic decadence and homosexuality, both of which were then associated with physical degeneration. Historian George Mosse argues that decadence played a key role at the turn of the twentieth century in "defining the enemies against which manliness and society measured itself" (81). Art historian Lisa Tickner makes the case that virility becomes a staple metaphor that distinguishes modernity from 1890s aestheticism ("Men's Work" 56). In the meantime, publications by Edward Carpenter, who embraced his homosexuality and championed women's rights, and Havelock Ellis, whose sexological tracts catalogued a variety of sexual practices and gender identifications, contributed to a sense of radical shifts in gender sensibilities. With the increased visibility of agentic women and homosexual males, "Masculinist modernism," Rachel Blau DuPlessis claims, "is a form of concealed moralism in response to erosions of male hegemony, which are hardly attributable to females or homosexuals ... but are nevertheless symptomatically focused on them" (*Purple Passages* 21).

Ezra Pound was a key participant in this strand of homophobic hypermasculinity. As evidence, Colleen Lamos points to Pound's contempt for "Bloomsbuggers" (9) and Tickner notes that Pound's phallic Vorticism relies on the assertion of heterosexual virility, as in his praise of "art before it has spread itself into a state of flaccidity" ("Popular" 170). DuPlessis argues that Pound and T. S. Eliot's imagist program of 1914, which dismisses feminine embellishment and sentiment in favor of manly stylization, "was a specific choice upholding a claim of male cultural hegemony, particularly an insistence on originality as opposed to imitation" (*Purple Passages* 33). Lamos argues that T. S. Eliot participates in this tradition when he "disavows his gender and sexual anxieties, like his Americanness, subsuming them within a European, Patriarchal and anti-Semitic literary tradition; [and that] abjuring feminine and queer alterity, he positions himself as the adoptive heir of his self-appointed fathers" (9). DuPlessis also draws a connection between the male vitalism of Pound and that of D. H. Lawrence, whose 1929 book of poetry, *Pansies*, "argues from nature ... about the natural curative qualities of phallic heterosexuality" ("Virile Thought" 30). The curative qualities of phallic heterosexuality are, of course, the theme of his 1928 novel *Lady Chatterley's Lover*. As Lawrence wrote in a letter at the time of its composition, "I do believe the phallic reality is good and healing, in a world going insane" (*Letters* 319–20).

Bloomsbury's sensibility was a counterpoint to this strand of modernist hyper-masculinity. As Tickner observes, "Its homosexual component ironized hearty masculinity, and, for all the intricacies of its sexual relationships, sexual conquest and a sense of virility did not permeate its work" ("Men's Work" 53). While Bloomsbury masculinity did not share the anxious virility of Futurists, Vorticists, Eliot or Lawrence, Barbara Caine counters that "the men of

Bloomsbury may not have been at the forefront of muscular or strenuous masculinity, and they may have been calling into question the ways in which men related to each other, but," she points out, "they were still enjoying—in a very real and practical sense—what R.W. Connell termed the patriarchal dividend" (280), a dividend Virginia Woolf's body of work illustrates as available to men again and again, perhaps most poignantly in her representation of the ultimate patriarch, Mr. Ramsay in *To the Lighthouse* (1925).

If Bloomsbury's ironic masculinity is one counterexample to the phallic modernism that in its mid-twentieth-century valuation was called high modernism, Henry James's versions of masculinity are another. Leon Edel's monumental biography of Henry James concludes that James suffered from a confused, "weak" masculinity and "troubled sexuality" (87). James's male characters rarely assume conventional masculinity. As Michael Kimmel noted in his cultural history of manhood, "James's male characters seemed to embody everything that real men were not" (108). Kelly Cannon's *Henry James and Masculinity: The Man at the Margins* (1994) explores the unconventional masculinity of James's "marginal male" characters, such as Hyacinth in *The Princess Casamassima*, who vows not to marry, Strether in *The Ambassadors*, who ultimately rejects marriage, and Ralph Touchett in *Portrait of a Lady*, who never marries. Cannon's logic is that by refusing marriage, as did James himself, these characters were choosing to remain outside of the social structure and to occupy a marginal social position. Leland S. Person's 2003 book, *Henry James and the Suspense of Masculinity*, reinterprets what presenting non-hegemonic masculinities in his fiction might mean. Person argues that James's fiction mirrors the unstable gender and sexual boundaries of his time: "Writing during this period of transition, James illustrates the ambiguities and confusions—the multivalence—of gender and sexuality, and his fiction it seems to me conducts a series of experiments in gender/sexual construction and deconstruction" (7). Critics agree that James's works offer dissent from uniform masculinity and present complicated, nonnormative masculine characters that, depending on the critic, are either marginalized (Cannon) or offer unresolved spaces of play (Person).

If aggressive, reactionary masculinity was a significant thread woven into modernist writing, it was of course not the only one. In the United States and Europe, mainstream writers championed either an individualist model of hard work and restraint, often figured as the cowboy or the imperialist, or the brotherly model of brave endurance in the form of soldiers.

Imperialists, cowboys, and soldiers

In answer to the loss of masculine hegemony, some modernists presented the redemptive figures of the imperialist, the cowboy, or the soldier, whose masculinity, even when ironized, was simultaneously celebrated and mourned as rare, fragile, and all but lost. What these figures share is that their masculinity is shaped, in part, through geography, a masculinity that can only be so by departing from the domestic sphere to be tested against the elements and hostile others. At the turn of the twentieth century, England's most famous imperial writer, Rudyard Kipling, wrote poems such as "If" (1895) and "The White Man's Burden" (1899) that characterize imperial endeavor as a testing ground to prove one's "manhood." The poem "If" makes conditional the status of masculinity—"you'll be a man"—if, when surrounded by ungrateful and unknowing colonized subjects, "you" show stoicism and self-restraint. Imperial masculinity of the mainstream Kipling variety was predicated on discipline, because to rule others, one must be able to rule oneself. An unmasculine lack of control was frequently attributed to non-Englishmen, even when European, as the depiction of the rapacious imperialism of the Belgian Congo and the European-created Kurtz in Joseph Conrad's novella *Heart of Darkness* (1899) demonstrates.

The gendered workings of Joseph Conrad's imperialist figures have received critical attention from Joseph Bristow, Sarah Cole, Robert Hampson, Jeremy Hawthorn, Scott McCracken, Padmini Mongia, Andrew Michael Roberts, Elaine Showalter, and Rebecca Stott, among others. In his book *Conrad and Masculinity* (2000), Andrew Michael Roberts highlights that Conrad's "fondness for setting up chains or groups of male tellers and listeners creates structures which, by implication, can extend beyond the bounds of the fiction to include both author and readers" (8) and thereby exclude women. Roberts observes that just as the narrative structure excludes women, so does the work of empire, which is the subject of Conrad's writing. *Heart of Darkness* for instance "is a story about the gaining and passing on (or failure to pass on) of knowledge and about relationships between men" (126). Male friendship, Sarah Cole argues, is not incidental to colonial relations but fundamental to their workings (77). Cole further shows that Conrad's texts "have come to mark an important moment in a literary tradition defined not by its heroic break with bourgeois conventionality, as the modernists themselves might have had it, but by its adherence to a masculine, European, global hegemony" (92). McCracken offers that "the 'boys' own' nature of Conrad's narratives constructs a romance of lonely masculinity, where ultimately self-sufficiency, the ideal of Heyst's island in *Victory*, is an unattainable utopia" ("Hard and Absolute" 8). The romance of masculinity shaped through exploration (and exploration shaped by masculinity) is an important turn of the century narrative. Cole and Roberts detail Conrad's adaptations of adventure narratives beloved by huge readerships of late-Victorian males featuring rugged, masculine explorers, as in the novels of R. L. Stevenson, Rider Haggard, and Rudyard Kipling, or the exploration narratives of Richard Burton or H. M. Stanley. Roberts describes *Nostromo*'s Gould, for instance, as "the ideal English gentleman colonial administrator: resolute, dignified, restrained, inscrutable, knowledgeable in the ways of his adopted country yet indelibly English" (94). Cole claims that *Heart of Darkness* … stages the imperial encounter repeatedly, as it adopts, reshapes, and yearns for the traditions of male heroism and comradeship epitomized by Stanley's writing" (101). Certainly there are multiple masculinities at play in any of Conrad's texts, and they are not divided solely on racial lines: Conrad approves of the restrained men willing to make sacrifices such as Lord Jim, Marlowe or, ironically and pointedly, the cannibals in the "heart of darkness," suggesting that masculinity is a set of traits one chooses to adopt.

Colonial empire can itself be, as Praseeda Gopinath calls it in *Scarecrows of Chivalry: English Masculinities after Empire* (2013), "a theatre of manliness" (34) in modernist literature. In E. M. Forster's *A Passage to India* (1924), for instance, Gopinath argues that Ronny Heaslop tries to project his metropolitan gentlemanly ethics onto his imperial duty, but his adherence to British law strips him of his masculine-imperial authority. In contrast, Fielding refuses to follow the codes of the pukka sahib and disrupts English manliness by transgressing racial lines in his articulation of public school, gentlemanly values. For Gopinath, political instability in the empire manifests itself as a crisis in masculinity. Forster's novel depicts the separation of "the personal-ethical code of gentlemanliness from the ethno-national code of gentlemanliness in empire" (46).

Even outside of the colonies, the imperialist model of acquisitive masculinity affects modernist narrative. For instance, Karen Hoffman claims acquisitive imperialism as the shaping impulse that drives John Dowell's incessant revisions to his identity in Ford Madox Ford's *The Good Soldier* (1915):

> Throughout the novel, Ford presents the operative definition of patriarchal masculinity in late Victorian/Edwardian England as inextricably linked to the assumptions and practices of imperialism, likening the expectations that men transgress boundaries in order to possess ever more women to the scramble for colonies among colonial powers .... Ford depicts late Victorian/Edwardian literature offering no alternatives to this definition of masculinity: the male characters either follow the definition compulsively, even at times against their explicitly stated wishes, or they do not compete and consequently are emasculated or destroyed. (30)

Colonizing and ruling the colonized was a testing ground of masculinities for European literature during the modernist period, but US literature had its own colonized frontier in the American West.

In American literature, portrayals of cowboys and what was by then a mythological Western frontier were responsible not just for representing a style of masculinity but for producing one. Daniel Worden claims in the introduction to *Masculine Style: The American West and Literary Modernism* (2013) that "cowboy masculinity," though not often linked to modernism due to the frontier's association with nostalgic regionalism and modernism's congruity with the cosmopolitan, should be considered a "mode of aesthetic embodiment in modernist texts from the 1910s to the 1930s" (2). Michael Kimmel describes modernist cowboy heroes as a vehicle for male escapist fantasy through which men can retrieve their "pure masculinity" by shedding the trappings of modernity (112, 154). The fantasy, he contends, originates from the many "weak and puny" eastern city men such as Theodore Roosevelt, Owen Wister, Frederic Remington, and Thomas Eakins, who went West to find cures for a now obsolete but commonly diagnosed condition at the turn of the century called neurasthenia, the cause of which was believed to be overactivity of the nerves due to advanced civilization. The cure for neurasthenia was believed to be a better conformity with bodily expectations for one's gender norms. Women neurasthenics were treated with bed rest and inactivity, while men were prescribed rugged activity. America's most classic Western novel, *The Virginian* (1902), which sold 300,000 copies in its first two years, is a result of the diagnosed neurasthenia of its author, Owen Wister. Wister's doctor, the famed S. Weir Mitchell, prescribed a trip to a Wyoming dude ranch during which Wister wrote the novel. The similarities between imperial and cowboy masculinity, both founded on white supremacy, are on full display in a 1902 review of the novel, which states, "To catch the deeper meaning of our life, one's path must be toward that Western verge of the continent where all white men are American born" (in Kimmel 111).

No less important, but chronologically subsequent to imperial and cowboy masculinities, the Great War had equal claim to making men. The soldier was celebrated as the epitome of both the imperial ideal and appropriate masculinity (Meyer 5). Although one hardly needs to furnish proof of such a concept, literary examples abound. In Ernst Jünger's *In Stahlgewittern* (*Storm of Steel*, 1920), the narrator relates the young German soldiers' fantasy of war as one of an aestheticized, masculine rapture: "We thought of it as manly, as action, a merry dueling party of flowered, blood-bedewed meadows" (5). Not surprisingly, Adolf Hitler was always clear that public power should be aggressively male; indeed that it should rely on the type of soldierly community of men that he fondly recalled from the years of the First World War (Timm and Sanborn 153). English soldier Siegfried Sassoon's 1915 poem "Absolution" equally shows war as a masculine right of passage that admits one to the privileges of power, "War is our scourge; yet war has made us wise, / And, fighting for our freedom, we are free." Although Sassoon would later revise his attitude to the war, his early poetry aligns the experience of battle with masculinity. The idea that being a soldier *made* one a man, and endowed one with the privileges of manhood, was exploited for nationalist, recruitment purposes, as the recruitment poster featuring a rugged soldier in a position of dominance over a sexually willing girl in Figure 6 shows. George Orwell later commented on what it had meant to miss the experience of being a

"YOUR MOTHERLAND WILL NEVER FORGET"

FIGURE 6 *"Your motherland will never forget" from* Canada in Khaki *(1916), a tribute to the officers and men who served in the overseas military forces of Canada, suggests a warm welcome home. British Museum.*

soldier in the First World War: "As the war fell back into the past, my particular generation, those who had been 'just too young', became conscious of the vastness of the experience they had missed. You felt yourself a little less than a man, because you had missed it" (qtd in Meyer 1). British society had thought of the Great War as an answer to the presumed physical degeneracy of the working classes and the moral degeneracy of the middle classes. Much of the European and American literature produced in the 1920s refers at least implicitly to the state of masculinity during and after the war. But there was also a war books boom between 1928 and 1931 with the publication of Robert Graves's *Goodbye to All That* (1929), Richard Aldington's *Death of a Hero* (1929), and Siegfried

Sassoon's *Memoirs of an Infantry Officer*, among others. In writing about what it meant to be a soldier, these writers were reflecting on the changes to the status of masculinity. In her book *Men of War: Masculinity and the First World War in Britain* (2009), Jessica Meyer differentiates imperial masculinities from martial masculinities as the difference between self-control and endurance: "Unlike self-control, a quality of masculinity that had its roots in Victorian prescriptions about masculinity, the quality of endurance, so much a part of the narratives of warfare constructed in letters and diaries, was more specifically the product of war" (142). Wilfred Owen's poems, such as "Disabled" and "Dulce et Decorum Est" (1917), are exemplars of an alienated but enduring soldierly masculinity, that of the wizened onlooker.

Multiple critics point out that in the context of war, love between men was encouraged and expected (Cole, Timm, Meyer). Cole reads Robert Graves's poem "Two Fusiliers" (1917) as a model of heroic intimacy:

Show me the two so closely bound
As we, by the wet bond of blood,
By friendship blossoming from the mud,
By Death.

Virginia Woolf's *Mrs. Dalloway* (1925) equally portrays soldierly intimacy in her depiction of the bond between shell-shocked First World War veteran Septimus Warren Smith and his war buddy, Evans. Although their bond would have been normative within the context of war, Annette Timm and Joshua Sanborn argue that a different story of gender begins with soldiers' homecoming, which often was a protracted and difficult transition, as *Mrs. Dalloway* exemplifies. The fact that many critics find in Smith's and Evans's relationship homosexual overtones may have as much to do with modern critical expectations of masculinity and Smith's emasculated state after the war as the language Woolf uses to depict their bond. The narration of Septimus Smith's shell shock disrupts the heroic masculinity of the soldier and exposes his fragility. There were approximately 80,000 shell shock victims treated by the end of the Great War and the malady was felt by its sufferers to be intensely shaming and emasculating (Mergenthal 192–3). Because of masculine ideals of courage and self-control, military psychiatrists were slow to understand and admit that shell shock was something other than a lack of discipline, for doing so would be to admit to the emotional and psychological vulnerability of men. Elaine Showalter has theorized shell shock as a form of complaint against the outsized demands of wartime masculinity:

> If the essence of manliness was not to complain, shell shock was the body language of the masculine complaint, a disguised male protest not only against the war but against the concept of 'manliness' itself. [It was] a protest against the politicians, generals, and psychiatrists. The heightened code of masculinity that dominated wartime was intolerable to surprisingly large numbers of men. (175)

Cole observes that while resisting the emasculating categorization of helpless beings, "soldiers often found themselves falling in between seemingly opposed social categories, such as adult and child, patriot and rebel, masculine icon and debilitated relic" (201). Inasmuch as the public was eager to celebrate the soldier as the embodiment of the masculine ideal, soldiers' ultimate fragility as human beings did much to unmask the impossible demands of masculinity, and this informed an important strand of the literature of the 1920s.

The others of white middle-class masculinities: Jews, blacks, and imperial subjects

Within any ethnicity, race, or social strata, there are of course competing or alternative masculinities available. If some Jews living in Western Europe in the early twentieth century embraced athleticism and acculturation, there were others who focused solely on intellectual pursuits and religious insularity, and both emphases negotiated authentic masculinities in relationship to different sources of power. However, in looking at the literatures of Europe and the United States in the modernist period, what becomes obvious is how Christian, white middle-class masculinity relied on male others to define itself. The German Nazis adopted a eugenicist, essentialist model of gender and became trapped in a binary model of hyper-masculinity such that anything that resonated of the feminine, whether homosexuals, the eugenically imperfect, or Jews, became a threat that through their elimination further defined Nazi perfection. George Mosse argues that "never before or since the appearance of fascism was masculinity elevated to such heights: the hopes placed upon it, the importance of manliness as a national symbol and as a living example played a vital role in all fascist regimes" (155). Texts such as Otto Weininger's popular 1903 *Geschlecht und Charakter (Sex and Character)*, which described all Jews and women as creatures of passion and emotion, incapable of evolving to a state of self-control and chastity, as real men did, revealed the general purchase of such ideas while also providing textual cover for those who sought to act on eugenic ideas.

The primacy of self-control as a masculine virtue is evident in any of the ascriptions to nonwhite, nondominant European or North American men. To the English, those ethnicities under the British Empire, whether Indian, Irish, or Ibo, were defined by their unrestrained and ungovernable traits. Imperial subjects were in need of true British gentlemen to civilize them and teach them to control their impulses. That hegemonic masculinity was the channel through which ideal Englishness was distinguished as different from black/brown men, from white women, and from the working classes is, for instance, what makes the educated, middle-class Muslim Dr. Aziz vulnerable when accused of attacking the British Adela Quested in E. M. Forster's *A Passage to India* (1924).

To a majority of white Americans in the early twentieth century, black American men were hypersexual primitives, either too much or not enough of whatever made a real man, which was of course linked to his whiteness. As Gail Bederman has argued in *Manliness and Civilization: A Cultural History of Gender and Race in the United States, 1880–1917* (1995), white America shared a pervasive belief in male power as stemming from white supremacy (5). Bederman explains that in nineteenth-century America, the middle class defined itself through its gentility and respectability and that it used the term "manliness" to describe "honor, high-mindedness, and strength stemming from this powerful self-mastery" (12). This discourse was challenged by new medical diagnoses of neurasthenia that led many to believe that white middle-class men had become decadent while black, working-class, and immigrant men, who lived lives of the body and had so-called primitive customs, appeared to possess a virility and vitality that made them masculine in comparison with these now "overcivilized" and effeminate neurasthenic men. Bederman observes that the terms "masculine" and "masculinity" were relatively new and came into increased use in the 1890s "precisely because they could convey the new attributes of powerful manhood which middle-class men were working to synthesize" (18). By 1930, "masculinity" had come to represent ideals common to the twentieth century such as aggressiveness, physical force, and male sexuality (19). However, until then there was an uneven application of the discourse of civilization, which depicted African-Americans as unsexed and unevolved primitives or, as Philip Brian Harper terms it, "the savage 'walking phallus'" (9).

In her book *Race Men* (1998), Hazel Carby acknowledges the historical arc from Victorian ideologies of manliness to modernist discourses of masculinity but says, "I would add to Bederman's insights, however, an insistence that within the framework of modernist cultural texts, the generalities of reference to a discourse of civilization are replaced by the specificities of reference to national belonging, as both black and white intellectuals and cultural producers increasingly represented the fate of the nation and black people as interdependent" (47). She points in part to *The Souls of Black Folk* (1903), by W. E. B. DuBois, which had the premise that black people did not exist in opposition to national ideals but embodied them. Carby also notes, however, that DuBois created a conceptual framework that applied exclusively to men who enacted rigidly determined codes of masculinity.

Martin Summers's *Manliness & Its Discontents: The Black Middle Class & The Transformation of Masculinity, 1900–1930* (2004) points to the pressures of class and segregation that made it difficult for most black men to assimilate to middle-class masculine ideals and obtain manhood by dominant cultural standards. Summers notes of some of the Harlem literati of the 1920s:

> Where adherents to manliness talked of character, reason, production, self-denial, and respectability as being constitutive values of manhood, these iconoclasts constructed and performed their gender subjectivity through the elevation of the physical and sexual potency of the body, consumption and self-gratification,

and an individual self-expression that was not confined by the black bourgeoisie's standards of propriety. Where proponents of manliness predicated their claims to manhood on the public-private organization of gender roles and hetero-normativity, many of these rebels resisted procreative heterosexuality and—in practical terms if not in principle—patriarchy as the norm. (128)

Summers further argues that rebellion against this restrictive approach to manliness can be found in jazz, blues, and literary expressions of the Harlem Renaissance. The repudiation of bourgeois manliness and the birth of a modern black masculinity can be seen most obviously in the authors whose works appear in *Fire!!*, the single-issue magazine published by Wallace Thurman in 1926. Alongside Thurman, a host of writers that included Zora Neale Hurston, Countee Cullen, Langston Hughes, and Richard Bruce Nugent explored homosexuality, bisexuality, interracial relationships, promiscuity, and prostitution among other topics, and in doing so they celebrated the very thing that had been used against blacks previously, the potent primitivism of African and black folk culture over the spiritually enervated, less virile cultures of Europe and Anglo-America. Not surprisingly, Alain Locke's review of *Fire!!* accused it of being a "hectic imitation of the 'naughty nineties' and effete echoes of contemporary decadence" (qtd in Schwarz 40), thus attempting to feminize such works in contrast to then-normative ideals of black middle-class masculinity.

Summers argues that other writers modeled alternative masculinities outside of the decadent tradition. Jean Toomer's utopian view of black folk culture as expressed in *Cane* (1923), for instance, reconfigures black masculinities by critiquing the effects of industrialization on black masculinities, seeking to uncouple the connection between the marketplace and manliness constituted by nineteenth-century gender conventions (177–181). Claude McKay's novel of black proletarians, *Home to Harlem* (1928), critiques the unnatural constraints placed on sexuality and virile masculinity by bourgeois gender conventions (182). Gary Edward Holcomb has engagingly contrasted the depiction of masculinities through Jake Barnes in *The Sun Also Rises* (1926) with that of *Home to Harlem*'s Jake Brown, also a First World War veteran who never saw any military action as a result of US discrimination. Holcomb argues that, in contrast with Jake Barnes's sexual and modernist impotence, Jake Brown's lusty appetite for copious sexual activity figures as the antithesis of teleological modernist disintegration—of Hemingway's winner take nada. For McKay the condition of being a constituent of the black proletariat and the inevitability of the struggle against racism and imperialism ironically provide the means for dodging the bullets of modernist impotence and its inexorable consequence, masculine incapacitation. (71)

Where white American and European authors relied on a discourse of civilization to assert their masculinity and hegemony over nonwhites and non-Christians, nonwhites discovered alternative masculinities that challenged white middle-class masculinities and refuted the value of them. Of particular grievance to the 400,000 African-American men who served the United States in the First World War, military service had seemed to affirm their identity as true men and true Americans, but they found that they received unequal treatment during the war and discrimination after. Chad Williams describes the sexual bravado of McKay's slighted veteran Jake Brown not as "an embodiment of African American patriotism and respectability but ... a transnational working-class symbol of black social, political, cultural, and sexual rebellion" (338).

Whether in Europe or the United States, the overriding narrative of white modernist masculinities emerges as a response to a sense of encroaching feminine influence that forces authors to reassert forms of masculine hegemony. Modernist masculinities brim with examples of how power is both exercised and sustained by controlling the meaning of what it is to be a man and, thus by extension, redefining forms of subordination. The legacy of the early critical canonization of a white, masculine strain of modernism as high art and therefore true art, and the still-lingering effect these early shapers of modernism had in defining the terms on which what is modernism is judged, is exemplary of the strength of masculine hegemony to define and shape reality.

4

Sex, Politics, and Law

Overview

To be entirely free, and at the same time entirely dominated by law, is the eternal paradox of human life that we realise at every moment.
—OSCAR WILDE

Modernists worked at a historical moment in which, as Oscar Wilde wrote in a prison cell in 1897, the freedom to live and create was nevertheless circumscribed and even thwarted by the force of the law. This ongoing realization is one that characterizes modernist literature as writers struggled to understand what freedoms they, and others, might reasonably enjoy. Political and legal structures shaped literary modernism from its inception. Because men had made and administered the laws for centuries, it was no surprise that women's literature—and representations of female sexuality—were particularly unpopular with powerful political and legal figures. Modernist authors often took aim at what writers saw as repressive legal norms and used their work to challenge divorce laws, contraception bans, the prohibition of (or simple distaste for) homosexual acts, and, quite simply, sexual pleasure. Writers as varied as Henrik Ibsen, James Joyce, Radclyffe Hall, D. H. Lawrence, Bernard Shaw, Henry Miller, Theodore Dreiser, and many others would find their work censored. Other writers like Wyndham Lewis would run afoul of libel laws, while Ezra Pound, Virginia Woolf, and their contemporaries would struggle to navigate the vicissitudes of copyright laws that gave (or denied) the right to profit from their creative work. Modernist writers and their contemporaries also represented the actions of the law in their literary work, putting the legal system and its strictures figuratively on trial in their poems, fiction, and plays.

Modernist writers also wrote nonfiction about the legal system, working to make their audiences understand the ways in which the law created horizons that shaped their work. In September of 1928, for example, E. M. Forster and Virginia Woolf wrote a letter to *The Nation and Athenaeum* in which they expressed their anger and frustration at the destruction order issued against Hall's *The Well of Loneliness* (1928). Hall's novel, which traced the coming of age and young adulthood of a lesbian (Hall used the term "invert") novelist, was famously decorous in its treatment of the main character's sexual relationships. It expressed, however, a call for toleration and understanding, and a British judge ruled that it might "deprave and corrupt" vulnerable readers. Forster and Woolf noted that the subject of lesbianism itself had been ruled obscene and protested: "What of other subjects known to be more or less unpopular in Whitehall, such as birth-control, suicide, and pacifism? May we mention these? We await our instructions!" (726). They expressed the concern that the result of such trials was to make a novelist "cling to subjects that are officially acceptable [...] and to shun anything original lest it lead him [sic] into forbidden areas" (726). The law, this letter suggested, could transform the very future of literature itself. The effects of this particular trial lingered: Vera Brittain, most famous for her memoir of the First World War, *Testament of Youth* (1933), would devote a whole book (*Radclyffe Hall: A Case of Obscenity?*) to the British and US trials of *The Well* in 1968.

Other modernist writers, like the famously irascible Lawrence, would come to their own defense in polemics that championed specific works. In the essay "A Propos of *Lady Chatterley's Lover*" (1929), he articulated his thoughts about his most scandalous novel, which was not initially published in Britain or the United States because the author knew it would be prosecuted. Calling *Chatterley* "an honest, healthy book" (307), Lawrence explained that "I want men and women to be able to *think* sex, fully, completely, honestly, and cleanly" (308)—to have what he called "a proper reverence for sex, and a proper awe of the body's strange experiences" (309).

If Forster and Woolf were concerned about the impact of the law on writers, Lawrence was concerned that the legal system would prevent readers from having access to work that might alter their perceptions of their own bodies, sexual experiences, and cultures. In both cases, the law limited what could be published; Lawrence suggested that it thus limited what could be thought as well.

Such passionate polemics have given modernism the reputation of an aesthetic libertarianism. Students might be tempted to assume that all experimental writers chafed at the restrictions the legal system imposed on the content of modern literature. But even writers who represented sexuality in their own creative works could be quite critical of how others did so. Joyce and Lawrence famously loathed one another's fiction. And Amy Lowell, creator of what we now read as frankly erotic poetry, expressed frustration that her American compatriots "could not see 'the difference between envisaging life whole and complete, physical as well as spiritual, and pure obscenities like those perpetrated by James Joyce'" (qtd in Vanderham 28). Balancing the physical with the spiritual was obviously in the eye of the beholder, with some very powerful readers able to limit how widely a work could circulate. Government censors did much of this work, but the heads of circulating libraries and vice societies also decided what books were available in different cities, states, and countries.

This chapter highlights how sex and gender were intimately involved in modernism's encounter with the law and, to a lesser extent, politics. As the creation of, and actor for, the state, law becomes one of the most visible ways in which politics makes itself felt. Although law may seem to lack the immediacy of politics, it represents the residuum of previous political decisions and acts. Politicians can choose to act upon laws that have fallen into obscurity, to encourage lawyers and judges to reinterpret existing laws, or to enact new laws. In the case of modernism and modernist studies, the interactions of politics, law, and literature reflect assumptions about who women and men are as writers, readers, and citizens. First, the chapter begins by highlighting the relationship between obscenity law and women, who were used as rationales for the prosecutions that haunted so many modernist writers. Next, we highlight scholarly approaches to modernism and its so-called others, obscenity and pornography, to illustrate how critics have complicated the story of modernism and censorship as well as the relationship between literature and "filth." Two texts that have received a great deal of attention, *The Well of Loneliness* and *Ulysses*, then serve to illustrate the kinds of arguments that emerge about *why* particular works were censored. The chapter next briefly explores other legal contexts for modernist literature, including libel and marriage laws. Finally, we turn our attention to politics and explore three areas in which modernism, sex, and gender squarely interacted with national and international politics: suffrage, empire, and fascism. Throughout these sections, one point remains at the forefront: politics and law were not neutral when it came to gender and sexuality.

Throughout this chapter, readers should understand that legal and political conflicts were originally shaped by the assumptions documented previously in this book. To read what judges, lawyers, critics, and reporters said about censored texts, or to revisit the question of whether women should have the right to vote, is to witness yet again the performance of a normative masculinity that was patriarchal, aggressively heterosexual, and bent on protecting and subordinating femininity along with lesbianism and biological women. To see that modernist writers, and later critics, averred that women should have political rights and had *always* written about national and international issues like empire and fascism is to understand the challenges modernism posed to gender and sex norms and the work critics had to do to underline modernism's own radicalism. Returning to the image of modernist studies as a palimpsest, we can say that all of the previous inscriptions on the manuscript (women and femininity, sexuality, and masculinity) needed to be excavated before the discoveries in this chapter could come to light. It is only after rethinking sex and gender that the story of their imbrication with law and politics could be told.

Women and censorship

Although modernist writers wrestled with different types of law, including libel, copyright, marriage, and property laws, censorship posed the most obvious and public threat to their livelihoods and reputations. A detailed account of censorship law is outside the scope of this book—for such a treatment, see Robert Spoo's

Modernism and the Law (2018)—but what we offer is an account that highlights the role that women, and assumptions about femininity, played in the selection of books to prosecute and the legal arguments that unfolded during obscenity trials. While censorship law may seem neutral to gender and sex in principle, modernist writers had to navigate a practice that treated women as vulnerable readers in need of masculine legal defense from books that might destroy them.

During the period, books could be censored for many reasons, including blasphemy, libel, and portraying public figures. But as Elisabeth Ladenson observes in *Dirt for Art's Sake: Books on Trial from Madame Bovary to Lolita* (2007), "Sexuality, and especially female sexuality, have always held a power to disturb" and to bring on obscenity charges (9). In *Modernism and the Theater of Censorship* (1996), Adam Parkes comes to a similar conclusion, describing censored experimental works as hinging on "questions of sexuality and gender" (17). Texts were censored if they presented unconventional visions of human, but especially female, sexuality. Examples examined by Ladenson, Parkes, and others include the censorship of Hall's novel but also of Lawrence's visions of women's sexual desire in homosexual (*The Rainbow*) and heterosexual (*Chatterley*) relationships, Joyce's vision of an exhibitionist Gerty McDowell ("Nausicaa") and unfaithful Molly Bloom ("Penelope"), the reading and desiring protagonist of *Madame Bovary*, the wayward and unpunished *Sister Carrie*, and many others. We'll return to some of these examples in more detail later. This section will demonstrate that while many modernists and critics of modernism have defended purportedly indecent literature, and many scholars have highlighted the role of sex and gender in prosecutions of individual works, some have paradoxically exaggerated the role of gender, as if to blame young women (and a feminized culture) for censorship. Female bodies thus become at once a reason to suppress work and take the blame for the men who conduct the actual prosecutions.

The odd position of women vis-à-vis censorship came about because of a Victorian trial that established a legal standard for the late nineteenth and early twentieth centuries. Under *Hicklin*, as well as rulings that explicitly or implicitly apply this standard, women were primarily envisioned as readers in need of protection. The 1868 case of *Regina v. Hicklin* might not, on the face of it, seem terribly relevant to *Ulysses* or *The Rainbow*. Henry Scott was charged with violating the 1857 Obscene Publications Act by reselling an anti-Catholic pamphlet that described clergy as engaging in various sex acts. Notably, the Hicklin of the trial's title was not the defendant but a minor official who had revoked a destruction order because he felt Scott's intentions were innocent in selling the pamphlet. On appeal, Scott's intention was found to be an irrelevant factor in his putative guilt; instead, the panel of judges ruled that all that mattered was whether the work was obscene. In what would come to be known as the Hicklin test, Chief Justice Cockburn opined that "the test of obscenity is this, whether the tendency of the matter charged as obscenity is to deprave and corrupt those whose minds are open to such immoral influences, and into whose hands a publication of this sort may fall." Cockburn did not detail *who* might be open to "immoral influences," but Victorian assumptions were that young, female, and working-class readers were especially vulnerable to corruption. Framing these constituencies as uncritical readers, the *Hicklin* ruling positioned a young, working-class woman as the most in need of legal protection against obscenity. In contrast, only comparatively well-off men were understood as able to decide what might corrupt a hypothetical reader.

Encounters between young women and modernist books were often the beginning of an obscenity prosecution. In 1916, Theodore Dreiser's *The "Genius"* came to the attention of the Western Society for the Suppression of Vice after a clergyman saw "a young girl" borrow the book from a library (de Grazia 118). The serial publication of Joyce's *Ulysses* in *The Little Review* came to an end when one of the journal's editors, Margaret Anderson, sent an unsolicited copy of the July–August issue, which included the episode that would later be known as "Nausicaa," to the daughter of a New York district attorney (Parkes 65). In that same city in 1924, Lawrence's *Women in Love* was prosecuted after a sixteen-year-old judge's daughter brought the book home from the lending library Womrath's (de Grazia 73). Although Joyce's reader alone brought the book to her father and triggered a prosecution, in the other cases, the sight of a young woman with a particular book was enough for men to start the work of suppression. Even—or perhaps especially—an *imagined* young girl was enough to stop modern novels from being published. In 1900, after Doubleday contracted to publish Dreiser's *Sister Carrie*, the publisher's wife "thought Carrie's fate not a denouncement that 'any young reader could possibly construe as advocating chastity as a way of life. Quite the contrary!'" (de Grazia 101). In these examples and others, the imagined or actual female readers of modern works slowed the progress of books to print or suppressed them once they were in circulation.

At the same time, women served as rhetorical figures to illustrate the difference between decency and obscenity. In 1883, the American purity crusader Anthony Comstock attempted to contrast a painted nude with the photographic reproductions he deplored, contending that "there is a marked difference between a woman in her proper womanly apparel and modest appearance, and when shorn of all these and posed in a lewd posture" (*Traps for the Young* 171). Although Comstock had his detractors (see Figure 7), this sentiment was widely held. Witness similar arguments that continued to be made in the 1930s: in his defense of *Ulysses*, lawyer Morris Ernst argued that "whereas a woman who bared her arms and legs on a beach in 1900 would have been arrested, the bathing suits of

FIGURE 7 *Glackens, L. M., Artist. "St. Anthony Comstock, the Village nuisance" (1906). Library of Congress, Prints & Photographs Division. This cartoon, published in* Puck, *demonstrates that censors received criticism from those who thought their actions unnecessarily prudish.*

the 1930s 'leave very little of the human form concealed'" (qtd in Vanderham 95). Ernst's argument, that obscenity standards needed to be contemporary, did not inherently require an illustration drawn from women's fashion, but the fact that he and Comstock reached for the figure of female clothing to make their points is telling. Women's bodies, and their dress or undress, were coded as sexual in ways that men's bodies were not. Those bodies, and the minds of readers who inhabited them, needed to be strictly monitored lest they be corrupted *or* corrupt others.

Most scholars have regarded these kinds of rhetorical flourishes, as well as defenses of young readers, with some humor as well as criticism. And yet, from a very early date, critics who defended modernist writers from charges of obscenity—or chronicled censorship with scholarly precision—also larded their own work with gendered assumptions and examples. Stuart Gilbert's 1930 *James Joyce's Ulysses: A Study* was of its historical moment when, during the chapter on "Nausicaa," he encouraged his "gentle reader" to pause and "acclaim the 'flappers' of Bloomsday, happy indeed [...] before the evil days befell of abridged skirts, when man no longer delights in any girl's legs" (284). As this remark makes clear, Gilbert did not imagine a female reader of his study or of *Ulysses* proper. Indeed, Gilbert made the opposite assumption about Joyce's audience than did the many men who prosecuted *Ulysses*: if the vice crusaders and prosecutors feared that young women might read the book, Gilbert responded by constructing a circle of male readers who could enjoy themselves, and their memories of flappers, in the safe company of *Ulysses*.

Scholarly studies of censorship published more recently have left such paeans to the female leg behind. Boyer's *Purity in Print: Book Censorship in America from the Gilded Age to the Computer Age* (2002), for instance, instead offers up the example of John Ford, a New York judge, as an exemplar of the hysterical heights to which some would-be censors aspired. Ford's *Criminal Obscenity—Plea for Its Suppression* (1926) was, Boyer notes, dedicated to his infant granddaughter "in the fond hope that her pure soul may not be tainted or her innocent mind defiled through contact with impure prints, plays, or pictures; and that her young life may unfold into noble womanhood immaculate as the heart of a rose unsullied by human touch" (qtd in Boyer 123). One can feel Boyer sneer as he documents the kind of rhetoric that was used against writers for decades. Immediately after quoting Ford, however, he writes of a legal crusade to create a "fool-proof instrument for the emasculation of serious literary expression" (123–4). Boyer's characterization of literature as "emasculated" may be a figure of speech, but it's certainly a subtle clue to the role of gender in assumptions about who writes important work. His diction (here and elsewhere [218]) makes it plain: women were used as pretexts to censor serious literature, which is gendered masculine, no matter the actual sex of authorship. De Grazia, whose extensive study *Girls Lean Back Everywhere: The Law of Obscenity and the Assault on Genius* (1992), parallels Boyer in both illustrating the rhetorical use of young girls by censors and uncritically gendering the battle over free expression. His introduction sketches out the *Hicklin* doctrine as "a test that subordinated the freedom of writers, publishers, and readers to the imagined effects books might have upon impressionable young girls" (xi). While young girls were often, as we have seen, ur-figures for vulnerable readership, de Grazia's description of *Hicklin* ignores the fact that working-class and young readers of both sexes were also regarded as having minds open to immoral influences. Throughout his excellent and entertaining account of famous literary trials, de Grazia's fervent defense of "the freedom of literature and art in this country [the United States]" (xiii) often treats women and femininity as though they, and not male vice society leaders, prosecutors, and judges, were responsible for banning books. While he recounts the sad case of Ida Craddock, who committed suicide after being found guilty of writing and publishing obscene work (5), for example, in his study, women are the passive tools and victims of censorship law, and male judges, lawyers, and publishers are "enlightened," "brave," and "wise and courageous" (xi, xii). Admittedly, de Grazia's project is primarily historical, and as a result, it reflects the biases of the period upon which he reports. A later generation of critics would work to unpack those biases and to analyze the role sex and gender played in many of the cases he chronicles.

As these scholars demonstrate, women were not only readers in need of protection (or figures of speech) but writers, editors, publishers, printers, and otherwise often connected to and responsible for works that suffered censorship. They endured a great deal of nastiness both from those who prosecuted and those who defended them. Parkes writes that censored female writers like Radclyffe Hall (who was threatened with ejection from the courtroom after she shouted "shame!" at a judge characterizing her work in an unflattering way) and *Little Review* editors Jane Heap and Margaret Anderson were forced to be silent in the courts, "not only by her [their] official antagonists but by her [their] own side" (151). Paul Vanderham's study *James Joyce and Censorship: The Trials of Ulysses* (1998) offers additional evidence of the often oppositional relationship between male lawyer and female client at an obscenity trial. John Quinn, lawyer and patron, described arriving at *The Little Review* trial and seeing his clients Heap and Anderson along with their friends in the courtroom. Quinn described them as looking like the occupants of a "fashionable whorehouse" (Vanderham 43); in correspondence with Ezra Pound, he also took issue with Heap and Anderson's lesbian partnership (Parkes 72–3). As Parkes and Vanderham both establish, women needed male expertise to defend the works they edited or published, but that defense was seldom accompanied by respect for the client. In fact, officials often acted as though women should not be in the courtroom at all, no matter what their relationship to the material under consideration. In the 1932 *Ulysses* case, as Vanderham notes, the lawyer for the prosecution did not read passages he thought obscene in court, "allegedly because of the presence there of a woman, who happened to be Ernst's [the defending attorney] wife" (5). The figure of a (young) woman might be the reason that a book was prosecuted, but *actual* women in a court of law were silenced or silencing.

Some of the most famous decisions in censorship trials also relied upon assumptions about which of the sexes were rational and therefore able to distinguish pornography from obscenity. The famed decision by Judge John M. Woolsey that allowed *Ulysses* to be published in the United States in 1934 overturned many aspects of the *Hicklin* precedent: Woolsey ruled that Joyce's intentions in creating the work were relevant; he ruled that the entire book needed to be taken into account, not just sexually explicit or suggestive passages in isolation; and most famously, he ruled that vulnerable readers should not serve as the standard for whether a work was obscene. Instead, Woolsey determined that a text's potential impact should be measured upon *l'homme moyen sensuel* (the man of average appetites): he positioned himself, and two friends to whom he had shown *Ulysses*, as said *hommes* and found that *Ulysses* did not excite sexual passion in any of them. As de Grazia notes, history has not preserved the names of the two other *hommes*, whom he describes as "two unknown and invisible men (certainly they could not have been women)" (31). While the Woolsey judgment freed *Ulysses* in the United States, and eventually in other countries that took their cue from the US legal system, this laudatory goal was accomplished not by *trusting* poor, working-class, or female readers but by rendering them irrelevant. Thus, the gender standards of an earlier era were not so much overcome as overwritten. Instead of worrying, as did the publisher George H. Doran, about the "'finer sensibilities' of women—particularly those who were mothers, sisters, or daughters" (qtd in Boyer 91), Woolsey posited men of his educated class as exemplary readers of modernist fiction.

Modernism and obscenity

Recent scholarship of modernism, obscenity, censorship, and pornography has navigated this gendered terrain to make three important arguments. First, that modernism and obscenity were not, as early critics claimed, binary opposites but rather imbricated discourses. Second, that modernists and their middlebrow contemporaries were not only subject to official, government censorship but experienced a variety of public and private oppressive mechanisms. Third, that censorship of modernism was not only or primarily "about" silencing particular beliefs, practices, or texts but rather worked to mitigate social anxieties over everything from the First World War to the reproductive futurity of Western countries. All three strands attend to sexuality and gender, albeit to different degrees.

The first critics to write about purportedly indecent works positioned them either as pure smut, and thus ripe for prosecution, or as works of art that could not by definition be obscene. Gilbert's study of *Ulysses* ignored the most explicitly sexual aspects of Joyce's work and even bowdlerized passages quoted from the novel, but he occasionally confronted the question of obscenity head-on. Of "Circe," he wrote, "the animal nature of man is laid bare in a manner never before attempted in literature. Still there is nothing 'indecent' in it, if the framers of the Irish Censorship Bill correctly construed indecency as 'anything calculated to excite sexual passion.' These passages are, in fact, cathartic and calculated to allay rather than excite the sexual instinct" (20). Although Gilbert would later acknowledge that "obscenity has its niche in the scheme of things and a picture of life in which this element was ignored or suppressed would be incomplete" (21), his study highlights the Homeric correspondences in *Ulysses* and makes every effort to position the epic as worlds apart from the pornographic. This kind of approach held well until the 1990s, when critics began to argue that works like *Ulysses* were not separate from but constellated with more straightforwardly pornographic tropes and ideas.

One of the critics to take this approach was Paul Vanderham, whose 1998 study of the US censorship trials of *Ulysses* analyzed them in light of previously unexamined government documents. His book includes an appendix ("The Censor's *Ulysses*") that identifies the specific passages "deemed obscene or otherwise objectionable by various governmental and editorial authorities" (169). Vanderham complicates the widely held assumption that *Ulysses* was solely censored because of its obscene content, demonstrating that political (anti-anarchist and communist) and religious objections to Joyce's work were also responsible for the text's suppression (6). At the same time, his appendix and a chart of offending passages broken down by episode indicate that American officials found "Circe" and "Penelope" by far the most objectionable (89 and 56 offending passages, respectively) with "Oxen of the Sun" (29) and "Cyclops" (25) running a distant third and fourth place. Because "Circe" and "Penelope" are the most sexually explicit episodes in *Ulysses*—and because they highlight women's sexuality through their representations of prostitution and the unfaithful Molly Bloom's sexual experiences and fantasies—Vanderham's research confirms that censors primarily objected to the work's presentation of female bodies and sexualities. Instead of arguing that Joyce's book is not pornographic or obscene, however, Vanderham builds on work by Leslie Fiedler and Richard Brown, who "attempt to appreciate the pornographic dimension of *Ulysses*" (119). In an effort to counter the critical tradition established by Gilbert, which emphasized Joyce's classical allusions, Vanderham states that "the inclusion of pornographic works among the satellites that illuminate *Ulysses* is warranted not only because Joyce read them but also because he embodied their vision in his novel." His study thus calls for a renewed attention to the penetration of pornography into high modernism as well as an appreciation for the overlapping publication histories of these two seemingly disparate genres (120).

Two years after Vanderham's archival approach to the question of modernism and obscenity, Allison Pease's *Modernism, Mass Culture, and the Aesthetics of Obscenity* (2000) would trace an evolution in aesthetic philosophy to demonstrate "not simply how modernist artists were influenced by popular pornography, but also the complex and conflicted ways in which they strove to incorporate mass-cultural pornographic representations of the body, sex, and sexuality into their works even as they affirmed the aesthetic value of their appropriations of pornography, thus redefining conceptions of the aesthetic" (xii). Writing about modernist precursors like Swinburne and Beardsley as well as Lawrence and Joyce, Pease posits "the aesthetic of the obscene," "a mode of sexual representation that, while potentially affecting the sexual interests of its readers, does not, as opposed to pornography, seek sexual arousal as its main purpose" (34). Instead, the "aesthetic of the obscene seeks to be accepted into the cultural mainstream, and it does so by mediating its own material interests with idealist artistic techniques that promote the kind of consumptive practices associated with the aesthetic" (35). Through readings that trace pornographic tropes and images in modernist work, Pease (again, contra Gilbert) argues that modernism *is* pornographic but disciplines that genre by subjecting it to a ruthless emphasis on form. While less interested in the legal mechanisms that writers negotiated than Vanderham and, as we will see, Ladensen, Pease's argument complements scholarship on modernism and law by diagnosing the cultural and aesthetic work authors accused of obscenity carried out with increasingly greater success across the twentieth century.

A final exemplar of criticism that dismantles the modernism/pornography binary is Ladenson, whose *Dirt for Art's Sake* (2007) traces the perceived relationship between her titular terms "dirt" and "art." Taking up Gustave Flaubert, Charles Baudelaire, Joyce, Hall, Lawrence, Henry Miller, and Vladimir Nabokov, Ladenson argues that the obscene-clean binary remains in place even after works that are censored are embraced by the wider public: "when apparently pornographic works become classic the categories of 'pornography' and 'classic' are still viewed as mutually exclusive"

(222). Throughout *Dirt for Art's Sake*, Ladenson draws attention to the role of sex and gender in censorship trials, noting that "women [...] posed the major problem in terms of the readership of novels, because of the idea that women in general, like the newly literate working classes, were unable to distinguish between fiction and reality" (11). Here and elsewhere in her study, one is reminded of the prolonged reliance on the *Hicklin* test, which implicitly placed female readers at the center of censorship law. In addition, *Dirt* draws attention to the role of literal dirt in inciting official repression; for example, Ladenson argues that what irked people about *Ulysses* was "Joyce's failure to draw a clear line of demarcation between two categories of shameful corporeality, between the sexual and the excremental" (93). This argument nicely dovetails with that of Vanderham, who argued that one of the first censors of *Ulysses* was Ezra Pound. Pound attempted to "clean up" Joyce's work for its serialization in *The Little Review* and was especially anxious to obscure Leopold Bloom's visit to the outhouse in "Calypso" (18–27). Pound's efforts to separate the erotic from excrement remind readers that some modernist writers were themselves uncomfortable with the lines their contemporaries would cross; Virginia Woolf, like Pound, expressed unease with the indecency of *Ulysses*. Such responses are not perhaps surprising—modernist writers were seldom unanimous on any given point—but they are reflected in a critical tradition that attempted to keep modernism and obscenity distinct from one another. Vanderham, Pease, and Ladenson have shown that this assumption, and the trials of modernist work, were often based on the false notion that art could not be what modernism sometimes is: sexually explicit, dirty, and arousing.

A second group of critics worked to complicate the field's understanding of how censorship of modernist work took place. While, as we have seen, many accounts of the encounter between literature and law focus on specific trials (de Grazia, Vanderham, Ladenson, Parkes, Medd, and others), these critics highlight a wider culture of censorship in which private individuals, organizations, and companies worked *with* government officials to initiate legal proceedings and to suppress literary works that somehow escaped destruction. Boyer's *Purity in Print* provided an early example of this approach. This study pays close attention to the political and legal agitation of American vice societies, which often brought books to government attention and generated public pressure for "Clean Books" legislation, as well as to the quietly censorious role of circulating libraries. Boyer's work is historical rather than critical, but it provides a broad context for what can otherwise seem like isolated acts of prosecution. His book also helpfully reminds readers that high modernism was not the sole target of censors' wrath: among other examples, he notes that Elinor Glyn's wildly popular 1907 novel *Three Weeks* (33) was banned in Massachusetts, an action that resulted in "little protest [...] from the literary community" (34–5). *Purity in Print* thus complicates the picture of censorship in the early twentieth century while also demonstrating that modernists, unlike popular authors, could count on support when their works were banned; writers such as Glyn, who were regarded as insufficiently literary, have had little scholarship devoted to them, although the recent interest in middlebrow and popular literature discussed in Chapter 1 may change this in the near future.[1]

Katherine Mullin's *James Joyce, Sexuality and Social Purity* (2003) focuses on the activities of the National Vigilance Association (NVA) in Ireland and Joyce's literary response to its ideas, assumptions, and campaigns. The NVA's initial purpose was to "ensure the enforcement" of the 1885 Criminal Law Amendment Act (24), a fact that demonstrates law's extralegal effects: the law not only criminalized particular behaviors, but it brought this private organization of citizens into being. Mullin reads across Joyce's *oeuvre*, covering short stories in *Dubliners* (1914) as well as *A Portrait of the Artist as a Young Man* (1916) and *Ulysses*, to argue that, paradoxically, "Joyce's writing is provocatively engaged with a Protestant evangelical social purity campaign which threatened his chances of publication" (19). Instead of focusing solely on Joyce's angered responses to the official and unofficial censors who suppressed his work, Mullin argues that "Joyce moved beyond simple reaction against the threat of censorship to weave such frustrations and proscriptions into the fabric of his art" (26). Mullin's repeated focus on Joyce's representation of women as sexually vulnerable or aggressive (in "Eveline," "Nausicaa," and "Circe") draws attention to the author's interrogation of the vice society's model of a passive (or predatory) femininity. Like Boyer, Mullin's work illuminates cultural forces invested in strict standards of public morality, but she differs in offering in-depth readings of canonical modernist texts that critique the ideological underpinnings of those same forces.

In *British Modernism and Censorship* (2006), Celia Marshik is similarly attentive to the social movements that worked to encourage prosecutions of modernist authors. Like Mullin, she uncovers how literary texts engaged with a culture of censorship that culminated in obscenity trials but also included circulating libraries, university curricula and libraries, and other private organizations. Positing a "censorship dialectic" in which authors anticipate the consequences of an obscenity trial and then self-censor or embrace oblique styles that might skirt censorship, Marshik writes about Bernard Shaw, Virginia Woolf, James Joyce, and Jean Rhys. Noting that the first three authors made public names for themselves by publishing anti-censorship polemics (and serving as literary martyrs), Marshik like Mullin positions modernism as not only being victimized by, but marketing itself through, engagements with censorship. Notably, *British Modernism and Censorship* points to modernists' repeated use of the prostitute as a way to confront censorship indirectly, representing a figure that embodied sexuality and obscenity without necessarily treating sex work directly. Here, too, criticism of modernism and obscenity law points to the centrality of female bodies in the battles over censorship even while complicating suppression as the work of government alone. Cathy Leeny's *Irish Women Playwrights 1900–1939: Gender & Violence on Stage* (2010) offers a parallel account of drama by writers such as Augusta Gregory, Eva Gore-Booth, and Dorothy Macardle, to argue that "the issue of censorship in Irish theatre in this period cannot be traced through official channels. With no direct censorship mechanism overseeing theatrical representation, censorship operated unofficially, through hidden networks, and was unpredictable and perhaps all the more restrictive on that account" (196). As Leeny, Marshik, Mullin, and Boyer demonstrate, censorship law was thus part of a much wider web of suppression, with a spectrum of individuals and organization arrayed against the publication and performance of works that represented gender and sexuality in nonconformist ways.[2]

Finally, an important strand of recent criticism demonstrates that censorship of modernism was not exclusively undertaken to silence particular texts; instead, obscenity trials served to manage dismay over the future of Western countries in a time of geopolitical uncertainty. There were multiple causes of such uncertainty, but it is worth noting that publications about contraception were frequently suppressed by the same individuals and groups that worked to censor modernism. Although activists' opinions on birth control varied, contraception was often associated with the cause of women's suffrage as both upset long-standing hierarchies of gender power. Censorship thus became a tool to reinforce compulsory heterosexuality and reproduction. Parkes's *Modernism and the Theater of Censorship* (1996), for example, explores how "modernism insinuates possibilities for expressing deviant and nonreproductive configurations of gender and sexuality" (19). He links the 1915 prosecution of Lawrence's *The Rainbow* with Marie Stopes's contraceptive advice manuals, noting that the nonreproductive and lesbian scenes in Lawrence's novel particularly alarmed readers in the throes of the First World War. Parkes argues that both contraception and lesbianism worried wartime readers, who questioned, "where might the next generation come from?" (56). In readings influenced by Judith Butler's theory of gender as performance (see Chapter 2), Parkes argues that Lawrence, Joyce, Woolf, and Hall "dramatized issues of sexuality, literary expression, and censorship that surfaced in contemporary responses to their work" (xi). Their challenge to heteronormative and reproductive models of sexuality was, Parkes's book shows, at least as responsible for their censorship as their purportedly obscene representation of specific sex acts.

More recently, Jodie Medd's *Lesbian Scandal and the Culture of Modernism* (2012) focuses on trials that took place between 1918 and 1928 and "that hinged on an accusation of lesbianism, encompassing trials for libel, slander, and obscenity" (1). While Medd's study points to the ways in which the word "'lesbian' occurs in discussions between men in legal and parliamentary documents, private letters, and male advice manuals, to be used against women with derogatory implications" (11), her study argues that lesbianism was less a stable signifier than an "unstable suggestion" (22). This suggestion, which emerges when lesbianism is brought into "legislative discourse," constitutes "lesbianism as a suggestion that simultaneously destabilizes systems of meaning, functions as a figure for postwar anxieties, and challenges the workings of the law" (88). Medd looks at the First World War Maud Allen libel trial, the treatment of Margaret Anderson and Jane Heap by John

Quinn during *The Little Review* obscenity trial (discussed earlier), and Bloomsbury reactions to *The Well of Loneliness* trial, among others, to highlight the ways in which the lesbian functioned in the courtroom as an unstable referent that nevertheless focalized concerns about sexuality's role in Western societies; the courtroom, Medd shows, became a battleground over not only people and sexual identities but what the future of the UK and the United-States might look like.

Two case studies: Radclyffe Hall (1880–1943) and James Joyce (1882–1941)

As the previous sections have suggested, many works on modernism and censorship have focused on the trials of a select few writers, with Joyce leading the pack and Lawrence, Hall, and Dreiser bringing up the rear. While a detailed treatment of any of these would take more time and space than we can give them here, it is illuminating to briefly touch on two very different cases to see how scholars have framed their cultural importance. We'll glance at the treatment of *The Well of Loneliness* and *Ulysses*, which together provide insight into the lingering cultural impact of the trials of modernist novels.

As the introduction to this chapter notes, Hall's *Well* was censored shortly after its publication in 1928 because it represented the novel's protagonist, the "invert" Stephen Gordon, as morally and creatively superior to many heterosexual characters who surround her. Although the novel was well reviewed after its initial publication in the UK, it came to the attention of British censors after James Douglas published an August 19, 1928, review in *The Sunday Express* under the inflammatory title "A Book That Should Be Suppressed" (for the full text of Douglas's review as well as other documents surrounding the trial, see Doan and Prosser). Douglas's judgment, that he "would rather give a healthy boy or a healthy girl a phial of prussic acid than this novel" (qtd in de Grazia 173), drew unwelcome attention to the book. The novel's publisher, Jonathan Cape, then made the error of sending copies of *The Well* to government officials as well as writing to the *Express* with the offer to withdraw it from circulation if the Home Office agreed with Douglas's assessment. The Home Secretary *did* agree; Cape stopped publishing *The Well* but secretly licensed the Parisian Pegasus Press to print the novel, and those copies were then used to fill orders in Britain and elsewhere that had been placed with Cape (176–7). The government seized copies from London booksellers, and Cape received a summons to appear in court. On the other side of the Atlantic, US publishers were initially reluctant to publish the book because of the prosecution, but eventually Covici-Friede took a chance and issued Hall's novel. That publisher too soon found itself in court.

The details of these trials are carefully documented in books by de Grazia and others; in the end, the British Magistrate Sir Chartes Biron found that *The Well* "would tend to corrupt those into whose hands it might fall" (de Grazia 197), and in New York, Magistrate Hyman Bushnel concurred. But after an appeal in the United States, a "court of special sessions dismissed the criminal charges" and *The Well* was able to circulate (201). Scholars then parsed the various reasons for the judges' quite varied decisions as well as the cultural impact of widespread news coverage of the British trial. Rebecca O'Rourke's *Reflecting on The Well of Loneliness* (1989) helpfully provides a chapter on criticism of Hall's novel to that date, and she concurs with "the argument that opposition to Radclyffe Hall came from a sense of moral outrage that she would neither offer homosexuality up for heterosexual mockery and entertainment, as Compton Mackenzie did, nor condemn it" (92). Parkes takes a parallel tack and argues that *The Well* was censored because it "pleads the cause of sexual inversion by taking up an aggressively polemical stance" (144); he further notes that Hall "seemed [...] guilty of speaking in the wrong tone of voice" (147) and compares *The Well* to Woolf's *Orlando*, which he believes escaped censorship because of its ironic, satirical manner. Ladenson in contrast argues that Hall tried to avoid censorship through the structure of her plot: "the unhappy fate of Stephen and her kind, foregrounded by Hall on every page of her book and especially in its title, represents, among other things, an unsuccessful attempt to conform to societal and literary expectations and ward off censorship even as the work pleads the case of inverts" (120). Ladenson points out that Hall herself did not have the pained relationships she chose to picture in her book and that *The Well*, while somewhat autobiographical, is thus structured to try to evade the very outcome it experienced. As these examples indicate, scholarship on literature and legal trials often draws attention to whether (and how) a text invited prosecution. By reading both Hall's novel *and* the comments of government and legal officials, scholars work to establish why this one novel was censored when others published in the same year that also represent lesbianism (*Orlando, Extraordinary Women*) were allowed to circulate.

In addition to providing critical readings of Hall's censored text and the legal arguments made against it, scholars have provided assessments of the trial that emphasize the cultural impact of what became a highly publicized event. Laura Doan's *Fashioning Sapphism: The Origins of a Modern English Lesbian Culture* (2001), for instance, demonstrates that the censorship trial—and the reportage thereof—rendered the author as a type, visible not as fashionable but as a mannish lesbian. Providing a study of a 1927 photograph of Hall and her partner Una Troubridge, Doan argues that before the trial, the image could have been read in many ways: by those "in the know" as lesbian but also as fashionable and modern (see figure 3, ch. 2) (186). *The Sunday Express*, however, cropped the same image around Hall's head and torso and used it with Douglas's screed; as a result, Doan writes, "Hall's famous image, previously the epitome of chic modernity for readers of magazines such as *Eve*, would gradually become the visual emblem of female sexual inversion" (187). Doan's argument demonstrates that the workings of the law can make particular sexual identities visible; a photograph that might be read in multiple ways is reduced to one sexual signifier. The "fact of the matter is that after the obscenity trial of *The Well* life changed utterly for *all* women who lived with other women, or *all* women drawn to masculine styles of dress, whether lesbian or not" (193). While Doan argues that this change wasn't entirely negative, her study highlights the fact that a trial can have unpredictable and widespread cultural outcomes. In a similar but more narrow argument, Medd's 2012 study asserts that the *Well* trial helped Bloomsbury consolidate what it was (and wasn't) doing in terms of sexual representation. Contrasting members of the coterie's public and private statements about putting sex acts into speech and writing, Medd argues that "the trial compelled Bloomsbury to negotiate its own boundaries, political commitments, and collective identity. It provided an opportunity for Bloomsbury not only to reassert its highbrow aesthetic in opposition to Hall's own middlebrow sincerity and sentiment, but also to distance its sexuality from Hall's scandal, while consolidating its members' identities as cultural authorities and publicly engaged intellectuals" (152). The trial of Hall's novel was therefore not incidental but central to Bloomsbury's, and thus modernism's, larger project.

A great deal of critical ink has also been spilled over the trials of *Ulysses*, including the American prosecutions of *The Little Review* (where the first episodes appeared serially) and later of the full novel. As mentioned earlier, *The Little Review*, which had earlier run-ins with censorship, was finally forced to stop serializing *Ulysses* after the July–August 1920 issue containing the episode now known as "Nausicaa" was brought to the attention of the New York County District Attorney by an angry father. After working its way through the courts, the issue's suppression was upheld in early 1921 (see Vanderham, chapter two, for an excellent account of this trial). Due in no small part to this prosecution, British and American publishers refused to take a risk and publish the entire novel, which was issued instead by Sylvia Beach's Shakespeare and Company (Paris) in 1922. Officials in America and Britain attempted to seize imported copies whenever they could, and it was not until 1933 that Judge John Woolsey ruled that *Ulysses* was not obscene and could be imported and published. Vanderham provides a detailed analysis of both the legal strategy that freed Joyce's novel and what he calls "the well-intentioned lies" of the Woolsey decision: in brief, Woolsey reasoned that a work of art could not be obscene; that a work's pornographic tendencies should be assessed by mature male (and not vulnerable female) readers; and that Joyce had not intended to write an obscene text, so *Ulysses* could not be obscene (115–131). Although this decision was later appealed, Circuit Court judges upheld Woolsey's decision by a 2/1 majority. The book was thereafter published in the United States; in Britain, readers had to wait until late 1936, when British officials decided to follow the example of their American counterparts and stop enforcing the ban (Marshik, *British Modernism* 163–4). While officials in the two countries did not invariably follow one another's lead, in the case of *Ulysses*, the Woolsey decision and changing mores made a continued British ban illogical.

The scholarship on *Ulysses* and the law is far-flung, with much of it focused specifically on the trials even as a minority looks at Joyce's representation of law *in* his text (an instance of the latter approach is Dale Barleben's 2017 *Staging the Trials of Modernism: Testimony and the British Modern Literary Consciousness*, which argues that Joyce "writes with an understanding of the law as culture" [116]). Readers will find many examples of studies that parallel work on *The Well of Loneliness*: critics provide readings of Joyce's text and argue that it paradoxically courted censorship through its representation of female sexuality. Other scholars have focused on "Nausicaa," the episode that resulted in the suppression of *The Little Review*, to argue that censorship of the issue (and later Joyce's full epic) was due to the characterization of Gerty McDowell as not only aware of, but complicit in, Bloom's masturbation. Vanderham argues that the offense this episode posed "undoubtedly lay not so much in Bloom's immorality as in the young person's impurity: she was not the innocent of the Victorian imagination" (3); Parkes writes that Gerty's "self-display is coupled with scandalous awareness of matters supposedly unintelligible to the minds of male New York judges, let alone to young girls" (78); Mullin similarly argues that the episode "argues for the belatedness and obsolescence of social purity's imagined 'young person'" (144). "Penelope" has received similar attention, with Parkes claiming that Molly Bloom's soliloquy "constructs sexuality as a performance, which proves to be the ground on which transformation is possible" (102), and Marshik demonstrates that British officials objected most to the episode because it was not only sexually explicit but narrated by a "working-class, female colonial" subject (161). In these and other studies, critics have established that Joyce's encounters with censorship were far from incidental: his work explicitly challenged officials' assumptions of *who* could express overtly sexual thoughts and desires and thus ran afoul of censorship law.

In addition to offering readings of *Ulysses* in light of assumptions upon which official censorship operated, scholars have been greatly interested in the sexual politics of the trials themselves. Vanderham, Parkes, and Medd draw attention to the disrespect with which the editors of *The Little Review* were regarded; as Medd concludes, although John Quinn acted as defense counsel during the trial, he cast Anderson and Heap as "only acting out their homosexual disposition toward self-exhibition and scandal, not legitimately resisting censorship" (144). If Quinn's nasty homophobia has been taken up by many critics, the 1933 reversal of the American ban has attracted even more attention because of its importance as a precedent and its dramatic role in allowing *Ulysses* to circulate in the United States. De Grazia, Boyer, Ladenson, Rachel Potter, Joseph Hassett, Kevin Birmingham, and many others have meditated on the trial with the Woolsey decision attracting the lion's share of attention. Vanderham's work offers the most detailed scholarly treatment of the legal strategies and trials, noting, for example, that when American officials decided to defend the customs ban on *Ulysses*, one cited "the latter part of the book, particularly the musings of the wife" (90), and during the trial, Woolsey "admitted that he, too, was troubled by parts of the novel, especially Molly's monologue" (110). His study not only highlights the continued role of sex and gender in the later court decision but provides an excellent example of scholarship on modernism and law, highlighting as he does not only the official court pronouncements but also the "behind the scenes" discussions and tactics that censors and Joyce's supporters employed. The archival turn of the New Modernist Studies is amply demonstrated by scholarship on censored modernist texts.

Copyright, libel, and other legal horizons

Although scholarship on modernism and law has most closely examined the impact of censorship, other legal fields have also received attention. In terms of copyright, Paul Saint-Amour (*The Copywrights: Intellectual Property and the Literary Imagination* [2003] and *Modernism & Copyright* [2011]) and Robert Spoo (*Without Copyrights* [2013]) are the main figures, and their work has illuminated both the interaction between censorship and copyright law—works suppressed for obscenity were not eligible for copyright protection and were often pirated—and the way in which copyright restrictions shaped modernist works. Although their studies are not primarily interested in the intersections among copyright, sexuality, and gender, essays by Carol Shloss and Marshik in Saint-Amour's *Modernism & Copyright* do attend to how copyright impacted work on female biographical subjects and Woolf's attempts to theorize a female literary tradition, respectively.

The impact of libel law on modernism has similarly attracted scholars. Medd's book (also discussed earlier) takes up the libel trials of Maud Allen and Radclyffe Hall, who both attempted to defend their reputations against charges of membership in "the cult of the clitoris" or of being a "grossly immoral woman," correspondingly. Medd and Doan, who also analyzes the Allen slander trial, agree that the very fact that women knew what lesbianism meant—that they understood what they were accused of in the purportedly libelous statements of others—was used against them; knowledge of so-called deviant practices meant that they seemed guilty regardless of their actual desires and relationships. Medd and Doan also draw attention to the debate over whether to criminalize lesbianism in the British Criminal Law Amendment Bill of 1921: the clause including a reference to female homosexuality "would eventually fail on the grounds that it would be unenforceable, would render women vulnerable to blackmail, and would only serve to increase lesbianism by advertising it," Doan writes (38). In both the case of libel trials and the discarded clause, it becomes clear that the law did not want to disseminate sexual knowledge and regarded women who possessed such knowledge as morally suspect.

Sean Latham's *The Art of Scandal: Modernism, Libel Law, and the Roman à Clef* (2009) is the most sustained study of the influence of libel law on modernism, particularly on writers whose work fictionalized biographical or autobiographical incidents. His study examines the work and careers of writers such as Joyce, Rhys, Wyndham Lewis, and Aldous Huxley, and he helpfully provides detailed information about the intersection between literature and libel in the period, including an appendix on "British and Irish Libel Law" (86–8). Although sexuality and gender are not Latham's primary foci, he examines sexologists' practice of concealing patients' identities in their case studies through the omission of names and other identifying information, and he links this practice to the *roman à clef* and its operation at "an increasingly fluid boundary between fact and fiction" (52). What sexology and the *roman* share, in Latham's terms, is that they titillate readers who know that a case study or character has a corresponding figure in the real world; libel law threatened both genres when readers were able to see the historical person behind the representation. Latham also provides an examination of novels that fictionalize the appearance, behavior, and personality of Ottoline Morrell, an aristocratic patron of the arts who was skewered by former friends in "at least ten romans à clef" (132). Becoming the abject bearer of anxieties about "the commodification of aesthetic culture" (136) and "the failure of aesthetic autonomy" (141), Morrell was thoroughly satirized in novels such as Lawrence's *Women in Love*. While she ultimately chose not to bring a libel suit against Lawrence or his publisher, Latham observes that Morrell could have done so (141); he argues that the author "resisted any attempt to root [the novel] in the events of his own life" because of "the fear that those he attacked would seek recourse in a libel court" (149). Indeed, he condemned Morrell "in starkly gendered terms as a vain and ignorant woman," suggesting that she was a bad reader in recognizing herself in his character Hermione Roddice (150). Like scholarship on censorship, Latham's work on modernism and libel law thus sheds light on how legal regimes shaped what authors said about their own work and how women—and representations thereof—became catalysts "for crucial narrative innovations" (155).

Compared to censorship, copyright, and libel law, other fields have garnered less attention from scholars of modernism. Occasionally, however, a book or article has illuminated a legal arena that profoundly shaped how individual texts and authors represented sex and gender. Janine Utell's work on Joyce, marriage, and adultery is a case in point. While her book *James Joyce and the Revolt of Love: Marriage, Adultery, Desire* (2010) primarily takes an ethical approach to her topic, a recent essay ("Criminal Conversation: Marriage, Adultery, and the Law in Joyce's Work") examines conversations between male and female characters throughout his oeuvre to illuminate "the extent to which such awareness of legal norms infiltrates intimate life. Yet we also see Joyce resisting that codification, pushing back against legal structures that overdetermine intimate relationships" (15–6). Through readings of *Giacomo Joyce, Exiles, Dubliners*, and *Ulysses*, Utell "suggest[s] that Joyce viewed men and women as caught up in a legal discourse that denied them the autonomy to shape their private lives the way they chose" (17), and she concludes that the author privileges "intimate moments, outside the realm of legal discourse" that "serve as an alternative to conventional, legally defined and determined unions" (28). Utell illustrates the latter claim by pointing to Leopold and Molly Blooms's shared memory of their courtship at Howth in *Ulysses*, with "the sensual sharing of seedcake taking the place of a civil ceremony or a joining at the altar" (28). This essay suggests that future scholarship on marriage in modernism might fruitfully engage with marriage and divorce laws, which authors had to navigate in their own lives and that shaped the horizons of the men and women they represented.

Utell's essay is published in the collection *Joyce and the Law* (2017), edited by Jonathan Goldman, which traces the impact of many other kinds of legal statutes and discourses on the author's work. Although only a few essays in the volume address sex and gender as squarely as she does, the range of essay topics—including finance, immigration, language, municipal corporation reform, property, and licensing laws, among others—demonstrates scholars' ever-expanding approach to the legal contexts that shaped modernism. There is a great deal of work yet to be done; while publications on Joyce lead the way, readings of literature by (or focused on) women, sexuality, and law will doubtless continue to reframe authors and texts we thought we knew well.

Navigating politics: Suffrage, empire, fascism

If the intersection of modernism and law has led to new understandings of modernism and sexuality, the interface of politics with modern literature has produced equally fruitful readings. As we have noted throughout this chapter, scholars have repeatedly demonstrated that particular legal regimes shaped specific texts as well as the careers of major and minor writers; it should therefore be no surprise that political systems similarly provided boundaries that writers had to navigate and that profoundly influenced their sense of self as well as art. Indeed, law and politics are inevitably linked: as Ewa Płonowska Ziarek observes in *Feminist Aesthetics and the Politics of Modernism* (2012), "the most frequently cited evidence of women's exclusion from political rights is taken from marriage, divorce, and family law regulating the private sphere" (27). In other words, the legal defines what is possible in the political realm, and laws were for centuries a mechanism of keeping women out of politics. At the same time, Plonowska Ziarek argues that legal regimes inspire political work: "Because the law articulates and preserves the historical victories of past generations, there is an irreducible temporal lapse between institutional rights and new demands for freedom" (37). Laws represent the achievements of previous political movements, and each new call for freedom comes into being out of frustration with dated statutes and the institutions that enforce them.

The term "politics" has enjoyed a rather expansive understanding since second-wave feminism articulated the idea that "the personal is political." For the present purposes, however, politics is parsed literally: as modernist engagement with political systems that seemed poised to remake the world stage. While writers and artists involved themselves in a myriad of movements around the globe, this section will focus on three arenas in which modernists and scholars focused their energies: the drive for women's suffrage; the role of empire in the national and individual imaginary; and the advent of fascism in the 1930s, which resulted in the Second World War.

Women's efforts to gain the right to vote were a prominent and often spectacular facet of early twentieth-century politics. Although the suffrage movement had its roots in the nineteenth century, it began to bear fruit toward the *fin de siècle*: New Zealand, a British colony, granted women the right to vote in 1893, with the British colony of South Australia following suit two years later. European countries began to make similar changes the following decade, with Finland granting women the right in 1906 and Norway in 1913. In the United States, women in individual territories were able to vote from an early date; Wyoming (1869) and Utah (1870) lead the way. As one might imagine, women in other territories and states—and other nations—took up the fight for suffrage in part because of their frustration with the disparities they saw around them. It was, they argued, patently unfair that women in colonies or Western territories could vote when those who lived in places with longer histories of democratic government could not cast a ballot. It wasn't until 1920 that the nineteenth amendment to the United States Constitution was ratified, guaranteeing the right to vote to adult women in that country; the UK, which gave women over thirty the franchise in 1918, did not grant the same right to all women until 1928.

The agitation over suffrage has been excellently chronicled by historians.[3] It took, however, some time for scholars of modernism to argue that suffrage had had an impact on literature. Elaine

Showalter's *A Literature of Their Own* (1977) was downright dismissive: "the suffrage movement was not a happy stimulus to women writers. If they participated in its militant phase, they did get some sense of effective solidarity, but not as writers" (236). It would take a decade, and the increasing activity of feminist literary scholars, to reverse this judgment. Jane Marcus's edited collection *Suffrage and the Pankhursts* (1987) led the way through an introduction that emphasized shared strategies, such as interruption, in the political and aesthetic realms. After addressing Christabel Pankhurst's invention of the practice of interrupting speeches by male politicians (9–10), Marcus turns to Woolf's *A Room of One's Own*, which she characterizes as "a permanent tribute to the suffrage movement's giving voice to women." Marcus describes *Room* as "constructed brilliantly around the literary tropes of interruption and absence" and as "eloquently enact[ing] the history of the struggle" (10). Although she does not offer an extended account of how modernism was shaped by women's suffrage, this pioneering essay served as encouragement for others to explore the relationships among suffrage, modernity, and modernism. The first two terms soon attracted attention in studies of the visual and cultural impact of suffrage spectacle; notable works are Lisa Tickner's *The Spectacle of Women: Imagery of the Suffrage Campaign 1907–1914* (1988) and Barbara Green's *Spectacular Confessions: Autobiography, Performance Activism, and the Sites of Suffrage 1904–1938* (1997). Green (also discussed in Chapter 1), for example, explores "the writings of militant suffragettes in relation to recent efforts to rethink the relations between gender, literary modernism, and modernity" (8). As Green notes, most of the authors she addresses "confronted and shaped modernity" but they were invested in "qualities literary modernism is said to have rejected" (8). Her work of recovery thus helps to reshape our understanding of the culture of modernity and therefore of modernism, although the latter is not her primary focus.

Modernism and the movement for women's suffrage has, however, been squarely addressed over the last two decades. The emphasis has been on strategies and aesthetic priorities that suffragists and modernists shared. Janet Lyon's *Manifestoes: Provocations of the Modern* (1999) juxtaposes the avant-garde work of F. T. Marinetti and Wyndham Lewis with the tactics of militant suffragists, uncovering a previously unremarked "dependence of the aesthetic avant-garde on the anti-bourgeois spectacle of suffragist violence" (6). Lyon demonstrates that "the rhetoric and tactics of the militant women's movement were enfolded into the foundations of English modernism" (94), noting, for example, that suffragettes and writers like Ezra Pound and Lewis turned "press accounts of militant lunacy and disease [...] back upon the accusers" (105). Both groups, she shows, "produced manifestoes and related polemical tracts designed to programmatize anger, to polarize readership, and to recalibrate their own group's revolutionary position within hegemonic liberalism" (106). Lyon's argument suggests that we might well reimagine British modernism as a creature *of* suffrage, no matter what individual writers felt about the franchise. Mary Chapman offers a parallel study of the situation on the other side of the Atlantic in *Making Noise, Making News: Suffrage Print Culture and U. S. Modernism* (2014). Although Chapman's study is deeply invested in the print ephemera of the American suffrage movement, she explicitly states that her book proves Lyon's argument "applies equally to U.S. modernism" (16). Tracing the connections between "radical politics' print cultural reform efforts and modernist literary experimentation" (13), Chapman pays sustained attention to modernists Marianne Moore and Gertrude Stein as well as to lesser-known popular writers such as Edith Eaton (Sui Sin Far) and Alice Duer Miller, and she concludes that "the shared genealogies of U.S. modernism and suffrage were not immediately forgotten in the wake of formalist-New Criticisms" (25). That these genealogies *were* eventually forgotten necessitates studies like Lyon's and Chapman's.

Students interested in the relationship between suffrage and modernism will find an exceptionally deft account in Płonowska Ziarek's *Feminist Aesthetics and the Politics of Modernism*. As she writes in her introduction, Plonowska Ziarek's approach is to juxtapose "suffrage militancy with aesthetic and political theory," a strategy that "allows us to rethink the pervasive modernist preoccupation with the new beyond mere formal experimentation for innovation's sake and address it instead in the context of political struggles" (20). In a study that traces the oscillation between revolutionary energies and melancholia, Plonowska Ziarek rereads suffrage not as a narrow movement with a single political aim—access to the franchise—but rather as the "suffragettes' redefinition of the right to vote as the right to revolt" (see Figure 8) (21). This

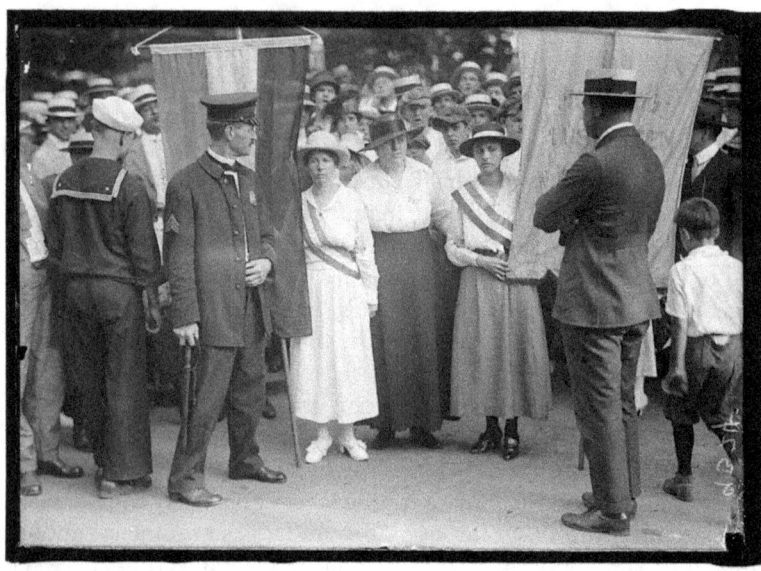

FIGURE 8 *Harris & Ewing, photographer. "WOMAN SUFFRAGE." Library of Congress, Prints & Photographs Division. This image, taken at a 1917 suffrage demonstration in Washington, DC, illustrates the right to vote as revolt. In a hostile crowd of male onlookers, only the woman in the center meets the male gaze.*

right, she argues, has political and aesthetic implications, because "revolt announces women's participation in a transformative, creative praxis, its inaugural temporality, and the plurality of political agents" (22). Even as suffrage thus positions women as autonomous political and artistic actors, she acknowledges that the slow pace of social change results in frustration and melancholy. Using Woolf and Nella Larsen as her primary literary examples, Plonowska Ziarek situates "modern literature [...] between political domination and the aesthetic promise of freedom" (43). Her readings of Larsen emphasize the qualified hope readers might find in work that ends with protagonists who are dead or dying (*Passing* and *Quicksand*): "Larsen's fiction suggests [that] women's art transforms the death of the feminine and the social death of blackness into a possibility of a black female renaissance yet to come" (84). *Feminist Aesthetics and the Politics of Modernism* is less invested in modernism's direct contact with or genealogies of suffrage than the other work discussed earlier, but the book highlights the profound interrelationship of "aesthetic novelty and the promise of a better praxis in women's writings" and the "inaugural force of freedom in the political," which was and is captured in the suffrage movement (48). One might distill Plonowska Ziarek's central claim as "the personal is the political *and* the aesthetic," as she casts modernist writing by women as a venue for the revolutionary energies expressed in the suffrage movement.[4]

As critics turned their eyes toward the intersection among politics, sex, and gender, the relationship among modernism, sexuality, and empire became a subject of investigation. Early work on modernism and imperialism like that by Fredric Jameson ("Modernism and Imperialism," [1988]) focused on male writers such as Joseph Conrad, who had personally explored Western empires during his career in the merchant marine and wrote about those spaces in (most notably) *Heart of Darkness* and *Lord Jim*, or Joyce, who was a product of the Irish colonial experience. It wasn't until the mid-1990s that scholars began to examine women writers' response to empire and particularly the ways that racial formations haunted ideologies of female sexuality and identity. This development was belated for the simple reason that women were not explorers, governors of colonies, or even members of the merchant marine; as a result, scholars ignored what many female writers had to say about empire. But say things they did. Witness Woolf's letter to Ben Nicolson in August of 1940:

> What puzzles me is that people who had infinitely greater gifts than any of us had—I mean Keats, Shelley, Wordsworth, Coleridge and so on—were unable to influence society. They didn't have anything like the influence they should have had upon 19th century politics. And so we drifted into imperialism and all the other horrors that led to 1914. Would they have had more influence if they had taken an active part in politics? Or would they only have written worse poetry? (*Letters* 6:421)

This letter, which raises the question of writers' ethical and moral responsibility to influence their fellow citizens, states Woolf's opinion of imperialism as a "horror" that her predecessors might have tried to mitigate. It is surprising that it took over fifty years to recognize Woolf's, and her female contemporaries', attempts to influence society on the same point.

As with work on suffrage, Jane Marcus was a pioneering voice through two essays, "Britannia Rules *The Waves*" (1992) and "Bonding and Bondage: Nancy Cunard and the Making of the *Negro* Anthology" (1995). These essays were later incorporated into Marcus's *Hearts of Darkness: White Women Write Race* (2004), which complicates some of her early arguments. "Britannia" made the bold claim that Woolf's 1931 novel functions as an anti-imperialist work (*Hearts* 5). *The Waves*, which contains one character (Percival) who works and dies in colonial India, now seems ripe for such an argument, but because Percival does not speak or narrate his experiences, readers can only see the workings of empire through the imagination of his childhood friends. Marcus argues that Woolf thus "interrogates the color problem, setting a metropolitan *whiteness* against the colored colonial world as a vast desert against which an intellectual elite like the Bloomsbury Group creates itself as culture" (64). Asserting that Woolf's fiction generally "connects imperialism to patriarchy" (62) and further links patriarchy to class consciousness, Marcus places gender at the center of these overlapping ideologies: "gender is often the site of [these] discourses, the place of articulation of the fear of difference" (68). While this essay occasionally points to women's complicity in imperialism, in 1992, Marcus was invested in positing a politically engaged Woolf whose writing resisted the forms of domination at work in the British Empire. Over the course of a decade, however, Marcus altered this approach, and while the 2004 *Hearts* includes her "Britannia" essay, it also includes a reassessment that *The Waves* "mourns the loss of empire" even as it criticizes the imperial project (13). Marcus notes that her original reading was premised on "the cultural need to produce a white English feminist voice of modernism that is not totally racist and makes a certain critique of imperialism" (13). *Hearts* thus offers readers not only examples of the early, rousing feminist work on modernism and empire, but also points out the limits of that work, which tended to read modernists as though they shared late twentieth-century political convictions. Other chapters in Marcus's book, such as one comparing Michael Arlen's *The Green Hat* (1924) and Mulk Raj Anand's *Coolie* (1936), reflect more recent efforts to root scholarship on empire in texts written by authors who came from outside the imperial center.

Marcus points to the rise of cultural studies as creating a context for analysis of the intersection of colonialism, patriarchy, and class prejudice, and in the mid-1990s, other scholars embraced not only the insights of cultural studies but also its method of reading across a range of literary and nonliterary texts. Anne McClintock's *Imperial Leather: Race, Gender, and Sexuality in the Colonial Contest* (1995) offered a "sustained quarrel with the project of imperialism, the cult of domesticity, and the invention of industrial progress" (4). Although many of McClintock's examples predate modernism, her argument that "imperialism is not something that happened elsewhere—a disagreeable fact of history external to Western identity" (5) is relevant to the field. *Imperial Leather* asserts that "imperialism cannot be fully understood without a theory of gender power" (6), and she traces, for example, the ways that new territories were envisioned as "virgin"—as feminized—thus yoking women to "a realm beyond history" (31) and placing them outside of narratives of historical agency and change. Reading advertisements for Pears' Soap alongside images of racial family trees and other texts, McClintock offered a model of exploring sex, gender, and empire through a methodology that did not privilege literature but treated it as one of many discourses that illuminated political formations.

Over the next decade, scholars built on Marcus's pioneering arguments and the insights of cultural studies to offer increasingly nuanced accounts of modernism, gender, sexuality, and empire. Jane Garrity's *Step-Daughters of England: British Women Modernists and the National Imaginary* (2003) and Robin Hackett's *Sapphic Primitivism: Productions of Race, Class, and Sexuality in Key Works of Modern Fiction* (2004), appearing just one year apart, uncovered the complex cultural pressures in texts by Woolf but also less well-known writers such as Dorothy Richardson, Sylvia Townsend Warner, Mary Butts, Olive Schreiner, and Willa Cather, among others. Both Garrity and Hackett locate the racial formations of empire as embedded within white female identity, particularly within figurations of reproduction (Garrity) and homoerotics (Hackett). Garrity's study examines experimental women's novels in which "the hegemony of and critical resistance to national identity formation are staged" (1). She places women as pivotal for studies of imperialism because "the white, middle-class, procreative female body was regarded as integral to the well-being of the nation and central to empire-building, key to conceptions of racial fitness and national stability" (2). Positioning writers as both resistant to *and* reinscribing the rhetoric of empire (3), *Step-Daughters* situates its readings within a broad account of women's history during the interwar period. Hackett, for her part, explores the late nineteenth and early twentieth century "overlap between markers of race, class, and sexuality in representations of female homoerotics" (1) and defines the keywords of her title, "Sapphic primitivism," as "a mode of writing in which figurations of blackness and working-class culture appear as constitutive elements of white-authored fictional representations of female sexual autonomy including homoerotics" (3). In Garrity's and Hackett's work, imperialism is not located elsewhere but within the self and inflected by sex and gender. Recent work on modernism and empire has been situated within a turn to the global in modernist studies. While very different in argument and approach, such studies have worked to dismantle the center and periphery ("motherland" and colonies) model that structured earlier scholarship as well as to continue to examine the crucial role that gender played in the imperial order.

Much like scholarship on modernism and empire, the treatment of modernism and fascism followed rather strict gender binaries for decades: the enthusiasm for or sympathy of male modernists (such as Pound, William Butler Yeats, Wyndham Lewis, David Jones, T. S. Eliot, and others) with Italian and German fascism was closely examined, while female writers such as Woolf were lauded for anti-fascist productions. After perusing this scholarship, a reader might easily conclude that political leanings mapped onto sexed bodies, with men inclined to embrace, and women to reject, fascism. In part, such a conclusion seems sensible because the modernists who embraced reactionary politics were often misogynist; as Charles Ferrall's *Modernist Writing & Reactionary Politics* (2001) notes, for example, "Yeats's and Marinetti's war machines fuse the mythic and the modern but they only do so by declaring war on women, untidy democracy, and the masses" (8). After providing an account of different reactionary factions, he observes that "all the members of these [...] movements were opposed to parliamentary democracy; most were hostile to the Suffragists" (14). Ferrall's book, which focuses on male modernists, thus suggests that political sympathies mapped somewhat straightforwardly onto sex and gender identity. Andrew Hewitt complicates this conceptual map by exploring the "anecdotal and theoretical [...] conflation and/or association of homosexuality and fascism" (3) in *Political Inversions: Homosexuality, Fascism, & the Modernist Imaginary* (1996). His argument that homosexuality became "a vehicle for representing the otherwise unrepresentable—fascism" (17) focuses, however, entirely on male homosexuality, and it thus offers a contribution to the history of sexuality without disrupting the sense of women as fascism's other.

When scholars initially took up fascism in the work and lives of female modernists, the initial tendency was to celebrate politically progressive publications and activities. As discussed in Chapter 1, this penchant is part of a general tendency to lionize (or even to construct hagiographic accounts of) women who have been left out of the canon for decades. Another important factor, however, is that some female modernists *did* write explicitly anti-fascist work, including the most famous, Woolf's 1938 polemic *Three Guineas*. This book, written in the context of global anxiety over what was occurring in Hitler's Germany, Mussolini's Italy, and the civil war in Spain, maps the fascism Woolf observed on the world stage onto the private sphere, comparing men who oppress or diminish women in Britain and elsewhere to dictators. Woolf advocated that "the daughters of educated men" form a "society of outsiders" who might work to undermine unequal power relations in all their forms, and one of her outsiders famously declares, "As a woman I have no country. As a woman I want no country. As a woman, my country is the whole world" (129). Many critics have unpacked Woolf's radical argument, including Marcus, whose introduction to the 2006 annotated edition hails *Three Guineas* for "Woolf's idea [...] that the gender issue was inseparable from the buildup to war and the power of fascism to rule the state" (xxxvi). "Woolf shows fascism at home in the English family," Marcus writes (xliv), and she notes that this argument generated resentment among Woolf's male contemporaries and even family members (liv). In a 1994 article and later her 2005 book *Virginia Woolf and the Bloomsbury Avant-Garde*, Christine Froula explains Woolf's still radical critique as exposing how women function as political and ideological scapegoats: "In attributing Englishwomen's exclusion from and subordination in the public sphere to the same scapegoat psychology that was fueling Europe's civil violence and its rising dictatorships, *Three Guineas* points to similar structures and dynamics at work in these very different instances of collective violence" (266). This singular text, and scholarship by Marcus, Froula, and others, provided and continues to provide evidence that women writers, and Woolf in particular, were furiously engaged in battling the fascism that many male modernists embraced.

Without discounting the importance of Woolf's argument or the scholars who have written about the anti-fascism of other female modernist and middlebrow writers (including Judy Suh, Mia Spiro, and others),[5] it's important to recognize scholars who worked to refine decades of criticism that framed male writers as regressive and their female counterparts as progressive. A groundbreaking example was Wanda Van Dusen's 1996 article "Portrait of a National Fetish: Gertrude Stein's 'Introduction to the Speeches of Maréchal Pétain' (1942)." Van Dusen was the first to write about Stein's efforts to interest her American publisher in bringing out an edition of the French Vichy official's speeches as well as to draw attention to Stein's general collaborationist stance. She acknowledges that Stein (who lived in France during the Second World War) and her lover Alice B. Toklas were, as Jews and lesbians, doubly vulnerable to the Vichy regime, and she argues that Stein claimed an essential Americanness in an effort to highlight aspects of her identity that the government might find less objectionable. Although Stein's introduction, and Pétain's speeches, were not published (her publisher found the idea of the project frankly disgusting), Van Dusen's article highlights Stein's "problematic relationship to modern history—a history that she liked to think she helped invent" even "as the 'Introduction' demonstrates, [she was] deeply caught in its fault lines" (87). This deft account of Stein's proposed publication adds much needed texture to accounts of women modernists and fascism.

Subsequent book-length studies would advance similarly nuanced readings of Stein and other female writers in relationship to fascism. Erin G. Carlston's *Thinking Fascism: Sapphic Modernism and Fascist Modernity* (1998) examines Djuna Barnes, Marguerite Yourcenar, and Virginia Woolf, "who wrote texts in the 1930s that engage, directly or indirectly, with fascist politics and ideology" (1). Carlston's goal was "not only to demonstrate that fascist discourses share a vernacular with non- and antifascist discourses of the same period, but also to argue that fascism itself could supply the vocabulary and the methodology of even the most rigorously antifascist critiques" (5). By focusing on shared discourses and diction, Carlston charts a closer relationship between the poles of what had seemed a binary. Annalisa Zox-Weaver's *Women Modernists and Fascism* (2011) similarly adds texture to our understanding of modernism and fascism, arguing as she does that female writers incorporate or identify with fascist leaders as a means of taking on (however figuratively) their power and authority. *Women* "concerns itself with the fascist dictator as constricted, reflected, and imagined by four artists," Stein, Leni Riefenstahl, Janet Flanner, and Lee Miller (1). Building explicitly on Van Dusen's article, Zox-Weaver argues, for example, that works from the last decade of Stein's life (such as *Four in America* and *Mrs. Reynolds*) "betray a fascination with masculine authority and authoritarian figures influenced by a deeply personal preoccupation with her own fame and influence. Even as Stein self-assuredly claimed her place as the literary genius of her time, she saw history's great men as figures with whom to identify and contend" (60). Stein's desire to write *herself* into history thus led her not to reject, but to imagine herself occupying, the position of absolute power fascist dictators assumed.

A final way in which the binaries male/female, fascist/anti-fascist have been unhooked from one another explores the role of fascism in the history of sexuality and the erotics of fascist style. Anyone interested in the sexual legacies of German Nazism should consult Dagmar Herzog's *Sex after Fascism: Memory and Morality in Twentieth-Century Germany* (2005), which provides insight into the often conflicting standards of the regime. "Nazism advanced often ribald and unapologetic celebrations of sexual activity; it avidly promoted most pre- and extramarital heterosexual sex" (4), Herzog writes, while making clear that such behavior was only advocated for men. Her attention to the Nazi Party's engagement with "sexually liberalizing tendencies" (5) renders the sexual politics of fascism in terms that will surprise most readers. While Herzog's work is not explicitly interested in modernism, Laura Frost's *Sex Drives: Fantasies of Fascism in Literary Modernism* (2002) unpacks the sex appeal with which fascism is inflected in so many works of the period. Frost argues that "antifascist, democratic culture has substantial, unacknowledged libidinal investments in fascism that need to be explored" (15). Touching on Lawrence, Georges Bataille, Hans Bellmer, Jean Genet, Marguerite Duras, and others, Frost traces the literary genealogy of eroticized images of fascism and explores why brutal European dictatorships became so widely associated with eroticism and sexual deviance that "fascinating fascism" came to constitute a major theme in twentieth-century fiction. These fictions [...] are complex explorations of how political and national identities are constructed around and shored up by particular sexual identities. They are as revealing of the democratic imagination as they are of fascism. (3)

In an argument that tracks the eroticization of fascism to representations of the enemy in the First World War (6), Frost explains how a political model came to be associated with erotic desire even by writers who did not embrace radical authoritarian nationalism.

Together, these studies suggest that national politics pervades sexuality even as they underline the complicated attractions fascism offered to writers of both sexes. If law sets normative horizons that individuals must navigate in their daily lives and creative activities, then different political systems became compelling to writers as they promised to set those horizons at quite different limits. The representations of sexuality and gender were deeply shaped by modernism's encounter with local and global political orders.

When examining modernism, law, and politics, it's important to remember the historical particularity of every debate over obscenity, empire, libel, or fascism: what a writer thought or a text meant to readers could change over the course of years or decades. One final example is illustrative: even the defenders of free expression expressed alarm about what was allowed to circulate as time passed. In 1929, Gilbert Seldes "took a more cordial view of censorship than he once had done." Seldes, the editor of the important vehicle for modernist literature, *The Dial*, had volunteered in 1922 to serve as an expert witness for an American publisher whose books were brought up on obscenity charges. Only seven years later, Seldes was "appalled to realize that the champions of free expression had 'fought for Ibsen and *Mrs. Warren's Profession*—and got Mae West'" (qtd in Boyer 247). West, the actress and writer famous for lighthearted bawdy banter and double entendres ("I used to be Snow White but I drifted," she quipped in 1933's *I'm No Angel*), seemed a dubious beneficiary of revised obscenity laws. As Seldes's comment indicates, even those individuals willing to go to the mat for modernist literature (*Mrs. Warren's Profession*, by Bernard Shaw, addressed the ways in which capitalism encouraged prostitution) were not entirely comfortable with the range of sexually explicit, and commercially popular, work encapsulated in Mae West's name. Women, and sexuality, continued to be a litmus test for legal and political positions, which would be renegotiated and relitigated for decades to come; indeed it still continues.

Scholarship of the relationship among modernism, sexuality, gender, law, and politics has added nuance to received notions of what modernist literature was and is. Where an earlier generation downplayed the sexual content of literary work or told uncomplicated stories about individual authors' triumphs over censorship, libel, or copyright laws, recent work has demonstrated that modernism, pornography, and libel are overlapping discourses *and* that many modernist writers may not have had the careers or stature they currently enjoy were it not for run-ins with the law. Where scholars once assumed that male modernists were the most likely to be invested in fascism as an idea or actuality, recent work has highlighted the libidinal and personal appeal of the dictator and of fascist style to women writers. In the palimpsest of modernist studies, for decades the relationship between modernism and the legal and political cultures it navigated was a fairly straightforward tale. Recently, however, scholars have uncovered details, documents, and contexts that were buried, obscured by the topmost story. These discoveries have enabled us to reframe the men and women of modernism; instead of one tale, we now have many, with additional layers no doubt left to be uncovered.

Notes

1 For exceptions, see Ingram and Marshik, "History's 'Abrupt Revenges.'"
2 Additional attention to these forces can be found in Nicola Watson's "Circulating Morals (1900–1915)" in David Bradshaw and Rachel Potter's collection *Prudes on the Prowl: Fiction and Obscenity in England, 1850 to the Present Day* (2013).
3 For accounts of the US suffrage movement, see, for example, Ellen Carol DuBois, *Harriot Stanton Blatch and the Winning of Woman Suffrage* (1997) and *Women's Suffrage and Women's Rights* (1998).

Accounts of the movement in the UK are ably offered by Susan Kingsley Kent, *Sex and Suffrage in Britain, 1860–1914* (1987) and Martin Pugh, *The March of the Women: A Revisionist Analysis of the Campaign for Women's Suffrage, 1866–1914* (2000).
4 In addition to these accounts, noteworthy additions to the scholarship on suffrage and modernism include Jane Eldridge Miller's *Rebel Woman: Feminism, Modernism, and the Edwardian Novel* (1994), which contains a chapter on "Suffragette Stories," and Mark S. Morrisson's chapter on the *Freewoman* and suffrage periodicals in *The Public Face of Modernism: Little Magazines, Audiences, and Reception, 1905–1920* (2001). Since the publication of Morrisson's book, interest in suffrage periodicals has exploded; a useful review of recent work is offered by Barbara Green in "The Feminist Periodical Press: Women, Periodical Studies, and Modernity." Readers interested in suffrage drama will want to consult the anthology *A Stage of Their Own: Feminist Playwrights of the Suffrage Era*, edited by Sheila Stowell (1992).
5 Suh's *Fascism and Anti-Fascism in Twentieth-Century British Fiction* (2009) examines the use of parody and comedy in middlebrow fiction by Olive Hawks, Phyllis Bottome, Woolf (*The Years*), Nancy Mitford, Elizabeth Bowen, and Muriel Spark. Spiro's 2013 *Anti-Nazi Modernism: The Challenges of Resistance in 1930s Fiction* provides an extended exploration of Woolf's *Between the Acts* (1941), Christopher Isherwood's *Goodbye to Berlin* (1939), and Djuna Barnes's *Nightwood* (1936). While Spiro's title suggests that her analysis only addresses the anti-fascist aspects of these novels, she also takes up the vexed question of their complicity with, for example, anti-Semitism.

CODA

Willa Cather, unlike many of the writers mentioned in this book, always received some critical attention. As early as 1938, scholars were publishing on the American author and essayist. The initial critics examined symbolism in Cather's fiction, debated the merits of her regionalism, and dissected the influence of the Spanish author Cervantes on her work. What one notices, however, is that while Cather was treated as a significant American novelist, she was not regarded as a modernist novelist. Malcolm Bradbury and James McFarlane's *Modernism: A Guide to European Literature 1890–1930* (1976), which included American writers in spite of its title, did not include any reference to Cather. Like the great tradition imagined by Eliot and Leavis, theirs was a male and masculine canon, although Dorothy Richardson, Marianne Moore, Gertrude Stein, and other female modernists are mentioned in *Modernism*. Cather's total omission from what Sean Latham and Gayle Rogers call "the most influential and certainly most enduring anthology of high modernism" (76) speaks to what modernism was before scholars detected the layers of inscription under the topmost ink of the palimpsest. As a woman, as a writer of nonmetropolitan fictions, as someone whose most intense relationships were with those of the same sex, and as an author who was interested in the minutiae of domestic life, she remained outside of the modernist canon.

The critical movements described in this book changed what scholars recognized and understood when looking at Cather. The author is anthologized in Bonnie Kime Scott's *The Gender of Modernism*, making Cather the beneficiary of a wave of feminist critics who worked to recover the lives and careers of female writers *and* to claim those writers for modernism specifically. Critical attention to feminized subjects and discourses next energized critical attention to Cather, and scholars began to produce work on her documentation of American (including immigrant) foodways, domestic arts, and daily rituals. As the history of sexualities became a critical interest, scholars debated whether Cather could or should be called a lesbian writer. They examined her use of male narrators, like Jim Burden, exploring whether this was a form of literary transvestism, and they celebrated her revision of nineteenth-century stereotypes such as "the fallen woman," which Cather challenged by writing a happy ending for a character who becomes pregnant out of wedlock. Cather's representations of masculinity were simultaneously dissected, with scholars identifying female masculinity in *O Pioneers* (1913) and *My Ántonia* (1918) and excavating her ideas of masculine style. In addition, Cather has been the subject of scholarship on progressive politics, settler colonialism, and labor relations, demonstrating that the political realm was always an aspect of her life and work. We just needed different critical eyes to see it.

All of the readings described earlier, and many others, have been available since Cather's works were first published. It took, however, the invention of new critical approaches before scholars could look beneath the top layer of the modernist palimpsest to recover Cather for modernism and to develop new readings based on increasingly nuanced understandings of sexuality and gender. The evidence was there, but critics needed tools to do that reading. Like the scientists and scholars who needed sophisticated microscopes and scanners to peruse the "erased" layers of a palimpsest, literary critics needed, for example, Jack Halberstam's theory of female masculinity before they could see Cather's assaults on binary gender identity. Because of decades of feminist and queer theory, we now have the tools, and the new readings, that make of modernist writers—and modernism—something far different than Eliot, Leavis, or even Bradbury and McFarlane could have conceived.

It is, however, at this point that the metaphor of the palimpsest begins to break down. Although there was always some overlap in when particular approaches to modernism gained and maintained traction—recovery of women writers remains a focus for many scholars, even as they fear the field's attention is directed elsewhere—it is no longer possible to speak of criticism on modernism, sex, and gender as unfolding in the orderly way in which one reads a palimpsest: layer by layer. Now scholars read with something akin to X-ray vision, a technology that was discovered in 1895, around the time that literary modernism was getting its start. With their metaphorical X-rays, scholars of modernism see not only how the layers interact with one another but also with critical concerns outside of the scope of this book. Thus, one finds work on the gender of the November revolution, on queer entomology, on the relationship between the transnational and the transgender, and on feminist inter/modernist studies. As a critical approach attuned to power differentials, and determined to undo the hierarchies of the old modernist studies, feminism has encouraged scholars to question binaries wherever they occur: male/female, masculine/feminine, gay/straight, public/private, animal/human, center/periphery, rich/poor, and others. The modernism of the future will surely be different because of this ongoing questioning as scholars "make it new" not in Ezra Pound's famous formulation but in our own.

CRITICAL BIBLIOGRAPHIES FOR *MODERNISM, SEX, AND GENDER*

Below we offer brief lists of key and representative studies in the areas we address in this volume. These lists are not comprehensive, and favor monographs over articles, but should serve as starting points for scholars seeking to delve into any of these topics.

Feminist Recovery

Benstock, Shari. *Women of the Left Bank: Paris, 1900–1940*. Austin: University of Texas Press, 1986.
Bradshaw, Melissa and Adrienne Munich, eds. *Amy Lowell, American Modern: Critical Essays*. Brunswick, NJ: Rutgers University Press, 2004.
Broe, Mary Lynn and Angela Ingram, eds. *Women's Writing in Exile*. Chapel Hill: The University of North Carolina Press, 1989.
DeKoven, Marianne. *A Different Language: Gertrude Stein's Experimental Writing*. Madison: University of Wisconsin Press, 1983.
DuPlessis, Rachel Blau. *Writing beyond the Ending: Narrative Strategies of Twentieth-Century Women Writers*. Bloomington: Indiana University Press, 1985.
Friedman, Susan. *Psyche Reborn: The Emergence of H. D.* Bloomington: Indiana University Press, 1981.
Friedman, Susan. "Who Buried H. D.? A Poet, Her Critics, and Her Place in 'The Literary Tradition.'" *College English* 36.7 (March 1975): 801–814.
Garrity, Jane. "Modernist Women's Writing: Beyond the Threshold of Obsolescence?" *Literature Compass* 10.1 (2013): 15–29.

Gilbert, Sandra M. and Susan Gubar. *No Man's Land: The Place of the Woman Writer in the Twentieth Century*, 3 vols. New Haven, CT: Yale University Press, 1988–1996.
Gruber, Ruth. *Virginia Woolf: The Will to Create as a Woman*. New York: Carroll & Graf, 2005.
Hull, Gloria T. *Color, Sex, & Poetry: Three Women Writers of the Harlem Renaissance*. Bloomington: Indiana University Press, 1987.
Kouidis, Virginia M. *Mina Loy: American Modernist Poet*. Baton Rouge: Louisiana State University Press, 1980.
Marcus, Jane, ed. *New Feminist Essays on Virginia Woolf*. New York: Palgrave Macmillan, 1981.
Nebeker, Helen. *Jean Rhys, Woman in Passage*. St. Albans, VT: Eden Press Women's Publications, 1981.
Patton, Venetria K. and Maureen Honey, eds. *Double-Take: A Revisionist Harlem Renaissance Anthology*. New Brunswick, NJ: Rutgers University Press, 2001.
Schlissel, Lillian, ed. *Sex, The Drag, The Pleasure Man*. New York: Routledge, 1997.
Scott, Bonnie Kime, ed. *The Gender of Modernism: A Critical Anthology*. Bloomington: Indiana University Press, 1990.
Showalter, Elaine. *A Literature of Their Own: British Women Novelists from Brontë to Lessing*. Princeton, NJ: Princeton University Press, 1977.

Feminine Genre Writing

Beauman, Nicola. *A Very Great Profession: The Women's Novel 1914–39*. London: Virago, 1983.
Botshon, Lisa and Meredith Goldsmith, eds. *Middlebrow Moderns: Popular American Women Writers of the 1920s*. Boston: Northeastern University Press, 2003.
Clark, Suzanne. *Sentimental Modernism: Women Writers and the Revolution of the Word*. Bloomington: Indiana University Press, 1991.
Hammill, Faye. *Women, Celebrity, and Literary Culture between the Wars*. Austin: University of Texas Press, 2007.
Hipsky, Martin. *Modernism and the Women's Popular Romance in Britain, 1885–1925*. Athens, OH: Ohio University Press, 2011.
Honey, Maureen, ed. *Shadowed Dreams: Women's Poetry of the Harlem Renaissance*. New Brunswick: Rutgers University Press, 1989.
Humble, Nicola. *The Feminine Middlebrow Novel, 1920s to 1950s: Class, Domesticity, and Bohemianism*. 2001. Oxford: Oxford University Press, 2004.

Keyser, Catherine. *Playing Smart: New York Women Writers and Modern Magazine Culture*. New Brunswick: Rutgers University Press, 2010.
Light, Alison. *Forever England: Femininity, Literature and Conservatism between the Wars*. London: Routledge, 1991.
Radway, Janice A. *A Feeling for Books: The Book-of-the Month Club, Literary Taste, and Middle-Class Desire*. Chapel Hill: University of North Carolina Press, 1999.
Sherrard-Johnson, Cherene. *Portraits of the New Negro Woman: Visual and Literary Culture in the Harlem Renaissance*. New Brunswick: Rutgers University Press, 2007.
Wall, Cheryl A. *Women of the Harlem Renaissance*. Bloomington: Indiana University Press, 1995.
Wallace, Diana. *The Woman's Historical Novel: British Women Writers, 1900–2000*. New York and Basingstoke: Palgrave Macmillan, 2005.

Genders of Modernity

Ardis, Ann L. and Leslie W. Lewis, eds. *Women's Experience of Modernity: 1875–1945*. Baltimore: Johns Hopkins University Press, 2003.
Conor, Liz. *The Spectacular Modern Woman: Feminine Visibility in the 1920s*. Indianapolis: Indiana University Press, 2004.
Felski, Rita. *The Gender of Modernity*. Cambridge: Harvard University Press, 1995.
Green, Barbara. *Spectacular Confessions: Autobiography, Performative Activism, and the Sites of Suffrage 1905–1938*. New York: St. Martin's Press, 1997.
Scott, Bonnie Kime. *Gender in Modernism: New Geographies, Complex Intersections*. Urbana: University of Illinois Press, 2007.

Modernist Lesbian and Gay Histories and Identities

Castle, Terry. *The Apparitional Lesbian: Female Homosexuality and Modern Culture*. New York: Columbia University Press, 1993.
Chauncey, George. *Gay New York: Gender, Urban Culture, and the Making of the Gay Male World 1890–1940*. New York: Basic Books, 1995.
Cohen, Ed. *Talk on the Wilde Side: Toward a Genealogy of a Discourse on Male Sexualities*. New York: Routledge, 1993.

Cohler, Deborah. *Citizen, Invert, Queer: Lesbianism and War in Early Twentieth-Century Britain.* Minneapolis: University of Minnesota Press, 2010.

Cook, Blanche Weisen. "'Women Alone Stir My Imagination': Lesbianism and the Cultural Tradition." *Signs* 4.4 (Summer 1979): 718–739.

Doan, Laura. *Disturbing Practices: History, Sexuality, and Women's Experience of Modern War.* Chicago: University of Chicago Press, 2013.

Doan, Laura. *Fashioning Sapphism: The Origins of a Modern English Lesbian Culture.* New York: Columbia University Press, 2001.

Faderman, Lillian. *Surpassing the Love of Men: Romantic Friendship and Love between Women from the Renaissance to the Present.* New York: William Morrow, 1981.

Lanser, Susan B. "1928: Sapphic Modernity and the Sexuality of History." *Modernism/Modernity Print Plus* 1.3 (October 25, 2016).

Lucey, Michael. *Never Say I: Sexuality and the First Person in Colette, Gide, and Proust.* Durham: Duke University Press, 2006.

Medd, Jodie. *Lesbian Scandal and the Culture of Modernism.* Cambridge: Cambridge University Press, 2012.

Newton, Esther. "The Mythic Mannish Lesbian: Radclyffe Hall and the New Woman." *Signs* 9.4 (1984): 557–575.

Schwarz, Christa A.B. *Gay Voices of the Harlem Renaissance.* Indianapolis: Indiana University Press, 2003.

Sedgwick, Eve Kosofsky. *Between Men: English Literature and Male Homosocial Desire.* New York: Columbia University Press, 1985.

Sinfield, Alan. *The Wilde Century: Effeminacy, Oscar Wilde and the Queer Moment.* New York: Columbia University Press, 1994.

Queer Modernism and Discourses of Sexual Otherness

Boone, Joseph Allen. *The Homoerotics of Orientalism.* New York: Columbia University Press, 2015.

Carby, Hazel. *Reconstructing Womanhood: The Emergence of the Afro-American Woman Novelist.* Oxford: Oxford University Press, 1987.

Frost, Laura. *Sex Drives: Fantasies of Fascism in Literary Modernism.* Ithaca, NY: Cornell University Press, 2002.

Glavey, Brian. *The Wallflower Avant-Garde: Modernism, Sexuality, and Queer Ekphrasis.* Oxford: Oxford University Press, 2016.

Herring, Scott. *Queering the Underworld: Slumming, Literature, and the Undoing of Lesbian and Gay History.* Chicago: University of Chicago Press, 2007.

Kahan, Benjamin. *Celibacies: American Modernism & Sexual Life.* Durham: Duke University Press, 2013.
Love, Heather. *Feeling Backward: Loss and the Politics of Queer History.* Cambridge: Harvard University Press, 2007.
Love, Heather. "Modernism at Night." *PMLA* 124.3 (May 2009): 744–748.
McClintock, Anne. *Imperial Leather: Race, Gender, and Sexuality in the Colonial Contest.* New York: Routledge, 1995.
Said, Edward. *Orientalism.* New York: Vintage, 1979.
Sedgwick, Eve Kosofsky. *Epistemology of the Closet.* Berkeley: University of California Press, 1990.
Sommerville, Siobhan B. *Queering the Color Line: Race and the Invention of Homosexuality in American Culture.* Durham: Duke University Press, 2000.

Modernist Masculinities

Bederman, Gail. *Manliness and Civilization: A Cultural History of Gender and Race in the United States, 1880–1917.* Chicago: University of Chicago Press, 1995.
Cannon, Kelly. *Henry James and Masculinity: The Man at the Margins.* New York: Palgrave Macmillan, 1994.
Carby, Hazel. *Race Men.* Cambridge: Harvard University Press, 1998.
Cole, Sarah. *Modernism, Male Friendship, and the First World War.* Cambridge: Cambridge University Press, 2003.
Gopinath, Praseeda. *Scarecrows of Chivalry: English Masculinities after Empire.* Charlottesville: University of Virginia Press, 2013.
Halberstam, Judith. *Female Masculinity.* Durham: Duke University Press, 1998.
Kane, Michael. *Modern Men: Mapping Masculinity in English and German Literature, 1880–1920.* London: Continuum, 1999.
McCracken, Scott. *Masculinities, Modernist Fiction and the Urban Public Sphere.* Manchester: Manchester University Press, 2007.
Meyer, Jessica. *Men of War: Masculinity and the First World War in Britain.* Houndmills, Basingstoke: Palgrave Macmillan, 2009.
Person, Leland S. *Henry James and the Suspense of Masculinity.* Philadelphia: University of Pennsylvania Press, 2003.
Roberts, Andrew Michael. *Conrad and Masculinity.* New York: Palgrave Macmillan, 2000.
Smith, Terry, ed. *In Visible Touch: Modernism and Masculinity.* Chicago: University of Chicago Press, 1998.

Summers, Martin. *Manliness and Its Discontents: The Black Middle Class and the Transformation of Masculinity, 1900–1930*. Chapel Hill and London: University of North Carolina Press, 2004.
Theweleit, Klaus. *Male Fantasies, Vol. 1: Women, Floods, Bodies, History*. Minneapolis: University of Minnesota Press, 1985.
Worden, Daniel. *Masculine Style: The American West and Literary Modernism*. Basingstoke: Palgrave Macmillan, 2013.

Women and Censorship

Boyer, Paul S. *Purity in Print: Book Censorship in America from the Gilded Age to the Computer Age*, 2nd edn. Madison: University of Wisconsin Press, 2002.
De Grazia, Edward. *Girls Lean Back Everywhere: The Law of Obscenity and the Assault on Genius*. New York: Vintage, 1992.
Doan, Laura and Jay Prosser, eds. *Palatable Poison: Critical Perspectives on* The Well of Loneliness. New York: Columbia University Press, 2001.
Ingram, Angela. "'Unutterable Putrefaction' and 'Foul Stuff': Two 'Obscene' Novels of the 1920s." *Women's Studies International Forum* 9.4 (1986): 341–354.
Ladenson, Elisabeth. *Dirt for Art's Sake: Books on Trial from Madame Bovary to Lolita*. Ithaca, NY: Cornell University Press, 2007.
Marshik, Celia. "History's 'Abrupt Revenges': Censoring War's Perversions in *The Well of Loneliness* and *Sleeveless Errand*." *The Journal of Modern Literature* 26.2 (2003): 145–159.
Medd, Jodie. *Lesbian Scandal and the Culture of Modernism*. Cambridge: Cambridge University Press, 2012.
Parkes, Adam. *Modernism and the Theater of Censorship*. Oxford: Oxford University Press, 1996.
Vanderham, Paul. *James Joyce and Censorship: The Trials of Ulysses*. New York: New York University Press, 1998.

Modernism and Obscenity

Gilbert, Stuart. *James Joyce's Ulysses: A Study*, 1930. New York: Vintage, 1955.
Leeny, Cathy. *Irish Women Playwrights 1900–1939: Gender & Violence on Stage*. New York: Peter Lang, 2010.

Marshik, Celia. *British Modernism and Censorship*. Cambridge: Cambridge University Press, 2006.
Mullin, Katherine. *James Joyce, Sexuality and Social Purity*. Cambridge: Cambridge University Press, 2003.
Parkes, Adam. *Modernism and the Theater of Censorship*. Oxford: Oxford University Press, 1996.
Pease, Allison. *Modernism, Mass Culture, and the Aesthetics of Obscenity*. Cambridge: Cambridge University Press, 2000.
Potter, Rachel and David Bradshaw, eds. *Prudes on the Prowl: Fiction and Obscenity in England, 1850 to the Present Day*. Oxford: Oxford University Press, 2013.

Copyright, Libel, and Other Legal Horizons

Goldman, Jonathan, ed. *James Joyce and the Law*. Gainesville: University Press of Florida, 2017.
Latham, Sean. *The Art of Scandal: Modernism, Libel Law, and the Roman a Clef*. Oxford: Oxford University Press, 2009.
Medd, Jodie. *Lesbian Scandal and the Culture of Modernism*. Cambridge: Cambridge University Press, 2012.
Saint-Amour, Paul. *The Copywrights: Intellectual Property and the Literary Imagination*. Ithaca, NY: Cornell University Press, 2003.
Spoo, Robert. *Without Copyrights: Piracy, Publishing, and the Public Domain*. Oxford: Oxford University Press, 2013.

Suffrage

Chapman, Mary. *Making Noise, Making News: Suffrage Print Culture and U. S. Modernism*. Oxford: Oxford University Press, 2014.
Green, Barbara. "The Feminist Periodical Press: Women, Periodical Studies, and Modernity." *Literature Compass* 6.1 (2009): 191–206.
Green, Barbara. *Spectacular Confessions: Autobiography, Performative Activism, and the Sites of Suffrage 1905–1938*. New York: St. Martin's Press, 1997.
Lyon, Janet. *Manifestoes: Provocations of the Modern*. Ithaca, NY: Cornell University Press, 1999.
Marcus, Jane, ed. "Introduction." *Suffrage and the Pankhursts*. London: Routledge & Kegan Paul, 1987.

Miller, Jane Eldridge. *Rebel Woman: Feminism, Modernism, and the Edwardian Novel*. Chicago: University of Chicago Press, 1997.
Morrisson, Mark S. *The Public Face of Modernism: Little Magazines, Audiences, and Reception, 1905–1920*. Madison: University of Wisconsin Press, 2001.
Tickner, Lisa. *The Spectacle of Women: Imagery of the Suffrage Campaign 1907–1914*. Chicago: University of Chicago Press, 1988.
Ziarek, Ewa Płonowska. *Feminist Aesthetics and the Politics of Modernism*. New York: Columbia University Press, 2012.

Empire, Fascism, Gender, Sexuality

Carlston, Erin G. *Thinking Fascism: Sapphic Modernism and Fascist Modernity*. Stanford: Stanford University Press, 1998.
Doyle, Laura. *Freedom's Empire: Race and the Rise of the Novel in Atlantic Modernity*. Durham: Duke University Press, 2008.
Ferrall, Charles. *Modernist Writing & Reactionary Politics*. Cambridge: Cambridge University Press, 2001.
Frost, Laura. *Sex Drives: Fantasies of Fascism in Literary Modernism*. Ithaca, NY: Cornell University Press, 2002.
Froula, Christine. *Virginia Woolf and the Bloomsbury Avant-Garde: War, Civilization, Modernity*. New York: Columbia University Press, 2005.
Garrity, Jane. *Step-Daughters of England: British Women Modernists and the National Imaginary*. Manchester: Manchester University Press, 2003.
Hackett, Robin. *Sapphic Primitivism: Productions of Race, Class, and Sexuality in Key Works of Modern Fiction*. New Brunswick, NJ: Rutgers University Press, 2004.
Herzog, Dagmar. *Sex after Fascism: Memory and Morality in Twentieth-Century Germany*. Princeton, NJ: Princeton University Press, 2005.
Hewitt, Andrew. *Political Inversions: Homosexuality, Fascism, & the Modernist Imaginary*. Stanford, CA: Stanford University Press, 1996.
Marcus, Jane. *Hearts of Darkness: White Women Write Race*. New Brunswick: Rutgers University Press, 2004.
McClintock, Anne. *Imperial Leather: Race, Gender, and Sexuality in the Colonial Contest*. New York: Routledge, 1995.

WORKS CITED

Acocella, Joan, "Cather and the Academy." *New Yorker* (November 27, 1995): 56–71.
Allen, Carol. *Black Women Intellectuals: Strategies of Nation, Family, and Neighborhood in the Works of Pauline Hopkins, Jessie Fauset, and Marita Bonner*. New York: Garland, 1988.
Ardis, Ann. "Making Middlebrow Culture, Making Middlebrow Literary Texts Matter: The *Crisis*, Easter 1912." *Modernist Cultures* 6.1 (2011): 18–40.
Ardis, Ann L. and Leslie W. Lewis, eds. *Women's Experience of Modernity: 1875–1945*. Baltimore: Johns Hopkins University Press, 2003.
Barleben, Dale. *Staging the Trials of Modernism: Testimony and the British Modern Literary Consciousness*. Toronto: University of Toronto Press, 2017.
Beauman, Nicola. *A Very Great Profession: The Women's Novel 1914–39*. London: Virago, 1983.
Bederman, Gail. *Manliness and Civilization: A Cultural History of Gender and Race in the United States, 1880–1917*. Chicago: University of Chicago Press, 1995.
Benstock, Shari. *Women of the Left Bank: Paris, 1900–1940*. Austin: University of Texas Press, 1986.
Berlant, Lauren. *The Female Complaint*. Durham: Duke University Press, 2008.
Birmingham, Kevin. *The Most Dangerous Book in the World: The Battle for James Joyce's* Ulysses. New York: Penguin, 2014.
Blackmer, Corinne E. "The Veils of the Law: Race and Sexuality in Nella Larsen's Passing." *College Literature* 22.3 (October 1995): 50–67.
Bone, Robert. *The Negro Novel in America*. New Haven: Yale University Press, 1958.
Boone, Joseph Allen. *Libidinal Currents: Sexuality and the Shaping of Modernism*. Chicago: University of Chicago Press, 1998.
Botshon, Lisa and Meredith Goldsmith, eds. *Middlebrow Moderns: Popular American Women Writers of the 1920s*. Boston: Northeastern University Press, 2003.

Bowler, Lisa and Claire Drewery, eds. *May Sinclair: Re-thinking Bodies and Minds*. Edinburgh: Edinburgh University Press, 2017.
Boyer, Paul S. *Purity in Print: Book Censorship in America from the Gilded Age to the Computer Age*, 2nd edn. Madison: University of Wisconsin Press, 2002.
Bradbury, Malcolm and James McFarlane. *Modernism: A Guide to European Literature 1890–1930*. London: Penguin, 1976.
Bradshaw, Melissa. *Amy Lowell: Diva Poet*. Ashgate, 2011.
Bradshaw, Melissa, and Adrienne Munich, eds. *Amy Lowell, American Modern: Critical Essays*. Rutgers University Press, 2004.
Bradshaw, Melissa, and Adrienne Munich. *Selected Poems of Amy Lowell*. Rutgers University Press, 2002.
Brittain, Vera. *Radclyffe Hall: A Case of Obscenity?* London: Femina, 1968.
Brown, Richard. *James Joyce and Sexuality*. Cambridge: Cambridge University Press, 1985.
Butler, Judith. *Bodies That Matter*. New York: Routledge, 1993.
Butler, Judith. *Gender Trouble: Feminism and the Subversion of Identity*. New York: Routledge, 1990.
Caine, Barbara. "Bloomsbury Masculinity and Its Victorian Antecedents." *Journal of Men's Studies* 15.3 (Fall 2007): 271–281.
Cannon, Kelly. *Henry James and Masculinity: The Man at the Margins*. New York: Palgrave Macmillan, 1994.
Carby, Hazel. *Race Men*. Cambridge: Harvard University Press, 1998.
Carby, Hazel. *Reconstructing Womanhood: The Emergence of the Afro-American Woman Novelist*. Oxford: Oxford University Press, 1987.
Carlston, Erin G. *Thinking Fascism: Sapphic Modernism and Fascist Modernity*. Stanford: Stanford University Press, 1998.
Caserio, Robert, "Queer Modernism." *The Oxford Handbook of Modernisms*. Eds. Peter Brooker, Andrzej Gasiorek, Deborah Longworth, and Andrew Thacker. Oxford: Oxford University Press, 2010.
Castle, Terry. *The Apparitional Lesbian: Female Homosexuality and Modern Culture*. New York: Columbia University Press, 1993.
Chapman, Mary. *Making Noise, Making News: Suffrage Print Culture and U. S. Modernism*. Oxford: Oxford University Press, 2014.
Chauncey, George. *Gay New York: Gender, Urban Culture, and the Making of the Gay Male World, 1890–1940*. New York: Basic Books, 1995.
Christodoulides, Nephie J. and Polina Mackay, eds. *The Cambridge Companion to H.D.* Cambridge: Cambridge University Press, 2012.
Clark, Suzanne. *Sentimental Modernism: Women Writers and the Revolution of the Word*. Bloomington: Indiana University Press, 1991.
Cohen, Ed. *Talk on the Wilde Side: Toward a Genealogy of a Discourse on Male Sexualities*. New York: Routledge, 1992.

Cohler, Deborah. *Citizen, Invert, Queer: Lesbianism and War in Early Twentieth-Century Britain*. Minneapolis: University of Minnesota Press, 2010.
Cole, Sarah. *Modernism, Male Friendship, and the First World War*. Cambridge: Cambridge University Press, 2003.
Collecott, Diana. "What Is Not Said: A Study in Textual Inversion." *Textual Practice* 4.2 (1990): 236–258.
Comstock, Anthony. *Traps for the Young*. New York: Funk & Wagnalls, 1883.
Connell, R.W. *Masculinities*. Berkeley: University of California Press, 1995.
Cook, Blanche Weisen. "'Women Alone Stir My Imagination': Lesbianism and the Cultural Tradition." *Signs* 4.4 (Summer, 1979): 718–739.
De Grazia, Edward. *Girls Lean Back Everywhere: The Law of Obscenity and the Assault on Genius*. New York: Vintage, 1992.
DeKoven, Marianne. *Rich and Strange: Gender, History, Modernism*. Princeton: Princeton University Press, 1991.
DeLauretis, Teresa. "Queer Texts, Bad Habits, and the Issue of a Future." *GLQ: A Journal of Lesbian and Gay Studies* 17.2– 17.3 (2011): 243–263.
Doan, Laura. *Fashioning Sapphism: The Origins of a Modern English Lesbian Culture*. New York: Columbia University Press, 2001.
Doan, Laura, and Jane Garrity, eds. *Sapphic Modernities: Sexuality, Women and National Culture*. New York: Palgrave Macmillan, 2006.
Doan, Laura and Jay Prosser, eds. *Palatable Poison: Critical Perspectives on The Well of Loneliness*. New York: Columbia University Press, 2001.
Douglas, Ann. *Terrible Honesty: Mongrel Manhattan in the 1920s*. New York: Farrar, Straus and Giroux, 1995.
Doyle, Laura. *Freedom's Empire: Race and the Rise of the Novel in Atlantic Modernity*. Durham: Duke University Press, 2008.
Doyle, Laura and Laura Winkel, eds. *Geomodernisms: Race, Modernism, Modernity*. Bloomington: Indiana University Press, 2005.
duCille, Ann. "Blue Notes on Black Sexuality: Sex and the Texts of Jessie Fauset and Nella Larsen." *Journal of the History of Sexuality* 3.3 (January 1993): 418–444.
duCille, Ann. *The Coupling Convention: Sex, Text, and Tradition in Black Women's Fiction*. Oxford: Oxford University Press, 1993.
DuPlessis, Rachel Blau. *Purple Passages: Pound, Eliot, Zukofsky, Olson, Creeley, and the Ends of Patriarchal Poetry*. Iowa City: University of Iowa Press, 2012.
DuPlessis, Rachel Blau. *Writing beyond the Ending: Narrative Strategies of Twentieth-Century Women Writers*. Bloomington: Indiana University Press, 1985.

DuPlessis, Rachel Blau. "Virile Thought: Modernist Maleness, Poetic Forms and Practices." *Modernism and Masculinity*. Eds. Natalya Lusty and Julian Murphet. Cambridge: Cambridge University Press, 2014. 19–37.
Edel, Leon. *Henry James: A Life*. New York: Harper and Row, 1985.
Eliot, T. S. *The Waste Land and Other Writings*. New York: Modern Library, 2002.
Empson, William. *Seven Types of Ambiguity*. 1930. New York: New Directions, 1966.
Faderman, Lillian. *Surpassing the Love of Men: Romantic Friendship and Love between Women from the Renaissance to the Present*. New York: William Morrow, 1981.
Felski, Rita. *The Gender of Modernity*. Cambridge: Harvard University Press, 1995.
Felski, Rita. "Introduction." *Sexology in Culture: Labelling Bodies and Desires*. Eds. Lucy Bland and Laura Doan. Chicago: University of Chicago Press, 1998. 1–9.
Fernald, Anne E. "Women's Fiction, New Modernist Studies, and Feminism." *MFS Modern Fiction Studies* 59. 2 (2013): 229–240.
Ferrall, Charles. *Modernist Writing & Reactionary Politics*. Cambridge: Cambridge University Press, 2001.
Fletcher, John. "Forster's Self-Erasure: Maurice and the Scene of Masculine Love." *Sexual Sameness: Textual Differences in Lesbian and Gay Writing*. Ed. Joseph Bristow. London: Routledge, 1992. 64–90.
Forster, E. M. *Virginia Woolf*. Cambridge: Cambridge University Press, 1942.
Forster, E. M. and Virginia Woolf. "The New Censorship." *The Nation & Athenaeum* XLIII (September 8, 1928): 726.
Forter, Greg. "Melancholy Modernism: Gender and the Politics of Mourning in *The Sun Also Rises*." *Hemingway Review* 21.1 (Fall 2001): 22–37.
Foucault, Michel. *History of Sexuality, Vol. 1*. New York: Vintage, 1990.
Fout, John C. "A Note from the Editor." *The Journal of the History of Sexuality* 1 (July 1990): 1.
Freedman, Ariela. *Death, Men, and Modernism: Trauma and Narrative in British Fiction from Hardy to Woolf*. New York: Routledge, 2003.
Friedman, Susan. *Planetary Modernisms: Provocations on Modernity across Time*. New York: Columbia University Press, 2015.
Friedman, Susan. "Who Buried H. D.? A Poet, Her Critics, and Her Place in 'The Literary Tradition.'" *College English* 36. 7 (March 1975): 801–814.
Frost, Laura. *The Problem with Pleasure: Modernism and Its Discontents*. New York: Columbia University Press, 2013.
Frost, Laura. *Sex Drives: Fantasies of Fascism in Literary Modernism*. Ithaca: Cornell University Press, 2002.

Froula, Christine. *Modernism's Body: Sex, Culture and Joyce*. New York: Columbia University Press, 1996.
Froula, Christine. "St. Virginia's Epistle to an English Gentleman: Sex, Violence and the Public Sphere in Woolf's *Three Guineas*." *Tulsa Studies in English Literature* 13 (1994): 27–56.
Froula, Christine. *Virginia Woolf and the Bloomsbury Avant-Garde: War, Civilization, Modernity*. New York: Columbia University Press, 2005.
Gale, Maggie B. and Gilli Bush-Bailey, eds. *Plays and Performance Texts by Women, 1880–1930: An Anthology of Plays by British and American Women from the Modernist Period*. New York: Manchester University Press, 2012.
Galvin, Mary. *Queer Poetics: Five Modernist Women Writers*. Westport, CT: Praeger, 1999.
Ganter, Granville. "Decadence, Sexuality, and the Bohemian Vision of Wallace Thurman." *MELUS* 28.2 (Summer 2003): 83–104.
Garber, Eric. "Spectacle in Color: The Lesbian and Gay Subculture of Jazz Age Harlem." *Hidden from History: Reclaiming the Gay and Lesbian Past*. Eds. Martin Mauml Duberman, Martha Vicinus, and George Chauncey, Jr. New York: New American Library, 1989. 318–331.
Garrity, Jane. "Found and Lost: The Politics of Modernist Recovery." *Modernism/Modernity* 15.4 (2008): 803–812.
Garrity, Jane. "Modernist Women's Writing: Beyond the Threshold of Obsolescence?" *Literature Compass* 10.1 (2013): 15–29.
Garrity, Jane. *Step-Daughters of England: British Women Modernists and the National Imaginary*. Manchester: Manchester University Press, 2003.
Gilbert, Sandra M. and Susan Gubar. *Madwoman in the Attic: The Woman Writer and the Nineteenth-Century Literary Imagination*. New Haven: Yale University Press, 1979.
Gilbert, Sandra M. and Susan Gubar. *No Man's Land: The Place of the Woman Writer in the Twentieth Century*, 3 vols. New Haven: Yale University Press, 1988–1996.
Gilbert, Stuart. *James Joyce's Ulysses: A Study*, 1930. New York: Vintage, 1955.
Gillespie, Diane F. "Introduction to Section on May Sinclair." *The Gender of Modernism: A Critical Anthology*. Ed. Bonnie Kime Scott. Bloomington: Indiana University Press, 1990. 436–442.
Glavey, Brian. *The Wallflower Avant-Garde: Modernism, Sexuality, and Queer Ekphrasis*. Oxford: Oxford University Press, 2016.
Goldman, Jonathan, ed. *James Joyce and the Law*. Gainesville: University Press of Florida, 2017.
Gopinath, Praseeda. *Scarecrows of Chivalry: English Masculinities after Empire*. Charlottesville: University of Virginia Press, 2013.
Green, Barbara. "The Feminist Periodical Press: Women, Periodical Studies, and Modernity." *Literature Compass* 6.1 (2009): 191–206.

Green, Barbara. *Spectacular Confessions: Autobiography, Performative Activism, and the Sites of Suffrage 1905–1938*. New York: St. Martin's Press, 1997.
Gruber, Ruth. *Virginia Woolf: The Will to Create as a Woman*. New York: Carroll & Graf, 2005.
Hackett, Robin. *Sapphic Primitivism: Productions of Race, Class, and Sexuality in Key Works of Modern Fiction*. New Brunswick, NJ: Rutgers University Press, 2004.
Halberstam, Judith. *Female Masculinity*. Durham: Duke University Press, 1998.
Hammill, Faye. *Women, Celebrity, and Literary Culture between the Wars*. Austin: University of Texas Press, 2007.
Hannah, Matthew N. "Desires Made Manifest: The Queer Modernism of Wallace Thurman's *Fire!!*" *Journal of Modern Literature* 38.3 (2015): 162–180.
Haralson, Eric. *Henry James and Queer Modernity*. Cambridge: Cambridge University Press, 2003.
Harper, Philip Brian. *Are We Not Men? Masculine Anxiety and the Problem of African-American Identity*. Oxford: Oxford University Press, 1996.
Hassett, Joseph M. "Literature Meets Law in Court: The Trials of *Ulysses*." *James Joyce and the Law*. Ed. Jonathan Goldman. Gainesville: University Press of Florida, 2017. 213–227.
Herring, Scott. *Queering the Underworld: Slumming, Literature, and the Undoing of Lesbian and Gay History*. Chicago: University of Chicago Press, 2007.
Herzog, Dagmar. *Sex after Fascism: Memory and Morality in Twentieth-Century Germany*. Princeton: Princeton University Press, 2005.
Hewitt, Andrew. *Political Inversions: Homosexuality, Fascism, & the Modernist Imaginary*. Stanford, CA: Stanford University Press, 1996.
Hipsky, Martin. *Modernism and the Women's Popular Romance in Britain, 1885–1925*. Athens, OH: Ohio University Press, 2011.
Hoffman, Karen A. "'Am I No Better than a Eunuch?': Narrating Masculinity and Empire in Ford Madox Ford's *The Good Soldier*." *Journal of Modern Literature* 27.3 (Winter 2004): 30–46.
Holcomb, Gary Edward. "The sun also rises in queer black Harlem: Hemingway and Mckay's modernist intertext." *Journal of Modern Literature* 30. 4 (2007): 61–82.
Hollander, Rachel. "Novel Ethics: Alterity and Form in *Jacob's Room*." *Twentieth Century Literature* 53.1 (2007): 40–66.
Honey, Maureen, ed. *Shadowed Dreams: Women's Poetry of the Harlem Renaissance*. New Brunswick: Rutgers University Press, 1989.
Horlacher, Stefan, ed. *Constructions of Masculinity in British Literature from the Middle Ages to the Present*. New York: Palgrave Macmillan, 2011.

Hough, Graham. *The Dark Sun: A Study of D.H. Lawrence*. New York: Macmillan, 1957.
Hull, Gloria T. *Color, Sex, & Poetry: Three Women Writers of the Harlem Renaissance*. Bloomington: Indiana University Press, 1987.
Humble, Nicola. *The Feminine Middlebrow Novel, 1920s to 1950s: Class, Domesticity, and Bohemianism*. 2001. Oxford: Oxford University Press, 2004.
Huyssen, Andreas. *After the Great Divide: Modernism, Mass Culture, Postmodernism*. Bloomington: Indiana University Press, 1986.
Ingram, Angela. "'Unutterable Putrefaction' and 'Foul Stuff': Two 'Obscene' Novels of the 1920s." *Women's Studies International Forum* 9.4 (1986): 341–254.
Irvine, Dean. *Editing Modernity: Women and Little-Magazine Cultures in Canada, 1916–1956*. Toronto: University of Toronto P, 2008.
Izenberg, Gerald N. *Modernism and Masculinity: Mann, Wedekind, Kindinsky through World War I*. Chicago: University of Chicago Press, 2000.
Joyce, James. *James Joyce's Scribbledehobble: The Ur-Workbook for "Finnegans Wake."* Ed. Thomas Connolly. Evanston: Northwestern University Press, 1961.
Joyce, James. *Ulysses*. New York: Vintage, 1961.
Jünger, Ernst. *Storm of Steel*. New York: Penguin Classics, 2004.
Kahan, Benjamin. *Celibacies: American Modernism & Sexual Life*. Durham: Duke University Press, 2013.
Kane, Michael. *Modern Men: Mapping Masculinity in English and German Literature, 1880–1920*. London: Continuum, 1999.
Katz, Tamar. *Impressionist Subjects: Gender, Interiority, and Modernist Fiction in England*. Urbana: University of Illinois Press, 2000.
Keyser, Catherine. *Playing Smart: New York Women Writers and Modern Magazine Culture*. New Brunswick: Rutgers University Press, 2010.
Kimmel, Michael. *Manhood in America: A Cultural History*. Oxford: Oxford University Press, 1996.
Kunka, Andrew J. and Michele K. Troy, eds. *May Sinclair: Moving Towards the Modern*. London: Routledge, 2006.
Ladenson, Elisabeth. *Dirt for Art's Sake: Books on Trial from Madame Bovary to Lolita*. Ithaca: Cornell University Press, 2007.
Lamos, Colleen. *Deviant Modernism: Sexual and Textual Errancy in T.S. Eliot, James Joyce, and Marcel Proust*. Cambridge: Cambridge University Press, 1998.
Lanser, Susan B. "1928: Sapphic Modernity and the Sexuality of History." *Modernism/Modernity Print Plus* 1.3 (October 25, 2016).
Latham, Sean. *The Art of Scandal: Modernism, Libel Law, and the Roman a Clef*. Oxford: Oxford University Press, 2009.

Latham, Sean and Gayle Rogers. *Modernism: Evolution of an Idea.* London: Bloomsbury, 2015.
Lawrence, D.H. "Apropos of Lady Chatterley's Love." *Sex, Literature and Censorship.* Ed. Harry T. Moore. New York: Twayne, 1953.
Lawrence, D.H. *The Letters of D.H. Lawrence.* Vol. 6. Eds. James T. Boulton and Margaret H. Boulton with Gerald M. Lacy. Cambridge: Cambridge University Press, 1991.
Leeny, Cathy. *Irish Women Playwrights 1900–1939: Gender & Violence on Stage.* New York: Peter Lang, 2010.
Lewis, Wyndham et al. "Manifesto I." *BLAST* 1 (6-20-1914): 11–29.
Light, Alison. *Forever England: Femininity, Literature and Conservatism between the Wars.* London: Routledge, 1991.
Lilly, Mark. *Gay Men's Literature in the Twentieth Century.* New York: New York University Press, 1993.
Lindemann, Marilee. *Willa Cather: Queering America.* New York: Columbia University Press, 1999.
Linett, Maren Tova, ed. *The Cambridge Companion to Modernist Women Writers.* Cambridge: Cambridge University Press, 2010.
Locke, Alain. "*Fire*: A Negro Magazine." *Survey* 58 (1927): 563.
Love, Heather. *Feeling Backward: Loss and the Politics of Queer History.* Cambridge: Harvard University Press, 2007.
Love, Heather. "Modernism at Night." *PMLA* 124.3 (May 2009): 744–748.
Lucey, Michael. *Never Say I: Sexuality and the First Person in Colette, Gide, and Proust.* Durham: Duke University Press, 2006.
Lusty, Natalya and Julian Murphet, eds. *Modernism and Masculinity.* Cambridge: Cambridge University Press, 2014.
Lyon, Janet. "Manifestos from the Sex War." *Gender in Modernism: New Geographies, Complex Intersections.* Ed. Bonnie Kime Scott. Urbana: University of Illinois Press, 2007. 68–74.
Lyon, Janet. *Manifestoes: Provocations of the Modern.* Ithaca: Cornell University Press, 1999.
Marcus, Jane. *Hearts of Darkness: White Women Write Race.* New Brunswick: Rutgers University Press, 2004.
Marcus, Jane, ed. "Introduction." *Suffrage and the Pankhursts.* London: Routledge & Kegan Paul, 1987.
Marek, Jayne E. *Women Editing Modernism: "Little" Magazines & Literary History.* Lexington: University Press of Kentucky, 1995.
Marinetti, F. T. "Manifesto of Futurism." *Modernism: An Anthology of Sources and Documents.* Eds. Vassiliki Kolocotroni, Jane Goldman, and Olga Taxidou. Chicago: University of Chicago Press, 1998. 249–253.
Marshik, Celia. *British Modernism and Censorship.* Cambridge: Cambridge University Press, 2006.

Marshik, Celia. "History's 'Abrupt Revenges': Censoring War's Perversions in *The Well of Loneliness* and *Sleeveless Errand*." *The Journal of Modern Literature* 26.2 (2003): 145–159.

McClintock, Anne. *Imperial Leather: Race, Gender, and Sexuality in the Colonial Contest*. New York: Routledge, 1995.

McCracken, Scott. "'A Hard and Absolute Condition of Existence': Reading Masculinity in *Lord Jim*." *The Conradian* 17.2 (spring 1993): 17–38.

McCracken, Scott. *Masculinities, Modernist Fiction and the Urban Public Sphere*. Manchester: Manchester University Press, 2007.

McDowell, Deborah E. "'That Nameless ... Shameful Impulse': Sexuality in Nella Larsen's *Quicksand* and *Passing*." *Black Feminist Criticism and Critical Theory*. Eds. Joe Weixlmann and Houston A. Baker, Jr. Greenwood, FL: Penkevill, 1988. 139–167.

McDowell, Deborah E. "The Neglected Dimension of Jessie Redmon Fauset." *Conjuring: Black Women, Fiction, and Literary Tradition*. Ed. Marjorie Pryse and Hortense J. Spillers. Bloomington: Indiana University Press, 1985.

Medd, Jodie. *Lesbian Scandal and the Culture of Modernism*. Cambridge: Cambridge University Press, 2012.

Mergenthal, Silvia. "A Man Could Stand Up: Masculinities and the Great War." *Constructions of Masculinity in British Literature from the Middle Ages to the Present*. Ed. Stefan Horlacher. New York: Palgrave Macmillan, 2011. 189–201.

Meyer, Jessica. *Men of War: Masculinity and the First World War in Britain*. Houndmills, Basingstoke: Palgrave Macmillan, 2009.

Miller, Jane Eldridge. *Rebel Woman: Feminism, Modernism, and the Edwardian Novel*. Chicago: University of Chicago Press, 1994.

Miller, Nina. *Making Love Modern: The Intimate Public Worlds of New York's Literary Women*. New York: Oxford University Press, 1998.

Millett, Kate. *Sexual Politics*. 1970. Urbana: University of Illinois Press, 2000.

Moffat, Wendy. "E.M. Forster and the Unpublished 'Scrapbook' of Gay History: 'Lest We Forget.'" *English Literature in Transition, 1880–1920* 55.1 (2012): 19–31.

Morrison, Mark S. *The Public Face of Modernism: Little Magazines, Audiences, and Reception, 1905–1920*. Madison: University of Wisconsin Press, 2001.

Mosse, George L. *The Image of Man: The Creation of Modern Masculinity*. Oxford: Oxford University Press, 1996.

Mullin, Katherine. *James Joyce, Sexuality and Social Purity*. Cambridge: Cambridge University Press, 2003.

Nadler, Stephen P., "Sweetback Style: Wallace Thurman and a Queer Harlem Renaissance." *MFS* 38.4 (Winter 2002): 899–936.

Neverow, Vara. "Contrasting Urban and Rural Transgressive Sexualities in Jacob's Room." *Woolf and the City: Selected Papers from the Nineteenth Annual Conference on Virginia Woolf*. Eds. Elizabeth F. Evans and Sara E. Cornish. Clemson, SC: Clemson University Digital Press, 2010.

Newton, Esther. "The Mythic Mannish Lesbian: Radclyffe Hall and the New Woman." *Signs* 9.4 (1984): 557–575.

O'Brien, Sharon. "'The Thing Not Named': Willa Cather as a Lesbian Writer." *Signs* 9.4 (1984): 576–599.

Oosterhuis, Harry. *Stepchildren of Nature: Krafft-Ebing, Psychiatry, and the Making of Sexual Identity*. Chicago: University of Chicago Press, 2000.

O'Rourke, Rebecca. *Reflecting on The Well of Loneliness*. London: Routledge, 1989.

Ostriker, Alicia. "What Do Women (Poets) Want? H. D. and Marianne Moore as Poetic Ancestresses." *Contemporary Literature* 27 (1986): 475–492.

Parkes, Adam. *Modernism and the Theater of Censorship*. Oxford: Oxford University Press, 1996.

Patton, Venetria K., and Maureen Honey, eds. *Double-Take: A Revisionist Harlem Renaissance Anthology*. New Brunswick, NJ: Rutgers University Press, 2001.

Pease, Allison. *Modernism, Feminism, and the Culture of Boredom*. Cambridge: Cambridge University Press, 2012.

Pease, Allison. *Modernism, Mass Culture, and the Aesthetics of Obscenity*. Cambridge: Cambridge University Press, 2000.

Penn Warren, Robert. *The Kenyon Review* IX. 1 (Winter 1947): 1–28.

Pero, Allan and Gyllian Phillips, eds. *The Many Facades of Edith Sitwell*. Gainesville: University of Florida Press, 2017.

Person, Leland S. *Henry James and the Suspense of Masculinity*. Philadelphia: University of Pennsylvania Press, 2003.

Pettipiece, Deirdre Anne McVicker. *Sex Theories and the Shaping of Two Moderns: Hemingway and H.D.* New York: Routledge, 2002.

Popp, Valerie. "Where Confusion Is: Transnationalism in the Fiction of Jessie Redmon Fauset." *African American Review* 43.1 (2009): 131–144.

Potter, Rachel. *Obscene Modernism: Literary Censorship & Experiment 1900–1940*. Oxford: Oxford University Press, 2013.

Pugh, Martin. *The March of the Women: A Revisionist Analysis of the Campaign for Women's Suffrage, 1886–1914*. Oxford: Oxford University Press, 2000.

Rado, Lisa, ed. *Rereading Modernism: New Directions in Feminist Criticism*. New York: Garland, 1994.

Radway, Janice A. *A Feeling for Books: The Book-of-the Month Club, Literary Taste, and Middle-Class Desire*. Chapel Hill: University of North Carolina Press, 1999.
Ransom, John Crowe. *The World's Body*. 1938. Baton Rouge: Louisiana State University Press, 1968.
Richards, I.A. *Principles of Literary Criticism*. New York: Harvest, 1925.
Richardson, Dorothy. *Pilgrimage 2: The Tunnel, Interim*. New York: Popular Books, 1976.
Roberts, Andrew Michael. *Conrad and Masculinity*. New York: Palgrave Macmillan, 2000.
Said, Edward. *Orientalism*. New York: Vintage, 1979.
Saint-Amour, Paul. *The Copywrights: Intellectual Property and the Literary Imagination*. Ithaca: Cornell University Press, 2003.
Saint-Amour, Paul, ed. *Modernism & Copyright*. New York: Oxford University Press, 2011.
Salvato, Nick. *Uncloseting Drama: American Modernism and Queer Performance*. New Haven: Yale University Press, 2010.
Schaffner, Anna Katharina. *Modernism and Perversion: Sexual Deviance in Sexology and Literature, 1850–1930*. New York: Palgrave Macmillan, 2012.
Schenck, Celeste M. "Exiled by Genre: Modernism, Canonicity, and the Politics of Exclusion." *Women's Writing in Exile*. Eds. Mary Lynn Broe and Angela Ingram. Chapel Hill: The University of North Carolina P, 1989. 225–250.
Scholes, Robert. *Paradoxy of Modernism*. New Haven: Yale University Press, 2006.
Schwarz, A.B. Christa. *Gay Voices of the Harlem Renaissance*. Bloomington: Indiana University Press, 2003.
Scott, Bonnie Kime, ed. *The Gender of Modernism: A Critical Anthology*. Bloomington: Indiana University Press, 1990.
Scott, Bonnie Kime. *Gender in Modernism: New Geographies, Complex Intersections*. Urbana: University of Illinois Press, 2007.
Scott, Bonnie Kime. *Refiguring Modernism, Volume 1: Women of 1928*. Bloomington: Indiana University Press, 1995.
Sedgwick, Eve Kosofsky. "Across Gender, across Sexuality: Willa Cather and Others." *South Atlantic Quarterly* 88.1 (Winter 1989): 53–72.
Sedgwick, Eve Kosofsky. *Between Men: English Literature and Male Homosocial Desire*. New York: Columbia University Press, 1985.
Sedgwick, Eve Kosofsky. *Epistemology of the Closet*. Berkeley: University of California Press, 1990.
Sheehan, Elizabeth M. "Fashioning Internationalism in Jessie Redmon Fauset's Writing." *A Companion to the Harlem Renaissance*. Ed. Cherene Sherrard-Johnson. Wiley Blackwell, 2015.

Sherrard-Johnson, Cherene. *Portraits of the New Negro Woman: Visual and Literary Culture in the Harlem Renaissance*. New Brunswick: Rutgers University Press, 2007.
Showalter, Elaine. *A Literature of Their Own: British Women Novelists from Brontë to Lessing*. Princeton: Princeton University Press, 1977.
Sinfield, Alan. *The Wilde Century: Effeminacy, Oscar Wilde and the Queer Moment*. New York: Columbia University Press, 1994.
Sitwell, Edith. *Letters 1919–1964*. Eds. John Lehman and Derek Parker. New York: Vanguard Press, 1970.
Smith, Terry, ed. *In Visible Touch: Modernism and Masculinity*. Chicago: University of Chicago Press, 1998.
Sommerville, Siobhan B. *Queering the Color Line: Race and the Invention of Homosexuality in American Culture*. Durham: Duke University Press, 2000.
Spiro, Mia. *Anti-Nazi Modernism: The Challenges of Resistance in 1930s Fiction*. Evanston: Northwestern University Press, 2013.
Spoo, Robert. *Without Copyrights: Piracy, Publishing, and the Public Domain*. Oxford: Oxford University Press, 2013.
Stowell, Sheila. *A Stage of Their Own: Feminist Playwrights of the Suffrage Era*. Ann Arbor: University of Michigan Press, 1992.
Suh, Judy. *Fascism and Anti-Fascism in Twentieth-Century British Fiction*. New York: Palgrave Macmillan, 2009.
Summers, Martin. *Manliness and Its Discontents: The Black Middle Class and the Transformation of Masculinity, 1900–1930*. Chapel Hill and London: University of North Carolina Press, 2004.
Sylvander, Carolyn Wedin. *Jessie Redmon Fauset, Black American Writer*. Troy, NY: Whitston, 1981.
Theweleit, Klaus. *Male Fantasies, Vol. 1: Women, Floods, Bodies, History*. University of Minnesota Press, 1985.
Thomas, Sue, "Thinking Through '[t]he grey disease of sex hatred': Jean Rhys's 'Till September Petronella.'" *Journal of Caribbean Literatures* 3.3 (Summer 2003): 77–90.
Thrailkill, Jane F. *Affecting Fictions: Mind, Body, and Emotion in American Literary Realism*. Cambridge, MA and London: Harvard University Press, 2007.
Tickner, Lisa. "Men's Work? Masculinity and Modernism." *Differences* 4.3 (1992): 1–33.
Tickner, Lisa. "The Popular Culture of Kermesse: Lewis, Painting, and Performance 1912–13." *In Visible Touch: Modernism and Masculinity*. Ed. Terry Smith. Chicago: University of Chicago Press, 1998. 139–171.
Tickner, Lisa. *The Spectacle of Women: Imagery of the Suffrage Campaign 1907–1914*. Chicago: University of Chicago Press, 1988.

Timm, Annette F., and Joshua Sanborn. *Gender, Sex and the Shaping of Modern Europe: A History from the French Revolution to the Present Day*. Berg Publishers, 2007.
Trask, Michael. *Cruising Modernism: Class and Sexuality in American Literature and Social Thought*. Ithaca: Cornell University Press, 2003.
Utell, Janine. "Criminal Conversation: Marriage, Adultery, and the Law in Joyce's Work." In Goldman 15–30.
Vanderham, Paul. *James Joyce and Censorship: The Trials of Ulysses*. New York: New York University Press, 1998.
Van Dusen, Wanda. "Portrait of a National Fetish: Gertrude Stein's 'Introduction to the Speeches of Maréchal Pétain' (1942)." *Modernism/modernity* 3.3 (1996): 69–96.
Vicinus, Martha. *Intimate Friends: Women Who Loved Women, 1778–1928*. Chicago: University of Chicago Press, 2004.
Wall, Cheryl A. *Women of the Harlem Renaissance*. Bloomington: Indiana University Press, 1995.
Wallace, Diana. *The Woman's Historical Novel: British Women Writers, 1900–2000*. New York and Basingstoke: Palgrave Macmillan, 2005.
Watson, Nicola. "Circulating Morals (1905–1915)." *Prudes on the Prowl: Fiction and Obscenity in England, 1850 to the Present Day*. Eds. David Bradshaw and Rachel Potter. Oxford: Oxford University Press, 2013.
Wilde, Oscar. *De Profundis*. Mineola, NY: Dover, 1996.
Williams, Chad. *Torchbearers of Democracy: African American Soldiers in the World War I Era*. Chapel Hill: University of North Carolina Press, 2010.
Wimsatt, Jr., W. K. *The Verbal Icon: Studies in the Meaning of Poetry*. University of Kentucky Press, 1954.
Woolf, Virginia. *Jacob's Room*. 1922. San Diego: Harcourt Brace, 1950.
Woolf, Virginia. *The Letters of Virginia* Woolf, *1936–1941*. Ed. Nigel Nicolson and Joanne Trautmann. Mariner Books, 1982.
Woolf, Virginia. *Orlando: A Biography*. 1928. San Diego: Harcourt Brace, 1956.
Woolf, Virginia. *Three Guineas*. 1938. Ed. and annotated by Jane Marcus. Orlando: Harcourt, 2006.
Worden, Daniel. *Masculine Style: The American West and Literary Modernism*. Basingstoke: Palgrave Macmillan, 2013.
Ziarek, Ewa Płonowska. *Feminist Aesthetics and the Politics of Modernism*. New York: Columbia University Press, 2012.
Zimmerman, Bonnie. "What Has Never Been: An Overview of Lesbian Feminist Criticism." *Feminist Studies* 7.3 (1981): 451–475.
Zox-Weaver, Annalisa. *Women Modernists and Fascism*. Cambridge: Cambridge University Press, 2011.

INDEX

abortion 2
Acocella, Joan 87
affect theory 48
African American(s) 11, 28, 42–5, 78–9, 119–20
Akiko, Yosano 56
Aldington, Richard 115
Allen, Maud 12, 139, 146
Anand, Mulk Raj 154
Anderson, Margaret 3, 6, 68, 128, 132, 139
Ardis, Ann 41, 44
Arlen, Michael 154
Auden, W. H. 59, 73

Barleben, Dale 144
Barnes, Djuna 2, 10, 49 n.1, 53, 58, 67, 79, 82–4, 158
  Ladies Almanack 2
  Nightwood 2, 162 n.5
Barney, Natalie 23, 67
Bataille, Georges 159
Baudelaire, Charles 135
Beach, Silvia 3, 23, 68, 143
Beauman, Nicola 36
Beckett, Samuel 93
Bederman, Gail 118
Bell, Clive 54
Bellmer, Hans 159
Bell, Quentin 49 n.1
Bell, Vanessa 54–5
Bennett, Arnold 31
Benstock, Shari 22–4, 49
Berlant, Lauren 32

Birmingham, Kevin 145
Blackmer, Corinne 66
Blackmore, David 106
Bloomsbury Group, the 109–10, 142–3, 154
Boccioni, Umberto 107
Bone, Robert 43
Boone, Joseph Allen 64–5, 83–4
Bottom, Phyllis 162 n.5
Bournet, Edouard 76
Bowen, Elizabeth 37, 67, 162 n.5
Boyer, Paul 130–1, 136–7, 145
Bradbury, Malcolm 163
Bradshaw, David 161 n.1
Bradshaw, Melissa 14, 29–30
Brecht, Bertolt 104
Bristow, Joseph 111
Brittain, Vera 124
Brooks, Cleanth 93
Brown, Richard 55, 57
Brown, Sterling 66
Bruce, Kennilworth 76
Bryher 23, 58, 68, 70, 74
Burton, Richard 112
Bush-Bailey, Gilli 50 n.5
Butler, Judith 63–4, 77, 80, 87–8, 100
Butts, Mary 155

Cannon, Kelly 110
Carby, Hazel 65, 119
Carlston, Erin G. 158
Carpenter, Edward 57, 70, 109
Caserio, Robert L. 82–4

INDEX

Castle, Terry 69–70
Cather, Willa 25, 79, 80, 82, 83, 86–9, 92, 155, 163–4
  "Paul's Case" 86–9
celibacy 83
censorship. *See* law
Chapman, Mary 151
Chauncey, George 75–6, 79
Cheney, Russell 76
Chisholm, Anne 49 n.1
Chopin, Kate 25, 56, 84
Christie, Agatha 37
Chughtai, Ismat 56
Cixous, Hélène 25
Clark, Suzanne 33–4
cognitive approaches to literature 48
Cohen, Ed 74–5
Cohler, Deborah 72
Cole, Sarah 91, 111, 112, 116
Colette 23, 76
Collecott, Diana 73, 74
Comley, Nancy 106
Comstock, Nancy 129
Connell, R. W. 94, 100–1
Conor, Liz 41
Conrad, Joseph 64, 83, 93, 104, 111–12, 153
contraception 139
Cook, Blanche Weisen 12, 67
Corelli, Marie 39
Corvo, Baron 83
cowboys 111–17
Crane, Hart 15, 86, 99
Cullen, Countee 42, 66, 76, 120
cummings, e. e. 52
Cunard, Nancy 49 n.1

Darwin, Charles 56
de Grazia, Edward 6, 131, 145
DeKoven, Marianne 6, 20
  Rich and Strange: Gender, History, Modernism 6

Dickson, Lovat 49 n.1
Doan, Laura 58, 70–2, 142, 146
Doran, George H. 133
Douglas, Ann 98–9
Dreiser, Theodore 56, 123, 128–9
DuBois, Ellen Carol 161 n.3
DuBois, W. E. B. 42, 66, 92, 119
duCille, Ann 43, 66
Dunbar-Nelson, Alice 27
DuPlessis, Rachel Blau 22, 107–9
Duras, Marguerite 159

Eakins, Thomas 113
Eastman, Max 104–5
Eaton, Edith (Sui Sin Far) 151
écriture feminine 16
Edel, Leon 110
Eliot, T. S. 2, 3, 7, 12, 15, 27, 58, 92, 93, 108, 109, 156
  "The Metaphysical Poets" 14–15
  "Tradition and the Individual Talent" 3–5
  The Waste Land 2, 13, 99
Elliott, Ira 106
Ellis, Havelock 2, 57, 58, 70, 109
Ellison, Ralph 59
Empson, William 15

Faderman, Lillian 67, 79
fascism 156–9
fashion 42
Faulkner, William 84, 92, 93
Fauset, Jessie Redmon 16, 27, 42–5, 66
Felski, Rita 6, 50 n.4, 58–9
  The Gender of Modernity 6, 39–41
female difference 16–18, 26
female masculinity 101–2
femininity 1–2, 8, 10, 17, 39–42, 126–33
feminism 6, 14
  methods of 47

recovery work 8, 16–33
  second-wave 7–9, 19, 149
Ferber, Edna 83
Ferguson, Rachel 37
Fernald, Anne 48
Ferrall, Charles 156
Firbank, Ronald 83
Fire!! 82, 120
Fitzgerald, F. Scott 58, 92
Flanner, Janet 23, 159
Flaubert, Gustave 135
Ford, Charles Henry 84
Ford, Ford Madox 113
Ford, John 130
Forster, E. M. 2, 14, 58, 59, 83, 93, 112–13, 124
  Maurice 2, 73
  A Passage to India 118
Forter, Greg 92, 106
Foucault, Michel 77, 83–6
  History of Sexuality, Vol. 1 9, 61–3
Freedman, Ariela 91
Freud, Sigmund 25, 58, 61, 68, 80, 84, 94, 99, 100
Freytag-Loringhoven, Baroness Elsa von 81
Friedman, Susan Stanford 19–20, 45–7
Frost, Laura 49, 66, 159–60
Frost, Robert 93
Froula, Christine 99–100, 157
Futurism 107–8

Gale, Maggie 50 n.5
Garber, Eric 69
Garrity, Jane 29, 47–8, 72, 155
gay men 73–7
gender
  Butler on 63–4, 100
  defined 1–2
  Felski on 39–41
gender studies 8–9

Genet, Jean 60, 82, 159
Gibbons, Stella 37
Gide, André 64, 76
Gilbert, Sandra M., and Susan Gubar 24–6, 49, 69, 93
Gilbert, Stuart 130, 133–4
Gillespie, Diane 31
Glasgow, Ellen 25
Glavey, Brian 74
Glyn, Elinor 137
Goldman, Emma 34
Gopinath, Praseeda 112
Gore-Booth, Eva 138
Graves, Robert 115, 116
Green, Barbara 41, 50 n.4, 150, 162 n.4
Gregory, Augusta 138
Grimké, Angelina Weld 27
gross indecency 108
Gruber, Ruth 18–19
Gubar, Susan. *See* Gilbert, Sandra M.

Hackett, Robin 155
Haggard, H. Rider 112
Halberstam, Judith (Jack) 101, 164
Hall, Radclyffe 2, 12, 49 n.1, 53, 58, 67, 70, 71–2, 80, 102, 123, 124, 132, 135, 140–3, 146
  The Well of Loneliness 12, 67, 70, 72, 78, 80, 102, 124, 140–3
Hammill, Faye 37–8
Hampson, Robert 111
Hannah, Matthew N. 82
Hardy, Thomas 56
Harlem Renaissance 11, 27, 34–5, 42–5, 65–6, 69, 76, 82, 92, 119–20
Harper, Philip Brian 119
Hassett, Joseph 145

Hawks, Olive 162 n.5
Hawthorne, Nathaniel 2
Hawthorn, Jeremy 111
H.D. (Hilda Doolittle) 2, 15, 16, 18, 19–20, 23, 27, 31, 58, 59, 68, 74
Heap, Jane 3, 6, 132, 139
Hemingway, Ernest 58, 92, 99, 104–6
  The Sun Also Rises 92, 105–6, 120–1
Herring, Scott 79, 80, 88–9
Herzog, Dagmar 159
heterosexuality 54, 70
Hewitt, Andrew 156–7
Hicklin (Regina v. Hicklin) 127–8, 131, 132, 136
Hipsky, Martin 41
Hirschfeld, Magnus 57, 58
Hitler, Adolph 114
Hoffman, Karen 113
Holcomb, Gary Edward 120–1
homosexuality 2, 6, 57, 66–77, 87, 108, 120, 157
Honey, Maureen 43
Hopkins, Pauline 78
Hough, Graham 58
Howard, Sidney 99
Hughes, Langston 42, 58, 76, 83, 120
Hull, Gloria T. 26–7
Humble, Nicola 36
Hurston, Zora Neale 7, 17, 43, 59, 120
Huxley, Aldous 146
Huyssen, Andreas 98

Ibsen, Henrik 55, 123
imperialism 111–17, 153–6
intersectionality 45–6
inversion 75, 76, 95, 140
Irvine, Dean 50 n.2
Isherwood, Christopher 58, 162 n.5

James, Henry 68, 86, 92, 93, 110
Jameson, Fredric 153
Jewett, Sarah Orne 25
Jews 11, 95, 98, 117–18, 158
Johnson, Georgia Douglas 27
Johnson, James Weldon 78
Jones, David 156
Joyce, James 2, 27, 55, 57–9, 83, 93, 99–100, 123, 125, 127, 135, 137–8, 146, 147, 153
  Ulysses 6, 9, 13, 23, 51, 84, 92, 129–30, 132–4, 136, 143–5
Jünger, Ernst 114

Kafka, Franz 83, 104
Kahan, Benjamin 66, 83, 84–5
Kane, Michael 103–4
Katz, Tamar 50 n.4
Kent, Susan Kingsley 162 n.3
Kermode, Frank 93
Keyser, Catherine 38
Kimmel, Michael 101, 110, 113
Kipling, Rudyard 111, 112
Kouidis, Virginia 20
Krafft-Ebing, Richard von 56–7, 68, 70
Kunka, Andrew J. 32

Labouchere Amendment 108
Ladenson, Elisabeth 127, 135–6, 141, 145
Lambert, Deborah 86
Lamos, Colleen 108, 109
Lanser, Susan 67, 72–3
Larsen, Nella 2, 10, 43, 44, 65–6, 152
Laski, Marghanita 48
Latham, Sean 146, 163
law(s) 123–61
  British Criminal Law Amendment Bill (1921) 146
  censorship 2, 6, 123, 126–33
  copyright 145–6

Criminal Law Amendment Act
  (1885) 137
libel laws 123–4, 146
Obscene Publications Act
  (1857) 128
Lawrence, D. H. 2, 9, 27, 51–2,
  55, 58–60, 84, 92, 93, 104,
  108, 109, 123, 124–5, 127,
  135, 159
  Lady Chatterley's Lover 2, 49,
    58, 109
  The Rainbow 127–8, 139
  Women in Love 128, 147
Lawrence, T. E. 83
Leavis, F. R. 3, 7, 12, 93
LeBlanc, Georgette 68
Leeny, Cathy 138
Lehmann, Rosamond 69
lesbian(s) 8, 12, 24, 26, 56, 58,
  66–77, 124, 126, 139,
  140–3, 146, 158, 164
  mannish lesbian 71, 142
Lessing, Doris 22
Levenson, Lew 76
Lewis, Leslie 41
Lewis, Wyndham 2, 15, 97, 107,
  108, 146, 156
  Tarr 97
Light, Alison 36
Lilly, Mark 69
Linett, Maren Tova 50 n.5
little magazines 3, 8, 43
Little Review, The 6, 136, 140, 143
Locke, Alain 76, 120
London, Jack 101, 104
Lorca, Federico García 83
Lorrain, Jean 76
Love, Heather 73, 79–80, 82
Lowell, Amy 2, 4, 14, 16, 29, 52,
  125
Loy, Mina 7, 20, 59
Lucey, Michael 76
Lyon, Janet 107, 150–1

Macardle, Dorothy 138
MacDiarmid, Hugh 27
Mackenzie, Compton 67, 72
Mailer, Norman 60
manliness 118–19
Mann, Thomas 59
Mansfield, Katherine 21, 31, 47
Marcus, Jane 20, 150, 154, 157
Marek, Jayne 50 n.2
Marinetti, Filippo Tommaso 14,
  107–8, 156
Marshik, Celia 138, 144, 145
masculinity 1–3, 10–11, 91–121,
  126
  hegemonic masculinity 94–5
  reactionary 106–11
Mason, Charlotte Osgood 3
Mathiessen, F. O. 76
Maugham, W. Somerset 64
McClintock, Anne 155
McCracken, Scott 94, 102–3, 111,
  112
McDowell, Deborah 10, 43, 66
McFarlane, James 163
McKay, Claude 58, 76, 81, 92–3,
  120
  Home to Harlem 120–1
Medd, Jodie 72, 139–40, 142–4,
  146
Meeker, Richard 76
Mendès, Catulle 76
Messerli, Douglas 49 n.1
Mew, Charlotte 27, 35
Meyer, Jessica 116
Meynell, Alice 35
middlebrow 8, 12, 17, 36–9, 42,
  43
Millay, Edna St. Vincent 15, 34
Miller, Alice Duer 151
Miller, Henry 59, 60, 123, 135
Miller, Jane Eldridge 162 n.4
Miller, Lee 159
Miller, Nina 50 n.3

Millett, Kate 60–1
Mirrlees, Hope 16
Mitford, Nancy 37, 162 n.5
Moddelmog, Debra 106
Mongia, Andrew 111
Monnier, Adrienne 23, 68
Moore, Marianne 16, 151, 163
Moore, Olive 48
Morrell, Ottoline 146–7
Morrison, Mark S. 162 n.4
Mosse, George 108, 118
Mullin, Katherine 137–8, 144

Nabokov, Vladimir 135
Nardi, Marci 25
National Vigilance Association 137
Naturalism 56
Nebeker, Helen 20
neurasthenia 113–14, 118–19
New Critics 15
Newton, Esther 71
Niles, Blair 76, 84
Nin, Anaïs 59
Nordau, Max 104
Norris, Frank 56
Nugent, Richard Bruce 76, 79, 82, 84, 120

O'Brien, Sharon 86–7
obscenity 133–45
Oosterhuis, Harry 55
O'Rourke, Rebecca 141
Orwell, George 114–15
Ostriker, Alice 13, 16
Owen, Wilfred 116

Paris Was a Woman (film) 23
Parkes, Adam 127, 132–3, 139, 140, 144
Pater, Walter 80
patriarchy 10
Pease, Allison 32, 49, 66, 135, 136
Pero, Allen 50 n.5

Persephone Press 37
Person, Leland S. 110
Phillips, Gyllian 50 n.5
pornography 61, 133–5
Potter, Rachel 145, 161 n.2
Pound, Ezra 14, 27, 108, 109, 124, 132, 136
prostitution 138
Proust, Marcel 76, 77, 83, 108
Pugh, Martin 162 n.3

queer theory 9, 11, 75, 77–83

Rachilde 39
Rado, Lisa 29
Radway, Janet 36
Raitt, Suzanne 32
Ransom, John Crowe 15, 93
Reid-Pharr, Robert 76
Remington, Frederic 113
Rhys, Jean 9, 20, 47, 59, 138, 146
Rich, Adrienne 22
Richards, I. A. 15
Richardson, Dorothy 7, 21, 25, 26, 30, 31, 49, 59, 69, 83, 155, 163
  Pilgrimage 1, 3, 18, 49, 102–3
Riefenstahl, Leni 159
Roberts, Andrew Michael 111–12
Rogers, Gayle 163
Roosevelt, Theodore 113
Rubin, Larry 87
Rukeyser, Muriel 22, 48
Rule, Jane 86

Sacher-Masoch, Leopold von 39
Sackville-West, Vita 58, 67, 69, 70
Said, Edward 64
Saint-Amour, Paul 145
Sanger, Margaret 2
Sassoon, Siegfried 114, 115–16
Schaffner, Anna Katarina 57
Schenk, Celeste 35

Schlissel, Lillian 20
Scholes, Robert 38, 106
Schreiner, Olive 22, 25, 155
Scott, Bonnie Kime 5, 31, 49
   Gender in Modernism: New Geographies, Complex Intersections 42, 45
   The Gender of Modernism 5, 27–9, 35, 163
Scully, Robert 76
Sedgwick, Eve Kosofsky 5, 74, 80, 88, 93
   Epistemology of the Closet 5, 51, 73–4, 77–8
   Between Men: English Literature and Homosocial Desire 96–7
Seldes, Gilbert 160
sentimental modernism 33, 43
sex
   biological 2, 42
   intersex 45
   non-binary 48, 75, 77–8
   transsexual 45
sexology 56–8, 68, 71, 78, 79, 108, 146
sexuality 9, 51–89
   female, linked to censorship 126–33
   as linked to identity 52–3, 67–8, 75
sexual orientation 2, 5, 52, 66–77
Shaw, Bernard 2, 55, 83, 123, 138
Sheehan, Elizabeth 44
shell shock 116–17
Sherrard-Johnson, Cherene 44
Shloss, Carol 145
Showalter, Elaine 21, 49, 69, 111, 117, 150
Silverman, Kaja 100
Simmel, Georg 39

Sinclair, May 7, 8, 27, 30–3, 59
Sinfield, Alan 74
Sitwell, Edith 2, 83
Smith, Terry 107
sodomy 73, 108
soldiers 111–17
Sommerville, Siobhan B. 78
Spark, Muriel 162 n.5
Spilka, Mark 106
Spiro, Mia 158, 162 n.5
Spoo, Robert 126–7, 145
Stanley, H. M. 112
Stead, Christina 84
Steinbeck, John 101
Stein, Gertrude 2, 15, 20, 23, 25–7, 49, 74, 86, 151, 158, 159, 163
Stevenson, Robert Louis 103, 112
Stoker, Bram 104
Stopes, Marie 70, 89, 139
Stott, Rebecca 111
Stowell, Sheila 162 n.4
Strachey, James 58
Strachey, Lytton 54–5
suffrage 41, 149–54
Suh, Judy 158, 162 n.5
Sylvander, Carolyn Wedin 43
Symonds, John Addington 57

Tellier, Andre 76
Theweleit, Klaus 93, 97–8
Thrailkill, Jane F. 48–9
Thurman, Wallace 11, 53, 58, 76, 79, 82, 92–3, 120
Tickner, Lisa 108, 150
Toomer, Jean 44, 78, 120
transgender 2, 80, 102
Trask, Michael 66, 85–6
Treadwell, Sophie 99
Troubridge, Una 71, 142
Troy, Michele K. 32
Tutton, Diane 37
Tyler, Parker 84

Ulrichs, Karl Heinrich 70
Utell, Janine 147–8

Vanderham, Paul 132, 134, 136, 143–5
Van Dusen, Wanda 158
Van Vechten, Carl 66, 76, 79
Vicinus, Martha 26
Virago Press 31, 37
Vivien, Renée 25

Wachman, Gay 72
Wallace, Diana 38
Wallace, Jeff 50 n.5
Wall, Cheryl A. 42–3
Walser, Robert 104
Warner, Silvia Townsend 35, 69–70, 80, 155
Warren, Robert Penn 92
Watson, Nicola 161 n.2
Weaver, Harriet Shaw 3
Weininger, Otto 118
Wells, H. G. 31
  Ann Veronica 9
Welty, Eudora 83
West, Mae 20, 76, 160–1
West, Rebecca 7, 20
Wharton, Edith 23, 25
White, Antonia 27
Wickham, Anna 27, 35

Wilde, Oscar 11, 39, 70, 74, 77, 82, 88, 103, 108, 123
Williams, Chad 121
Wimsatt Jr., W. K. 15
Wister, Owen 101, 113, 114
Woolf, Virginia 1–3, 7, 14, 16, 18, 20, 21, 25, 27, 31, 47, 53, 54–5, 58, 59, 67, 69, 110, 124, 136, 138, 145, 152, 153–4, 158
  Between the Acts 162 n.5
  Jacob's Room 13–14
  To the Lighthouse 110
  Mrs. Dalloway 84, 116
  Orlando 1–2, 14, 72, 141
  A Room of One's Own 4, 16, 26
  Three Guineas 8, 14, 157–8
  The Years 162 n.5
Woolsey, John (Judge) 143, 145
Worden, Daniel 113

Yates, Dornford 38
Yeats, W. B. 93, 156
Young, Tori 50 n.5
Yourcenar, Marguerite 158

Ziarek, Ewa Plonowska 148–9
Zimmerman, Bonnie 69
Zola, Émile 39, 56
Zox-Weaver, Annalisa 159

www.ingramcontent.com/pod-product-compliance
Lightning Source LLC
Chambersburg PA
CBHW050139240426
43673CB00043B/1731